RARE but SERIOUS

Interviews, Articles, and Commentary

ZACK KOPP

© 2024 Zack Kopp

All rights reserved.

Published by Red Penguin Books

Bellerose Village, New York

ISBN

Print 978-1-63777-690-2

Digital 978-1-63777-688-9

Versions of several of these articles have appeared at www.PleasekillMe.com, www.itspsychedelicbabymag.com, www.examiner.com, and www.campelasticity.com

All pictures taken by the author, from Public Domain, or used with permission of the interviewees.

Non-identical versions of some of these articles have appeared at www.PleasekillMe.com, www.itspsychedelicbabymag.com, www.examiner.com, www.raintaxireview.org, and www.campelasticity.com

No part of this book may be reproduced in any form or by any electronic or mechanical means, including information storage and retrieval systems, without written permission from the author, except for the use of brief quotations in a book review.

CONTENTS

1. "What's a counterculture? Is that like terrorism?"   1
   Question asked of the author at a variety show he hosts after he uses the word assuming everyone still knows what it means

2. Nicknames   6
   Lost Generation, Beat Generation, Hippies, Punks, etc., all the names given to the countercultures by media

3. Hospitality: the work of John Fante   9
   Essay from grad school about what makes Fante's writing special

4. Strange Tales of Jim Morrison   16
   Was he a secret agent? Did he fake his death? Is he still alive? etc. My first freelance writing article, including an interview with Floyd Bocox, manager at the time of Jim's presumptive son, Cliff Morrison

5. Through the Beat Time Machine with Eds. White, Cassady and Cayce   24
   Review of a collection of letters between Kerouac and Denver's Ed White and an overview of Neal and Carolyn Cassady's connection to Edgar Cayce via consideration of Carolyn's memoir Off the Road and other sources

6. The Hole-in-corner man: Bukowski as Outsider Artist   30
   Bukowski the literary artist considered as an example of the Outsider type per Colin Wilson

7. Lizard Son: A Conversation with Cliff Morrison   38
   Soundalike Cliff Morrison claims to be Jim's son

8. Dan Fante reads at Mutiny   42
   John Fante's son and inheritor of his writerly talents, Dan Fante, makes an appearance at Denver punk coffee house Mutiny Info Café

9. Johnny Strike on CRIME and Writing   44
   San Francisco punk band CRIME once played San Quentin dressed as police officers. Strike, who also wrote several novels, was the frontman

10. Beyond Writing with Paul Krassner   49
    Recently departed investigative satirist, prolific author and standup comedian Paul Krassner was a friend of the Merry Pranksters and the Chicago 8, founded the Yippies, once took acid with Groucho Marx and was my friend and longtime pen-pal

11. The fight over Charles Manson's will in the media market   56
    The author's investigation of Manson's leftovers post-mortem, including one question answered by Manson himself before dying and an interview with one-time Manson Estate claimant Michael Channels

12. A conversation with Gary Lachman about Grabbing Reality — 66
    Gary Lachman played bass in Blondie as Gary Valentine, later publishing several books looking into human consciousness Colin Wilson-style
13. Dear Dr. Gonzo — 71
    The author's personal connection to one of the last things Hunter Thompson did to subvert systemic protocol in response to a letter he received
14. His Brother's Keeper — 75
    Jim Morrison's brother-in-law for 22 years Alan Graham from Liverpool takes objection to my publishing Cliff Morrison's manager's remarks about him without consulting him first and becomes a new client of mine
15. Neal Cassady Denver Years Screening Sells Out — 86
    Heather Dalton has directed and produced a film on Neal's youth in Denver. This chapter gives a snapshot of its premiere in that city
16. No More Beatlemania: The Monks meet rock & roll — 89
    Conversation with multi-instrumental musician Eddie Shaw about his time playing bass with the Monks in Germany
17. The Central Joke: My Dinner with Fante — 98
    Dan Fante's first appearance in Denver at Mutiny Now! books before its transformation to Mutiny Information Café, followed by a dinner with other authors in attendance and bacon in the brownies
18. Used Books — 101
    Promoting events for Alan Graham after finding a publisher for Neal's son Bob Hyatt's book Beat Bastard, Denver used bookstore culture as backdrop
19. Self-made: Aram Saroyan on inventing his own tradition — 106
    A self-description of author Aram Saroyan's approach assembled from published passages and quotes and approved by him
20. Mike McQuate and Jami Cassady on the Joan Anderson Letter — 112
    McQuate who found it, Cassady whose late father Neal wrote it
21. The Invention of D.I.Y. — 116
    Promoting Al Graham's books in the Denver underground
22. 8th Annual Neal Cassady Birthday Bash, 2/10/2017, Denver — 124
    Until a few years ago, Denver's Mercury Café had a tradition of honoring Neal's birthday with annual literary-musical showcases
23. Reprinted — 126
    Promoting the reprints of Al Graham's books about growing up with the Beatles in Liverpool, and his friendship with his wife's brother Jim Morrison
24. Paul Williams: Remembered — 129
    Williams invented rock criticism with his Crawdaddy! Magazine

25. How I Met Antifolk　139
   A brief overview of the musical subgenre
26. Divine Madness with Philip K. Dick　144
   Philip K. Dick's 2/3/74 experiences and his inherent tolerance for amphetamines
27. Johnny Strike's Last Wish　148
   Johnny Strike of SF punk band CRIME sent me an email a few days before he died
28. Pretty tunes with sour, disassociated lyrics: a conversation with Jazz Butcher and Gentleman Adventurer Pat Fish　153
   My interview with the Jazz Butcher preceded his death by about one year
29. Juan F. Thompson at Mutiny　164
   Son of Hunter S. Thompson appears
30. Paul Krassner Goes Beyond Words　167
   My tribute in the form of a eulogy
31. A conversation with Gary Wilson about lucky breaks, Endicott, and pet ducks　173
   Mad pop genius talks about his influences and insights
32. Death to Dr. Madd Vibe: A Tale of Two Movies　178
   The first all black punk band and possibly the first punk band, Death, a movie about them, and a movie about one of their inheritors, the band Fishbone
33. Beyond Two Tone with Angelo Moore　184
   An email interview with Fishbone's Angelo Moore
34. Larry Flynt for President: Nadia Szold interviewed　188
   A conversation with director Nadia Szold
35. Andy Warhol and the Beats in Denver: A Conversation with Mark Sink　197
   Denver artist Mark Sink is Ed White's stepson and was a part of Warhol's Factory
36. San Francisco streets of A.D. Winans　203
   Winans is a great poet, peer of Bukowski, Micheline, Kaufman, and others
37. Altered Music with Eddie Shaw　212
   A conversation with Eddie Shaw about his musical career post-Monks
38. Neal Cassady Comes Back to Denver　216
   A conversation with Neal's daughter, Jami Cassady Ratto and his son-in-law, her husband, Randy Ratto
39. Happenings in Denver to promote Al Graham's Books　232
   Manic 79-year-old Al Graham as ageless rock and roll entrepreneur
40. A Conversation with Tamra Lucid　238
   Author and founding riot grrrl Tamra Lucid talks about punk metaphysics

41. Ronnie Pontiac on his American Metaphysical Religion (Inner Traditions, Rochester, VT, 2023)   245
   Author and former substitute lecturer for Manly P. Hall Ronnie Pontiac played lead guitar in Lucid Nation
42. Robert Anton Wilson: Who is the master who makes the grass green?   249
   Robert Anton Wilson satirizes countercultural paranoia as a guerrilla ontologist
43. Be the Apple you want to see in the Algorithm   255
   Approximate transcript of a podcast featuring A.I. metaphysician and US6 author T.E. Ross. Ross is the Transhumanist Party presidential candidate in this year's election
44. Gerald Nicosia's Beat Scrapbook: A Ride Home from a Lonely Party   262
   Nicosia is author of Kerouac bio Memory Babe and champion of Jack's daughter Jan's legacy
45. From the Back Bay to the Bluebird: In the Bread with Jonathan Richman   267
   An overview of Richman's incomparable career
46. Theater of the Mind   278
   David Byrne and Mala Gaonkar's Theater of the Mind
47. Something is happening here   284
   Paul is Dead never died
48. Billy Burroughs at Prakriti Junction   293
   Son of Naked Lunch
49. Punk Metaphysics with Ronnie Pontiac   302
   Approximate transcript of a podcast
50. Alan Graham is Dead. Long Live Alan Graham.   307
   My eulogy for a fallen friend, followed by an update on Cliff Morrison and Floyd Bocox's current activities
51. Not the kind of Animals you think   312
   What it means to be a counterculture and where the edge lies presently

About the Author   315

1 "WHAT'S A COUNTERCULTURE? IS THAT LIKE TERRORISM?"

QUESTION ASKED OF THE AUTHOR AT A VARIETY SHOW HE HOSTS AFTER HE USES THE WORD ASSUMING EVERYONE STILL KNOWS WHAT IT MEANS

WHEN I was a teenager, all you had to do was choose which previous countercultural style to identify with. They were all right there. Costumes of the bygone countercultures were easily found in thrift stores. Cast-off symptoms of the clash between freedom and power lying draped over the furniture of Western culture. I discovered the Beats as a teen in the mid-to-late 1980s, about 30 years after their heyday—starting with Jack Kerouac, who'd been inspired to write spontaneously by a letter he received from future Merry Prankster, Neal Cassady. By the time I entered high school, rebellion had become a commodity consumers identified with by hairstyles and listening preferences. And maybe it always had been that in part, but now maybe that's all it was. I started high school as a heavy metal kid, wearing the standard heavy metal uniform of denim jacket and long hair. I got into punk, I slashed a vent in the back of the jacket, wrote THE SEX PISTOLS in black magic marker below it, then spray painted it red as if I'd been stabbed in the back, and shaved hair off the sides of my head with disposable razors in my parents' bathroom. "You look like an idiot," said my Dad, and I stuck a safety pin through my nose, which hurt like hell and didn't last long. A year later, I got into ska and became a "rude boy" which entailed a whole new style of dress. I dropped out of high school in my junior year as a punk/ska/mod who sometimes wore a black Beat turtleneck.

In the 90s, I went by Henry Alarmclock and hosted three or four readings and art-jams every week, and when I finished grad school in 2008, I started hosting a variety show at Mutiny. I met a lot of creative writers and musicians. Some of the younger ones had never heard of the Beat Generation or Bukowski (let alone Fante) or even the seventies punk scene. In some cases people world-famous as recently as twenty years back were unknown to them. "How do you start a counter-culture?" one kid asked. "Is that the same thing as terrorism?" He was wearing a polka dot miniskirt, a pair of plastic antennae, and butterfly wings. I told him the story of an artists' collective called Bleeding TVs of Angels Alarmclock co-founded in the 90s. [How we got the name: one day at the coffee house, my friend Devin Scheimberg said "Bleeding," then told me and our friend James

Gonzalez to pick a word]. We hosted events without specified performers full of donated typewriters, art supplies, and instruments and hung signs reading YOU ARE THE SHOW to inspire improvised jams. I think we had seven or eight of them over a period of five or six years. That was our attempt to start our own Denver-specific counterculture. The events were well-attended, but never went beyond local underground history.

We all grow up encompassed by the doings of various bygone bigshots, and as an artist, I've always felt like the product of some previous counterculture in an endless war between law and joy or some other cops-and-robbers conflict, and maybe you have, too. I read all the Beat stuff I found, Corso being my favorite because of his humor. I read Kerouac's *On the Road*. I read Neal Cassady's self-conscious *The First Third* (I prefer his unedited *Collected Letters*), about growing up in Denver flophouses when Larimer Street was all pool halls, flops and bars and wondered why there wasn't a statue of Neal anywhere. A few years ago, I wrote an informal connection of the Beats' multiple connections to Denver, mostly through Neal, and now I'm connected to several of the Beats' offspring and grandchildren myself. I'm friends with Neal's latest-discovered orphan, artist Robert Hyatt, whose memoir *Beat Bastard: An Adoptee's Portfolio* was published by Boston's Big Table Publishing in 2017. Denver artist Mark Sink introduced me to his stepfather, lifelong Kerouac friend-and-correspondent architect Edward Divine White. I gave him a copy of *The Denver Beat Scene* and he quipped, "Can't beat that!" ["See? He's still got it." put in Mark from the side *sotto voce*]. My interview with Neal's daughter Jami Cassady Ratto and her husband Randy was recently published at campelasticity.com, and is reproduced later in this book.

John Fante (April 8, 1909 – May 8, 1983), a writer who preceded the Beats, was most famous in the 1930s before disappearing (with a few exceptions) into screenwriting. Fante became known to me via anti-Beat Charles Bukowski's description of finding his *Ask the Dust* in a Los Angeles Library as having been "like finding gold in the city dump." I was working for the Denver Examiner and became aware of a writer named Dan Fante (February 19, 1944 – November 23, 2015), found his email address somewhere, and sent him one asking if he was John's son, and would he like to do an interview? We became pen pals for a number of years. He wrote a blurb for one of my books and I set up a couple of events for him at Denver's Mutiny Information Café on Broadway before he died. Judging by his impeccable poise, I'd say Dan died at peace with the demons of his self-destructive youth, but it's a guess. The late investigative satirist and first zinester (The Realist editor) Paul Krassner (April 9, 1932 – July 21, 2019) was another pen pal of mine who was extremely supportive. Paul wrote me a couple of great blurbs and introduced me to Intrepid Traveler Ken Babbs and other Pranksters, including the late Lee Quarnstrom, who died last year (2021). I've edited two books for poet/Doors frontman Jim Morrison's ex-brother-in-law Alan Graham so far—one on growing up with the Beatles in Liverpool, one on his years as Morrison's drinking buddy, and someday maybe we'll do the one about Al working as a fixer for pornographer Larry Flynt in 1983 when Flynt ran for president from inside a madhouse, if he feels like unearthing those memories.

In grad school I co-edited a zine called The Gut. One of my first unsolicited interview requests was sent to Handsome Family lyricist and author of the books *Evil* and *Wilderness*, Rennie Sparks, who knew my anti-comic friend Brian Potrafka, author of *Small and Wrong*, from when she and husband Brett Sparks lived in Chicago. Ms. Sparks is an excellent writer of hard boiled prose and genius lyrics like "butterflies are monsters when you look at them too close," who deserves more recognition, by the nerves of this hard-boiled brain. Around this time I did an interview with former City Lights employee V. Vale, who founded RE/Search Publications with donations from Ferlinghetti and Ginsberg.

I might have been one of the last people author and CRIME bassist Johnny Strike sent an email to, urging me to recommend his final book, *The Exploding Memoir* to my local library. CRIME was one of the first punk bands in San Francisco circa 1976, and once played a free show for San Quentin inmates dressed as cops. That email trailed off inconclusively, and in the next day or so, I heard Strike had died.

That got me my first article in the recently departed www.pleasekillme.com founded by oral historians Legs McNeil (Legsville.com) and Gillian Welch, who put together a lot of it sourced from principals in the New York punk scene in a book called *Please Kill Me* before moving on to other projects. The originals of a lot of these interviews appeared on that site.

2 NICKNAMES

LOST GENERATION, BEAT GENERATION, HIPPIES, PUNKS, ETC., ALL THE NAMES GIVEN TO THE COUNTERCULTURES BY MEDIA

MAINSTREAM American culture is rooted in conflict, beginning with the pilgrims versus redcoats, then invaders versus natives, North versus South, the Civil War–it's a culture of separation breeding racial bias of every imaginable nature, and gender bias and sex-preference bias; old versus young; counterculture versus culture. Anything new and popular and unusual is typically reacted to by the establishment as an invasion. The whole thing might have started with nicknames. Another foundational norm in America is consumerism, selling things and advertising, which takes public relations and flash, and over the years the authorial vantage, formerly thought of as commentary above and beyond the drag of normalcy, has become increasingly united with entertainment because of this influence, perhaps to avoid hostility.

The Lost Generation in the 1920s consisted of writers including Ernest Hemingway, Gertrude Stein, E.E. Cummings and others noted for their nonconformity. I'm not sure who came up with the name, some newspaper columnist probably. Maybe a critic. The Beat Generation ("Beat" from Black American slang quoted by Times Sq. hustler Herbert Huncke, popularized as literary tag by John Clellon Holmes, Jack Kerouac, Allen Ginsberg, others) started germinating in the 40s when Neal C visited Jack K and poet Allen G (*HOWL*) at Columbia U, and became famous in late fifties U.S. mass media stereotypes and cartoons were created. The Beats were mistakenly lumped in with the rock and roll juvenile delinquent scare of the time and dubbed with the "beatniks" slur by SF Chronicle columnist Herb Caen to link their scene with the Communists. This association was unfounded, as the Beats were apolitical in nature to begin with. Around the same time in England you had a literary movement known as the Angry Young Men including writers like Kingsley Amis and Colin Wilson, skiffle music and eventually rock and roll becoming popular with Teddy Boys or "rockers" in conflict with well-dressed, scooter riding Blue Beat and R&B loving mods. Guy Debord's Situationist International (SI), which inspired Bleeding TVs of Angels and European punk before it, was popular in France from 1957 to 1972

Back in America in 1964, Neal Cassady went on to drive Ken Kesey's bus from Acid Test to Acid Test, where samples of the then legal psychedelic LSD were distributed to the public. The word "hipster" began as a term for 1940s jazz fans. Hipsters were known for pot smoking and sarcasm. A few years later the "hippies" were born. Then came further commodification of the counterculture ethic with the Summer of Love, the Love Generation, The Beach Boys, Crosby Stills and Nash, The Beatles, The Rolling Stones. It wasn't really underground anymore but something in the air. This trend continued through the 1970s into album-oriented rock, with only a couple dramatic backfires, including punk, eventually numbing back down to the current hodgepodge of prefabricated boy bands and teen chanteuses.

I had lunch with Neal's son Bob Hyatt last week. I interviewed him about his art for a film I'm making. Others interviewed for this so far: Angela Black, who paints and drinks wine for weeks at a time, channeling art between shifts as a waitress who lives in an RV, Colfax Museum proprietor Jonny Barber. There are chapters coming up that go into more depth about the Hyatts (Bon's son Henry is a dead ringer for Neal and his daughter Vera is a Burning Man regular who keeps a blog about wanderlust, recalling her grandfather's need to be on the move all the time while working as a douala. I haven't met John Allen

Cassady yet, but there's an interview with Jami and Randy to come. You'll be meeting Jim Morrison's recently passed brother-in-law of 22 years, Alan Graham, to whom this book is dedicated, A.I. metaphysician Tom Ross, founding riot grrrl Tamra Lucid. The 20th century was a wildland where crime and art and spirituality frequently mixed and overlapped. This book even has a chapter on Charles Manson.

Neal Cassady's grandson, Henry Hyatt, beside a pic of young Neal.

3 HOSPITALITY: THE WORK OF JOHN FANTE
ESSAY FROM GRAD SCHOOL ABOUT WHAT MAKES FANTE'S WRITING SPECIAL

LIKE most readers of my generation, I came across John Fante's name during my exploration of the voluminous Bukowski catalog and first assumed they were contemporaries, later learning that Fante had in fact been a strong early influence on the young Bukowski, who felt starved for authenticity of emotion in literature. I bought a copy of *Ask the Dust* and was impressed, and after reading *The Road to Los Angeles,* I was hooked. Fante and Bukowski met as senior citizens, after Fante had gone blind and undergone double amputation of his legs due to the effects of diabetes, nevertheless telling Bukowski that the thing that happens to most people when they get old is they become bitter, and he hadn't succumbed.

John Fante was born in 1909, into Denver's then-thriving Italian-American community. He spent most of his youth in nearby Boulder, and moved to Los Angeles in the early thirties, where he died of diabetic complications in 1983. As a member of a predominantly Catholic ethnic minority, who lived through the Depression, and a talented writer never fully recognized as such in his lifetime who drifted into oblivion as a nameless, salaried Hollywood screenwriter, he's a true veteran of 20th Century American culture. In *Ask the Dust,* Fante's most famous novel, when protagonist Arturo Bandini develops a crush on the barmaid Camilla Lopez, he's immediately possessed of a sadistic desire to humiliate and insult her. He calls her a "Spick" and a "Greaser," even sneers at her huaraches. Lying in bed the same night unable to sleep, he remembers "Smith and Parker and Jones" back home in Colorado, "who hurt me with their hideous names . . . called me Wop and Dago and Greaser . . . because my name ends with a soft vowel, and they hate me and my father, and my father's father, and they would have my blood and put me down, but they are old now, dying in the sun and in the hot dust of the road, and I am young and full of hope and love for my country and my times, and when I say Greaser to you it is not my heart that speaks, but the quivering of an old wound, and I am ashamed of the terrible thing I have done."(47)

While Fante's prose is always colored by the politics and culture of its author, its artistry is uncorrupted by either. His father was a bricklayer, and this may have something to do with the incomparable hospitality of his work. He invites you into his tales as an honored guest and shows you around with an eye to your comfort. Here's a representative bit from an early story called "Bricklayer in the Snow," reprinted in the collection *The Wine of Youth*:

> "[My father's] fingers were like clumsy sticks. But he was a man of ceaseless activity, he had to be doing something, and the long pull of white days exasperated him and made him a dangerous man around the house. He smoked one cigar after another, cracked his knuckles noisily, and paced from room to room like a man in an iron cage. When he paced that way we children were terrified and crept away as soon as his short, big-muscled body appeared on quiet feet (21)."

Here's another, equally representative of the same considerate quality, from *The Brotherhood of the Grape*, written much later:

> "My first day in Los Angeles I took a job washing dishes at Clifton's Cafeteria. After a few days I was promoted to busboy and was sacked for 'socializing with the public,' in this case a girl carrying a volume of Edna St. Vincent Millay who invited me to her table for coffee and a

talk on poetry. Next day I found another dishwashing job at a saloon on the corner of Fifth and Maine. My room was upstairs for four dollars a week, shared by another dishwasher.

His name was Hernandez and he was crazy. He was the first writer I ever met, a tall, laughing Mexican sitting on the bed with a typewriter in his lap, guffawing at every line he wrote." (63)

I first heard of John Fante as "a friend of Charles Bukowski." Years later, after I'd become attached to Buk's spare and direct technique, I reinvestigated: in fact, he was more Bukowski's idol than his friend; John Fante was an up-and-coming writer in the late 30's and early 40's, a pick of H.L. Mencken. His first two published novels, *Wait Until Spring, Bandini* and *Ask the Dust*, both met with favorable reviews and respectable sales when released. It was the famous young Fante who most inspired and impressed the aspiring writer Henry Charles Bukowski, though the two never met until both were senior citizens. Fante made such an impression on the young Bukowski as a writer of uncommon originality that in the introduction to its reprint, Bukowski compared coming upon his first copy of *Ask The Dust* in the L.A. City Library to "finding gold in the city dump." Shortly after the first publication of *Ask the Dust* in 1939, Fante vanished into the netherworld of Hollywood screenwriters and as a result remained unrecognized as a creative talent in his own right until Bukowski's resuscitation of his name in the late seventies, which inspired Black Sparrow Press to reprint Bandini and Dust, even publish new Fante works, like Dreams From Bunker Hill and The Brotherhood of the Grape. While his work was never quite Italo-centric enough to preclude a near-universal accessibility, Fante never loses sight of

Catholicism's symbolic value. Here are a few lines from *Wait Until Spring, Bandini* (1938):

"Arturo Bandini was pretty sure that he wouldn't go to hell when he died. The way to hell was the committing of mortal sin. He had committed many, he believed, but the Confessional had saved him. He always got to Confession on time - that is, before he died. And he knocked on wood whenever he thought of it - he always would get there in time - before he died. So Arturo was pretty sure he wouldn't go to hell when he died. For two reasons. The Confessional, and the fact that he was a fast runner." (52)

And here are a few from *My Dog Stupid*, published in the early eighties:

"I could walk out into the night with my pipe and look from Stupid to the stars, and there was a connection. I liked that dog . . . He was childhood again, bringing back the pages of my catechism. Who is God? God is the creator of heaven and earth and of all things. Is God everywhere? God is everywhere. Does God see us? God sees us and watches over us. Why did God make us? God made us to know him and to love him in this world and to be happy with him in the next. I could sit on the grass with Stupid and believe every word of it. Sometimes as I sat there he would rise up and put his paws on my shoulders and try to screw me. So he loved me. How else could he express it? Write a poem, gather roses? I whacked him with an elbow, and that brought him down." (54)

From the beginning to the end of his career, the Church remains the perfect foil for its parishioner's ultimately humble (but no less snarky) wit. In *The Road to Los Angeles*, Fante's first novel, written in 1933 but deemed unpublishable when first presented to the publishers, the young Arturo Bandini (Fante's fictional alter-ego) is a self-professed and outspoken atheist - "You're a Christian, an Epworth Leaguer, a Bible-belter," he screams at his sister, "You're frustrated by your brummagem Christianity! You're at heart a scoundrel and a jackass, a bounder and an ass! (19)" This novel is one of the most ambitious satires I've read so far, in choice of targets. Below is a passage from *Road* wherein the aspiring writer Arturo surveys the results of his brutal massacre of a tribe of helpless crabs with an air-gun "for the good of the Fatherland." This sequence was written years before the U.S. entry into WWII, by the way, and it's eerily prophetic of the heartless extermination of non-Aryans carried out in secret by the Nazis, and as such is pointedly insightful, where otherwise it might seem merely grotesque.

> "The slaughter finally stopped when my head ached from eye strain. Before leaving I took another last look around. The miniature cliffs were smeared with blood. It was a triumph, a very great victory for me. I went among the dead and spoke to them consolingly, for even though they were my enemies I was for all that a man of nobility and I respected them and admired them for the valiant struggle they had offered my legions. "Death has arrived for you," I said. "Goodbye, dear enemies. You were brave in fighting and braver in death." To others I said, "Goodbye, thou coward. I spit on thee in disgust. Thy cowardice is repugnant to the Fuhrer. He hateth cowards as he hateth the plague. He will not be reconciled. May the tides of the sea wash thy cowardly crime from the earth, thou knave." (34-35)

This passage gets its laughs without naming any names or wringing its hands over any specific grievances, making an instructive cartoon out of stereotypical dictator-traits - vanity, aggression, extreme cruelty, a solipsistic romanticism - and in so doing, has a much greater effect in terms of satire without getting bogged in specifics. He did more than his duty as an artist by treating these issues symbolically rather than literally, thus hospitably offering them to his guest the reader as options for entertainment. "God, I was mad . . . I gathered some of the wounded into a pool and had a military conference and decided to court-martial them. I drew them out of the pool one at a time, setting each over the mouth of the rifle and pulling the trigger . . .

Even the princess had to die. It was unpleasant, but it had to be done (98-99)."

After returning to his job at the Soyo Fish Company and being accosted by a crowd of his co-workers, who stick a fish in his shirt to show him up for becoming nauseated by the cannery's smell, "Dictator Bandini" enacts his ultimate revenge with a crass display, this time for human spectators:

> "I reached into my shirt and felt the fish against my skin . . . I pulled the fish out, held him up and looked at him . . . Then I put him in my mouth and bit off his head. I was sorry he was already dead. . . . A bold fly landed on my arm and stubbornly refused to move, even though I warned him by shaking my arm. This made me insanely angry with him. I slapped him, killing him on my arm. But I was still so furious with him that I put him in my mouth and chewed him to bits and spat him out. Then I got the fish again, placed him on a level spot in the sand, and jumped on him until he burst open." (62)

During his first appearance at Mutiny Now! bookstore in Denver, John's son Dan related his discovery of the misplaced manuscript of *The Road to Los Angeles*, which would turn out to be his favorite of his father's works. He liked it so much that, after following directions given by an Italian medium in trance, he arranged for its republication by Black Sparrow Press in 1985.

The following passage from *Dreams From Bunker Hill*, a novel John Fante dictated to his wife Joyce after diabetes drove him blind, is also valuable as social commentary. The young screenwriter contemplates the reaction of his idol H.L. Muller - a fictional version of H.L. Mencken - to Arturo's sudden rise from privation, and his simultaneous loss of artistic integrity. It highlights Arturo the artist's willful incompatibility with the society around him:

> "I wondered what Heinrich Muller would say about my integrity. Integrity! I laughed. Integrity -balls. I was a nothing, a zero. To hell with it. I decided to go shopping for a pair of pants. I still had over a

hundred dollars. I would splurge and forget my troubles in profligate spending. What was money anyway? . . . The landlady sat behind the desk in the lobby. The first thing I noticed was a copy of The American Phoenix . . . Annoyed, I walked boldly to the desk and picked it up. "You haven't read it, have you?" She smiled, hostile. "No, I haven't." "Why not?" I said. "It bored me. I read the first paragraph and that was enough for me (155)."

No matter what the joke is, from self-perpetuated racism to unemployment to being an aspiring writer in bustling, money-mad America, Arturo is always the butt of his own shortcomings, which provides inexhaustible motive power for the narrator of his adventures. We learn success by watching him fail and fail, we're strengthened by his frailty. And he's the story's hero no less, as are we all of our own individual histories, in happy spite of distance from our dreams. From John Fante, I learned the importance and the magic of including the audience, whatever the topic. I hope someday he gets the recognition he deserves as one of the 20th century's greatest writers. My two cents.

Works cited (in order of citation): Fante, John. *The Wine of Youth*. Santa Rosa: Black Sparrow Press, 1999. - Fante, John. *The Brotherhood of the Grape*. Santa Rosa: Black Sparrow Press, 1999. -*The John Fante Reader*, edited by Stephen Cooper. New York, NY: First Ecco Paperback Version published 2003. - Fante, John. *The Road to Los Angeles*. New York, NY: First Ecco edition published 2002. - Fante, John. *Dreams From Bunker Hill*. Santa Rosa: Black Sparrow Press, 1999. - Fante, John. *Ask the Dust*. Santa Rosa: Black Sparrow Press, 1939, 1980.

4 STRANGE TALES OF JIM MORRISON

WAS HE A SECRET AGENT? DID HE FAKE HIS DEATH? IS HE STILL ALIVE? ETC. MY FIRST FREELANCE WRITING ARTICLE, INCLUDING AN INTERVIEW WITH FLOYD BOCOX, MANAGER AT THE TIME OF JIM'S PRESUMPTIVE SON, CLIFF MORRISON

LATE (?) comedian Andy Kaufman's recent reappearance in the news feed has reminded Americans of the prospect of faked death as a means of escaping the prison of fame. It's nice believing one of your heroes has escaped. In America, beloved celebrities are often venerated in this way postmortem. For example, legendary Doors frontman Jim Morrison supposedly died of heart failure in Paris in 1971, but Oregon rancher and rodeo photographer Gerald Pitts claims he faked his death. This was the first investigation I undertook as a citizen reporter a few years ago and there are a few chapters to it. It all happened a long time ago, and certain particulars are sure to have changed.

Jim as rodeo cowboy or crowd control agent

At the height of the Doors' success, Jim Morrison told reporters his parents were dead, and Jim's father said at the time he had probably done that "to protect his family." The elder Morrison made an addition to Jim's tombstone of a Latin phrase translating roughly, "True To His Own Mastermind."

According to Gerald Pitts, Jim faked his death to escape a French conspiracy to knock off influential protestors of the United States' involvement in the Vietnam War. They'd already taken down Janis and Jimi, Jim figured he might be next, and decided to split. Pitts claims Morrison appeared in 1998 to help him promote a shoot-'em-up rodeo movie called "Redeemed." His website, www.rodeoswest.com, still features photos and film footage attempting to prove the man in question is, in fact, Morrison, almost fifteen or more years after William James Loyer (who may or may not have been Morrison) denied all involvement with Pitts (who still claims to be his manager), even going as far as to offer "U.S. Government Jim Morrison Authentication Documents for Viewing by Appointment only."

If you accept the conventional portrait of Jim Morrison as one of several sixties era rock stars to die from lives of deliberate excess, all the rumors he faked his presumed death for one reason or another are easily dismissed as wishful thinking. But in Morrison's case, there's a whole other angle. Jim's dad, U.S. Naval Admiral Stephen Morrison, had top secret clearance, and thus would have known about the CIA's MK-ULTRA mind control program throughout its operation, whatever his degree of involvement. And whether or not Jim was any kind of "experimental individual," he was probably the recipient of lifelong secret service oversight because of his family ties. Once Jim Morrison's double existence in this sense is understood, his presumed death and seeming reappearance three decades later as a rodeo cowboy in Oregon is more easily swallowed— deep cover agents do that sort of thing all the time.

Rubio's first book examines the possibility that Morrison faked his death by ingesting Tetrodotoxin, a drug used to induce the "zombie" state and is still alive today. *The Jim Morrison Manual Case* is a further, more explicit investigation into this possibility, including the record of her acquaintance with the Oregon cowboy in question, and her correspondence by email with this man's wife, Marsha Loyer, who is referred to as "(AKA) Marsha Morrison" on Pitts's website. "Gerald Pitts is the kind of person who will do whatever to reach the goal," warns Rubio. "He made it clear to me in many telephone interviews we had in 2005, saying, 'This is a BILLION- dollars story!' I remember one of our conversations when I asked if his 'Jim' is still writing, and he just said: 'He told me that he wanted to publish a poetry book. I don't know much about books and to say the truth I don't care about that. I'm interested in breaking the news with this story!' Then he said that if I wanted further information I had to give him money! He is NOT a truthful person."

The following is excerpted from a 2005 mailing sent to Rubio by Marsha Loyer, "He was fired effective December 31st, 1999. We have completely disassociated ourselves from Mr. Pitts and his friends and his family. We have nothing to do with Gerald Pitts! 'A Current Affair' representatives came to our home unannounced on three days in a row this past March and were denied interviews or photos. They attempted to take photos from our neighbors' property. Their June 2005 episode on FOX TV featured Gerald Pitts and made a FARCE of the entire thing! . . . My husband previously had expressed an interest in meeting with Ray Manzarek. Unfortunately, Danny Sugerman interfered with that in 1996."

On her website, Adriana Rubio makes clear that she in no way wishes to confirm Gerald Pitts's allegations about the Oregon cowboy, having encountered a labyrinth of puzzles in her efforts to solve that particular mystery. And I don't either. William James Loyer's own apparent identification with Morrison, whether real or imagined, remains uncontested. In *The Jim Morrison Manual Case*, she says that after discovering the "false French name" this Oregon cowboy lives under, she contacted him. When Pitts found out, he became enraged, leaving a message with Rubio's publisher saying, "You are NEVER to call him again." She says she felt partially lucky for being in touch with the supposed Morrison and his wife Marsha for approximately a year and a half, even after being informed by his wife that the man in question, whatever his true identity, was undergoing chemotherapy treatments for "a liver illness." Was the whole thing really just an MK-ULTRA study of the effectiveness of rock music as crowd control tool, as has been alleged regarding Jim's in 1969 Miami obscenity bust?

The 1960s was a turbulent time for the United States in terms of transvaluation of values. Popular celebration of things formerly considered taboo set the established way of things on its ear, and the effect on successive generations has been prodigious. Highly questionable speculations and allegations about *what really happened* abound, two or three of which we'll look at briefly in this volume, and here's the first. Much has been made of the recurrent lizard references in Morrison's lyrics as evidence of his ties to sorcery. It has even been claimed that Jim was party to a top-secret government program involving reptilian aliens. When I asked Ms. Rubio the significance of those lyrics according to her research, she responded with a lengthy excerpt from *The Jim Morrison Manual Case* which stated that the agents involved in the highest echelons of the MK-ULTRA program were commonly referred to as "lizard men" or "lizard people." Declassified MK-ULTRA documents confirm that the relationship of personality to hypnotic susceptibility was studied in the early 1950s as a way of "creating anxieties," presumably in certain target personality types—i.e. the youth. The excerpt included some lyrics from Doors song, "The Celebration of the Lizard" which are highly suggestive of the introduction and onset of a hypnotic session when viewed in this light, at one point referring to the process as "a little game" just as it might have been introduced to Jim by his own spook father as a child. MK-ULTRA is well-known for its alleged use of hypnosis for the implanting of behavioral commands in scapegoat "lone nut" assassins like Lee Harvey Oswald and Sirhan Sirhan. On more than one occasion, Jim Morrison claimed he drank excessively to silence all the voices in his head, and maybe he wasn't just being colorful. Maybe his lyrics were a way of exorcizing the psychic trauma induced by years of hypnotic indoctrination. Paranormal theorist David Icke has remarked on this possibility in at least one essay. And there are weird loose ends. The "Z" classification (mostly used for wounded or injured persons in combat) Jim got for his army physical (according to Doors drummer

John Densmore, who saw him right after he got it) is another puzzling artifact in this connection. But there's nothing definite here.

On a previous version of his website, which has since been updated, Gerald Pitts apologizes for his inability at this time to answer emails and/or voicemails, providing a phone number he says is the best way to reach him directly. What's his angle? I wondered. Is he trying to promote the rodeo business or something? I wadded up some tissue paper and stuffed it between my lips and gums to disguise the tone of my voice, then I punched in the numbers and waited. It was gonna be great. Unfortunately, all I got was the operator's message saying the person I was calling had not yet set up a voicemail account. Says Dan Shaw in a blurb on YouTube, "I met Gerald Pitts, agent of the alleged Jim Morrison, and he seems sincere—naive perhaps, but he's just a rodeo photographer & auctioneer, not a slick con man. He may be being conned, but I'm still open to the possibility Jim's alive. I don't know much about Jim Morrison, not a big fan; I want to see more evidence, too."

With the passage of time, the amount of public interest in Jim's disputed death has lessened progressively. Director Oliver Stone's movie *The Doors*, released in 1991, made no mention of a faked death beyond an exposition of the rumors afoot when he died, none of which focused on his family ties. The same director's ambitious *JFK* was released the same year, leaving little if any doubt in the mass mind that Kennedy's death was most likely some kind of an inside job of some sort, but pop culture had outgrown the issues involved, if only in a superficial sense—the general public didn't care.

Lizard Sun

I found a phone number for Floyd Bocox, former president and CEO of Lizard Sun Entertainment, estranged former associate* of Jim Morrison's would-be son, Cliff, in Los Angeles. I asked him whether or not he believed Cliff was really Jim's son. Floyd paused and took a deep breath before answering, in an apologetic tone, as if he wasn't quite certain, "I'm being honest, no." Floyd bankrolled Cliff Morrison and his mother, Weiden, for a couple of years to the tune of hundreds of thousands a year, sincerely believing Cliff's story that he was Jim's son, and Lorraine's that she'd had an affair with the Lizard King. Waylon Krieger, son of Doors guitarist Robby Krieger, joined the Lizard Sun band for a while. Even Jim Morrison's brother-in-law, Cliff's "Uncle Alan" Graham, part of the Morrison family's inner circle who formerly served as Larry Flynt's bodyguard, believed it. But with his refusal to undergo DNA testing, times have changed. Even formerly credulous music journalist Al Bowman, founder of the LA Music Awards, who was present at the deaths of Morrison, Jimi Hendrix and Janis Joplin, Flynt's wife, Althea, and was even associated with Courtney Love near the time of Kurt Cobain's supposed overdose in 1994 (which ought to lend some weight to his position on the matter, whether or not you buy the line Bowman was in any way involved) has since retracted his endorsement of "the fraud Cliff Marsden Morrison," as has Bocox in a series of self-produced videos posted on YouTube.

Regardless of genetic heritage, Cliff's voice sounds exactly like Jim's in songs like "Rock Star" and "One Black Sheep" from his 1998 release, *Know Peaking*, so it seemed believable. But red flags began popping up indicating Cliff and Lorraine had Mafia connections, or were paid government snitches, causing even the formerly credulous Graham to warn Bocox, who'd by this time started a company called Lizard Sun Entertainment named after Cliff's band, away from association with the pair. Everything hit the fan when Floyd arranged a reality show for Cliff with the William Morris Entertainment Agency provided he would consent to a DNA test proving he was Jim's offspring. Negotiations broke off abruptly at this point, suggesting Cliff had something to hide. I can understand not wanting to cheapen the family name with a reality show. Perhaps relations between Cliff and Bocox were strained for another reason. In any case, why refuse a DNA test?

A hard copy of *Know Peaking*, allegedly financed by the Mafia, currently sells for roughly $100 on amazon, but free downloads appear to be available. Cliff and the Lizard Sun Band have a nice sound, even Floyd Bocox still agrees. Cliff and Lorraine were arrested for using an unauthorized recording of Jim's voice reading some of his poetry on their album, *Color of People*, which was bankrolled by Floyd and subsequently suppressed. They had enough juice to avoid being locked up in the general population somehow, and ultimately to avoid the charge itself, as a mysterious favor from prison officials. This is a gray area for students of the Morrison family's hidden history, in terms of evidence for or against Cliff's claim of kinship, since Jim's father. Admiral George S. Morrison, or "Steve," who died last month, may he rest in peace, often referred to by Cliff as "grandfather," had a lot of top-secret connections, which raises the question: were Cliff and Lorraine coddled this way because they were Admiral Steve's blood kin, because of their Mafia connections, or because of their prior status as paid "snitches," (as has also been alleged).

According to Floyd, "Uncle Al" Graham told him Lorraine was a past associate of the Manson Family whose only past association with Morrison was in an attempt to infiltrate his personal life in Paris for one government agency or another just before his death in 1971. This is another gray area for fans of weirdness generally, because of the evidence cited in prior articles suggesting Morrison's possible status as an "experimental individual" working consciously or unconsciously for MK-ULTRA and the CIA. Was she spying on him or bringing him information?

Cliff Morrison requested my phone number, which I sent him a few days ago. Floyd Bocox warned me he was dangerously unstable, a former pal of "Timothy Leary's son," with whom he once reportedly dosed all the ducks in Marina del Rey by dumping a vatful of acid to avoid a bust. Floyd strikes like a nice guy who was likely taken advantage of by opportunism on the part of Cliff and/or his mother. Still another possibility is that Lorraine knows more about things than she ever told Cliff. David Icke might propose another theory involving refusing the DNA test for fear of being exposed as reptilians.

The right side of Floyd's MySpace page is dedicated to promoting Cliff's music, (certainly forgivable considering all the money he's invested in Cliff and the Lizard Sun Band, not to mention their sheer listenability) and the left to his new artist, Jayo Felony, who has appeared previously with hip hop artists Snoop Dogg, Jam Master Jay and others. Do a search on "Lizard Sun Entertainment" and the link to a site with Floyd's name alongside Weiden's appears first, but a link to his taped protest of Cliff's appearance at the LA Music Awards, titled "Swindlers" is the next result. No call from Cliff Morrison yet. I want his side of the story.

*The two have been in and out of association several times and seem to be on good terms as of 8/2024.

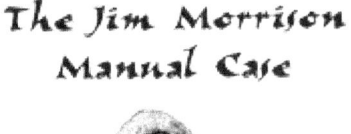

5 THROUGH THE BEAT TIME MACHINE WITH EDS. WHITE, CASSADY AND CAYCE

REVIEW OF A COLLECTION OF LETTERS BETWEEN KEROUAC AND DENVER'S ED WHITE AND AN OVERVIEW OF NEAL AND CAROLYN CASSADY'S CONNECTION TO EDGAR CAYCE VIA CONSIDERATION OF CAROLYN'S MEMOIR OFF THE ROAD AND OTHER SOURCES

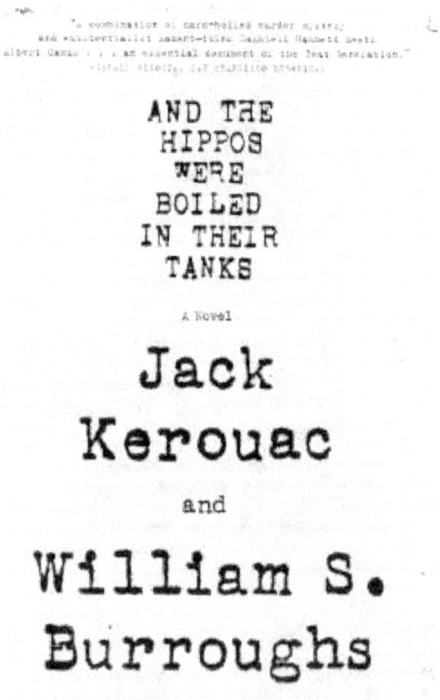

AND THE
HIPPOS
WERE
BOILED
IN THEIR
TANKS

A Novel

Jack Kerouac

and

William S. Burroughs

I'D heard of this early collaboration between Jack Kerouac and William S. Burroughs years ago and was impressed and pleased to find the published version readily available on a recent trip to the Colfax Tattered Cover in the form of a highly palatable plain spoken prose work. Far from sharing a rigid code, the so-called Beat Generation were united by their progressively contrarian stance as artists, despite glaring social and political differences which would surface and do them all a disservice later, as fans of their biographies might note. To the contrary, *And the Hippos Were Boiled in their Tanks*, which predates both books commonly considered to be either author's first novel, is a capable effort at hard boiled minimalism in the fictionalized retelling of the murder of David Kammerer by Kerouac's and Burroughs' mutual friend, Lucien Carr. Facts we knew from the biographers and Kerouac's own last published novel, *Vanity of Duluoz*—how Jack helped Lucien dispose of the murder weapon by dropping it down a sewer grate, how Burroughs advised Lucien turn himself in, how Jack was jailed as an accessory after the fact, and had to get married to get the bail money from Edie Kerouac Parker's parents after being turned down by his own Pop—but all those facts are given new grace and fictional form in this artwork, which I found especially enjoyable, despite the tendency of purists to find fault in internet forums.

Hippos was written before what was previously considered to have been Jack's debut, *The Town and the City*, thus lacking its sweeping Wolfean images or *On the Road*'s resultant spontaneous prose in conscious intuitive imitation of bop rhythms, both latter affectations. If anything, what hints there are of what may be considered Kerouac's signature long-windedness are purely constructive in what they add to the otherwise deliberately clipped narrative voice. Burroughs' pages resemble in tone his commonly acknowledged debut novel, Junky, a diary of his dealings with the New York underworld as a heroin addict. The interplay of these two voices is invariably complementary, providing a fair rendition of their friendship's mutually complementary nature in those early days, when Jack and Allen went to Columbia U, and Burroughs, not a student, lived off campus, and Herbert Huncke was hanging around. The publication of this early collaboration of Kerouac and Burroughs was postponed for sixty years at the wish of one of its principals, respected career UPI newshawk Lou Carr, who maintained friendships with Kerouac and Burroughs throughout their lives. Carr is recently deceased, making the details of his existence fair game, as seen in the film *Kill Your Darlings*, which can be said to have taken some liberties in its presentation of Carr's character. Even this reporter feels less than wholesome beating this particular dead horse, which remains the central social event synchronous with the development of that literary movement, in competition only with Henry Cannastra's accidental decapitation by attempting to climb out of a moving subway car through the window.

Another less-known Beat document is *Write a madder letter if you can*, a catalogue of the collected correspondence of On the Road author and Beat king Jack Kerouac and Colorado native artist and architect Ed White. White was a graduate of Columbia University in New York, who helped design the Boettcher Memorial Tropical Conservatory and Mitchell Hall in the Botanic Gardens, all located in Denver. The collection of correspondence between the two, published by Glenn Horowitz, Bookseller Inc. spans the years 1947 to 1969, covering the span of Kerouac's career as a novelist, all the ups and downs of his troubled life. Along with Neal Cassady, Ed White helped establish the portal connecting the East Coast-based first Beats to Denver, Colorado. The circle of Columbia University students who comprised the nucleus of what came to be known as the Beat Generation had a powerful, vital connection to Denver via postmodern supersucker Cassady, Ed White, Hal Chase and others, all with connections to Columbia. So close was Kerouac's relationship with Denver that he developed the code word "Elitch" to refer to marijuana smoking, having enjoyed that activity in a West Denver amusement park by that name on more than one memorable occasion. Each of Jack's letters is accompanied by White's illuminating commentary, characterizing the nuances of the friends' correspondence.

After my beats in Denver book was published, CO Rocky Mountain High Tours almost hired me as a Beat historian providing travelogue pertinent to the several remaining spots from Cassady's childhood and youth here in Denver. I reread Neal's widow Carolyn Cassady's excellent memoir, *Off the Road*. In this work, the recently transitioned Mrs. Cassady recounts her experience as a Bennington graduate in residence at what is now the Colburn Hotel on 10th and Grant while attending Denver University, upon meeting Neal Cassady eventually moving to California with him and bearing three of his children, in the process being introduced to all his teammates, from the riff raff to the artists and intellectuals like Kerouac and Ginsberg, providing over the next several years the closest thing to a stable family the troubled Neal had ever known, as evidenced by his repeated failures to comport himself appropriately in that placement.

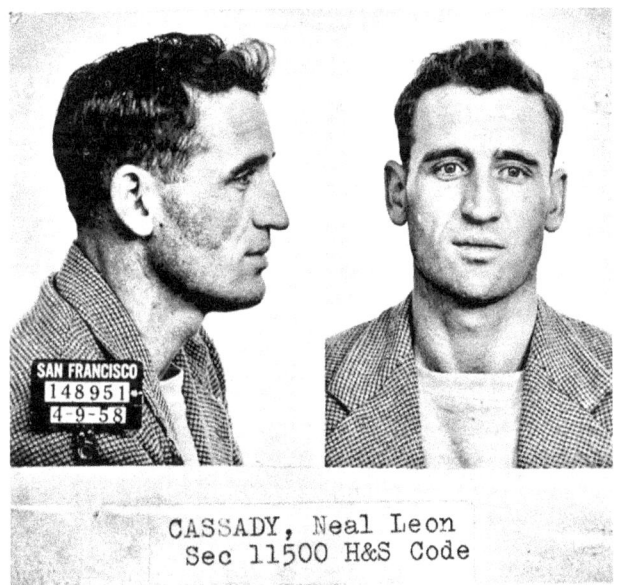

Neal Cassady mugshot

There followed twenty-some years of tumultuous relationship with Neal and the people drawn into his orbit, also including William S. Burroughs, Ken Kesey, Lawrence Ferlinghetti, Gordon Lish, and others. *Off the Road* is an interesting companion to Kerouac's *On the Road* (in particular the *Original Scroll*) and *Visions of Cody* since parts overlap, also Hunter S. Thompson's *Hells Angels* and Tom Wolfe's *Electric Kool-Aid Acid Test*, for the same reason. In the latter two, the majority of Neal's life at the time, occupied mainly by driving the bus for Ken Kesey's Merry Pranksters from Acid Test to Acid Test, was unknown to Carolyn (which produces an interesting effect when the two books are read simultaneously). In a sense, *Off the Road* is as much about Ms. Cassady's relationship with Kerouac as with Cassady, since the two were on-again off-again lovers, and their pairing represented an equal conflict or challenge as Jack's closing alcoholic period began to take the form of alcoholic phone calls insisting he was Jesus Christ and so forth. Equally valuable to the inspiration and enjoyment of life evoked by Wolfe or Kerouac's portrait of Neal C is the sensibility, endurance and positive aspiration of Carolyn Cassady as a mother and a spiritual seeker whose own road was more of a duty than any sort of fling. As a book reviewer, this reporter has long been familiar with the predictable objections of other readers loath to admit new aspects to their cherished authorial ideals (very much so in the case of the recently released Burroughs-Kerouac collaboration, *And the Hippos were Boiled in their Tanks,* to judge by the reviews on Amazon), and as fans, they're completely entitled, of course, but this reporter would earnestly plea that an equal amount of respect be given to Mrs. Cassady's account. She wasn't Neal's "One and Only," but let there be no doubt, she loved him very much, in spite or because of their dissimilarity as types, never losing sight of the momentous quality in terms of life lessons for both of them.

I had known about Neal's discovery of the book *Many Mansions* by psychologist Gina Cerminara while cleaning the train cars one day (he worked as a brakeman for the SP railroad until being sent to San Quentin for offering two joints as payment for a ride home). Said book detailed and analyzed the history and legacy of "sleeping prophet" Edgar Cayce, providing an understandable diagramming of the function of reincarnational karma. Edgar Cayce's miracle health cures delivered under hypnosis helped thousands until, after lengthy success, he was asked about reincarnation and delivered a lengthy response in the same calm voice. Cayce, a reverent Disciple of Christ in his waking life, was shocked to learn of what he'd said, since it didn't correspond with his habitual dogma, but in time came to peace with these utterances, since he felt they were doing people good, and in so doing, broadened his own understanding of the Bible. Neal was immediately captivated by Cayce's story and convinced of his philosophy's verity. His mania communicated to Carolyn, whose own pursuit of Cayceana was lifelong, and served along with her husband's to disharmonize them with the other Beats, who, beginning with Kerouac, had developed a fixation on Buddhist ideals, which, while not entirely dissimilar, were far less practical. In their time, Neal and Carolyn even met with Cayce's son, Hugh Lynn, early advocate Elsie Sechrist—Neal called her "See Christ" —and reformed reincarnation-believing convict Starr Daily in their vigorous efforts at salvation in the here and now. Carolyn's is the most thorough account we have of that aspect of Neal's life so far. It's worthy of note that in this sense, Neal Cassady, who inspired a revolution in literary expression, also provided the inspiration for an ongoing revolution in American spirituality because of countercultural influence.

6 THE HOLE-IN-CORNER MAN: BUKOWSKI AS OUTSIDER ARTIST

BUKOWSKI THE LITERARY ARTIST CONSIDERED AS AN EXAMPLE OF THE OUTSIDER TYPE PER COLIN WILSON

"At first sight, the Outsider is a social problem. He is the hole-in-corner man . . . the twentieth century simply alters the way of presenting him, feels the need to place him in his environment. The treatment of the theme becomes more clinical, more analytical. The hilltops and mountain caves disappear from the scenery props; [the] Outsider comes on, with his small room in a modern city. His main concern is still the fact that his surroundings seem incapable of fully satisfying his desires. He is afraid that the world was not created to fulfill the demands of the human spirit . . . the world into which he has been born is always a world without values. Compared to his own appetite for a purpose and a direction, the way most men live is not living at all; it is drifting (Wilson, 11, 49, 143)."

So wrote Englishman Colin Wilson in the 1950's, and thus a new psychological flavor was coined: the *Outsider*. Wilson was still in his twenties when the book was published and became quite famous briefly for his youthful erudition. The above quote sums up the attitude and methodology of American writer Henry Charles Bukowski (1920-1994). Not for almost thirty or forty years after the events chronicled in his fictionalized autobiography, *Ham On Rye*, did Charles Bukowski begin to gain any significant acclaim as a writer, and only then for his deliberately sleazy column in the L.A. weekly *Open City*, which popularized his name and launched the groundswell of support which would ultimately make him famous, but seems simultaneously to have poisoned him against serious consideration by the academics. Bukowski, if he cared at all, was likely pleased by this. He died in San Pedro, California at the age of seventy-three. The inscription on his tombstone reads: DON'T TRY . . .

Ham on Rye, titled in homage to Salinger, and also as a metaphor for the young Bukowski's feelings of being sandwiched between his parents, and the author's tendency to ham it up when drinking rye whiskey, is an overlooked landmark in the grand tradition of the *bildungsroman*, a masterpiece of modern fiction. In one sense it's the story of a boy's coming-of-age during the depression and into the first days of WWII, in another it's the story of the incompatibility of the World Outside with the developing artistic temperament.

The narrator, Henry Chinaski, comes quickly to the perception of himself as an outsider:

> "The first thing I remember is being under something. It was a table. I saw the table leg. I saw the legs of the people, and a portion of the tablecloth hanging down. It was dark under there, I liked being down there . . . Nobody seemed to know that I was there.
> . . . There was sunlight upon the rug and upon the legs of the people. I liked the sunlight. The legs of the people were not interesting, not like the tablecloth which hung down, not like the table leg, not like the sunlight (*Rye*, 9)."

Hank's instinctive wariness of the other people is confirmed as he grows older. His father— an unemployed ex-soldier who leaves every morning for an imaginary job and returns every evening at the same time for the sake of appearances— gives him regular beatings with a razor strop for such minor infractions as missing a single blade of grass with the mower. His mother is eerily present-yet-absent in these passages, like a ghost. Though totally dominated by her brutal, insensitive husband, we get the sense she is culpable in Hank's abuse by her complacence.

> "MAMA! MAMA!" He ran into the house. "What is it?" "I found a hair." "You did?" "Come, I'll show you." He came out of the house quickly with my mother following. "Here! Here! I'll show you!" He got down on his hands and knees. "I can see it! I can see *two* of them!" My mother got down with him. I wondered if they were crazy... "Yes, daddy, I see them..." They both got up. My mother walked into the house. My father looked at me... "Into the bathroom... Take your pants down (*Rye*, 69,70)."

When he touches on politics, he does it indirectly, with his eye on the greater importance of the story he's telling, dropping some dry social commentary in describing his high school R.O.T.C. squad as mostly consisting of guys from rich neighborhoods who didn't care who won the war since they knew they'd be okay. Fired from his demeaning job at "Mears-Starbuck" shortly after graduating high school, Henry enrolls at L.A. City College at the urging of his parents, where he discovers politics and flirts briefly with Nazism "out of sheer alienation and a natural contrariness (*Rye*, 236)," but is quickly disillusioned once he realizes the Nazis are just like all the other people he's known— "restrictive and careful, all alike. And I've got to live with these fuckers for the rest of my life, I thought. God, they all had assholes and sexual organs and their mouths and their armpits. They shit and they chattered, and they were dull as horse dung... Was I the only person who was distracted by this future without a chance?" (*Rye*, 262) Forcibly evicted from the family home after his father's discovery of a drawer full of short stories, finally separate from the poisonous family dynamic, Chinaski rents a room in a cheap rooming house and embarks on what was to become (for Bukowski) a lifelong career of drinking recklessly and living for his art. *Factotum* is a novel that begins by detailing the young Bukowski's experiences on the job-market. Hapless resident of a world ill-suited to his accommodation, he works at a number of jobs, but never quite fits in. Bukowski was also a poet, but his poetry has such a prose-y rhythm sometimes, one wonders why he never published it as prose.

> *something*
> I'm out of matches.
> the springs in my couch
> are broken.
> they stole my footlocker.
> they stole my oil painting of
> two pink eyes.
> my car broke down.
> eels climb my bathroom walls.
> my love is broken.
> but the stock market went up
> today (*Dog,* 156).

Barfly came out in the eighties, a film approximation of Bukowski's hardscrabble youth on skid row (where he went on purpose) drinking and watching and dreaming and wishing for fame as a writer. It quickly became a cult favorite. It's another reason most people know him best as a drunk and might be surprised to consider him a worthy commentator. Per Russel Harrison, "There are several reasons why we may be tempted to regard Bukowski as an apolitical novelist . . . [but] the representation of politics in [his] novels must be seen as involving more than just the protagonist's views, no matter how central he is to them (Harrison,160)."

Linda King and Charles Bukowski

Hank might have hated this book, the voice is way too clunky, but

Harrison makes a valid point: Bukowski somehow manages to *seem* objective, even when he's kidding, and thereby more convincing. He describes this distinctive semi-detached perspective in his posthumously-published poem, "the joke is on the sun," apparently equating it with personal integrity:

> as the game continues you
> should seek to say ever more clearly
> what you truly
> believe
> even if what you truly
> believe
> turns out to be
> wrong. (*Madness,* 105)

An extremely prolific writer, Bukowski produced poems, short stories, novels, even one screenplay, as we've seen. He was often unabashedly autobiographical, but never hesitated to change his facts for the sake of a better fiction. Regardless of the balance between these two ingredients, his voice remains essentially the same throughout his catalog. He was qualified unfit to serve in WWII because of a condition called "extreme sensitivity of character." In this passage from the short story *Remember Pearl Harbor?* he gives young Chinaski's quirky reaction:

> Now that I couldn't be in the war I almost wanted the war. Yet, at the same time, I was glad to be out of it. My objection to war was not that I had to kill somebody or be killed senselessly, that hardly mattered. What I objected to was to be denied the right to sit in a small room and starve and drink cheap wine and go crazy in my own way and at my own leisure (*South,* 85).

To quote Colin Wilson once more, "This is the Outsider's

wretchedness, for all men have a herd instinct that leads them to believe that what the majority does must be right. Unless he can evolve a set of values that can correspond to his own higher intensity of purpose, he may as well throw himself under a bus, for he will always be an outcast and a misfit (Wilson,142)." Bukowski has his own de-facto system of values, one that favors those parts of himself he feels are most essential: comfort and style, and coolly disdains all attempts at regimentation and conditioning— "I didn't want to make friends, I didn't want to make enemies, I just didn't want them or it or the thing. To kill or be killed hardly mattered (*South of no North*, Bukowski, 86)."In this poem, "my favorite movie," after watching a bargirl depart with a returning soldier as an unconcerned pianist accompanies, he qualifies this self-evolved barometer of right and wrong:

> the piano player then moves slowly into another
> tune and I used to think, jesus, he should have
> her, but he's certainly not in a hurry
> about anything, seems to have more sense than most, he
> doesn't worry about nazis or a better world
> or how to act tough enough to deserve a woman
> in a banana dress;
> he has that satisfied smile,
> wears old-fashioned and comfort-
> able suspenders and you realize all he finally wants
> is that drink on the piano and
> then to play another tune, he knows the price of
> every-thing else:
> too much (*Open*, 85-86)

He's in love with the miraculous. It's one of my favorite things about his writing. He's more than just a shirker of unwanted tasks. The choice he's made is aesthetic. He's more interested in leisurely artistic pursuits than common, sad human habits like politics, and all their ill-gotten gains (like fawning bargirls). His work abounds with references to bars and alcohol, which may explain his lack of popularity with the mainstream. In the words of recently passed Cal. State Long Beach English professor, Gerald Locklin:

> "As everyone knows, Bukowski drinks a bit, and he can be unfair, in person and in print, at certain levels of the bottle, but there is also a purity in his unsparing view of humanity . . . Only those who have read *Ham On Rye* can appreciate how for someone with Bukowski's childhood . . . booze represented not destruction but salvation, an alternative to suicide . . . or homicide. Furthermore, he admits to the heresy of having a drink while writing. He says that he enjoys writing and he enjoys drinking, so why shouldn't he enjoy them at the same time? (Locklin, 7,18)"

I'm barely a drinker myself, and I've never been to a race-track (Bukowski loved to play the horses), so I have to pick and choose my favorite bits, but he published more than forty books during his lifetime, and the posthumous poetry keeps on coming. Considering the volume of his output, not to mention the scope of his influence, Charles Bukowski's absence from current college textbooks on postmodern American fiction and poetry (at least that's how it was at Metro State) is both puzzling and unfortunate. He was a jack-of-all-trades, an outsider, a drunk, a poet, a comic. More than anything else, he was an artist, as evidenced by "my favorite movie"'s benedictory conclusion:

The piano player seems content enough
and then somebody asks for
a new tune and he runs it off, first sipping the
drink, lighting a cigarette, and then his fingers
run up and down the keys, up and down, it's
good and easy, it asks for nothing, asks for so little
that it gives hope to all those who ask
for no chance, who ask for nothing at all,
who just ask for someplace to sit quietly and wait
for the slanting sun moving on the wall
and for the peace of soft rain
spread out all over the place (*Open All Night,* Bukowski, 86).

7 LIZARD SON: A CONVERSATION WITH CLIFF MORRISON

SOUNDALIKE CLIFF MORRISON CLAIMS TO BE JIM'S SON

Shot from YouTube by the author.

JIM Morrison's alleged son Cliff called me back the afternoon before the U.S. led detonation of the moon purportedly in search of water on Friday, October 9th, 2009. He said he was about to start rocking the world. According to him, the U.S. was sitting on top of a super- volcano in Yellowstone Park, and crazy shit was gonna happen when it blew. "That's why I'm doing it now." His voice was steely and determined.

"Are you talking about 2012?"

"More like mid-13."

I kept telling Cliff I had no way of recording our conversation and asking if he'd let me send him some questions by email. "What about the moon mission?" I hazarded. "They're gonna crash two spaceships into the moon tomorrow—what's that all about?"

"It has to do with the earth's alignment. I'm just going by government files of what they're doing, you know."

"Okay."

"All that stuff Floyd's been saying about my mother and I getting arrested, it's just bullshit he spreads around the internet to make himself feel powerful. He's the one who's going to jail. He's been hanging around with crips, and those people are not as forgiving as I used to be. He might end up losing his life."

"I'm glad you called, I want to get your side of the story, too. What do you have to say about William James Loyer, the cowboy in Oregon who Gerald Pitts says is Jim Morrison?"

"Jim Loyer's a good guy."

"Is he Jim Morrison?"

"He can be anyone he wants to be."

"Is he your father?"

"He's not my father, but he can be anyone he wants to be. On earth you can be anyone you want to be."

This statement could be taken in a humorous light given the speaker's contested identity but had the ring of concession to a greater need on the fixated Loyer's part he couldn't mention. Cliff denies his former manager Floyd Bocox's claims that he and his mother were ever imprisoned, which he says are nothing but blatant slander. "I think Gerald Pitts was just trying to make money. A man walked the earth thousands of years ago, and he was very forgiving. You know who that man was?"

"Jesus?"

"Jesus. And you know where a man gets sent when he sins. Who does the punishing there?"

"The devil?"

"The devil. And who does he work for?"
"Uh, God?"
"But I'm not as forgiving as he was."
"You're not as forgiving as Christ?"
"Nowhere near. Floyd Bocox is gonna burn. Tonight's going to be a very interesting night," he promised.
"What's happening tonight?"
"Do you not have access to the internet?"
"Sure, I just don't know what's happening."

By the author & friend(s).

Cliff told me there was an invitation-only performance of his Lizard Sun Band at the Whisky a Go Go that night. "I've been holding a grudge for 45 years." The Doors were banned from the Whisky because their song "The End" contained scatological lyrics inspired by the Greek myth of Oedipus and the movie In Cold Blood. Cliff says he'll call again and let me know in advance by voicemail before he does. I should have asked why he refused the DNA test. I've also heard it was the Morrison Estate who refused to allow it, and not Cliff's doing at all. I received an email from Alan Graham asking how dare I go to press with such slanderous third-party allegations, meaning the slander by Bocox, without consulting him first. We exchanged a few emails, and he asked me to help him edit the re-release of his book on Morrison. "Sure."

8 DAN FANTE READS AT MUTINY

JOHN FANTE'S SON AND INHERITOR OF HIS WRITERLY TALENTS, DAN FANTE, MAKES AN APPEARANCE AT DENVER PUNK COFFEE HOUSE MUTINY INFO CAFÉ

DAN Stafford and Luke Janes, owners of Kilgore Books, were in attendance. My friend Kat Works showed up. Tom Piccirilli was there, rest him, author of several horror, action and adventure books (including *The Coldest Mile* and *Nightjack)*, a mountainous presence slow to smile, feet planted widely apart. I kept looking around for Sam Dent, formerly Sam Kane (both pseudonyms), who'd been the first to recommend I read Dan's father's work several years previously, but Sam was known to be a late-night drinker and general recluse, so his absence from this early afternoon event didn't surprised me.

Dan Fante alternated readings from his new memoir and a book of poetry, telling stories of his childhood among great drunk writers sucking money out of Hollywood as Hollywood sucked their creative juices, Nat Wests and Faulkners and Fantes. He told one about the happy gambler William Saroyan (who, according to Dan, always spoke at "megaphone volume") jumping up on his publisher's desk and saying, "Double or nothing, you son of a bitch!" when offered his first $25,000 contract. "And once he gave me his Cadillac. Just tossed me the keys and said, 'Here you go, kid.' Back then, writers were the rock stars!"

Things sure have changed, I thought.

Several churches and schools in the Denver-Boulder area were built by Dan's grandfather, Nicola Fante, before the family's migration to California, but no one seemed to know exactly which ones anymore. Ask the dust.

Dan told about the time he'd been given a message by his late father via a medium in Italy to publish a novel he'd find at the bottom of a certain filing cabinet in Point Dume, Malibu, which turned out to be *The Road to Los Angeles*. I watched him as he spoke, realizing only two generations back in the same bloodline it would have been a bricklayer from Torricella Peligna talking to us.

"Thanks for writing that article," Fante told me after the reading was over. He meant the one announcing the event.

"Oh, sure. Whatever good it did. Hardly anyone came."

"That's okay, I had a good time."

"I never knew you had a hand in the publication of *The Road to Los Angeles*. That's one of my favorite John Fante books."

Dan said it was his personal favorite, which made sense, given his own deliberately unrestrained voice, and his father's ultimate reluctance to publish a novel he'd once felt might "singe the hair off a wolf's rear" it was so explicit.

9 JOHNNY STRIKE ON CRIME AND WRITING

SAN FRANCISCO PUNK BAND CRIME ONCE PLAYED SAN QUENTIN DRESSED AS POLICE OFFICERS. STRIKE, WHO ALSO WROTE SEVERAL NOVELS, WAS THE FRONTMAN

HAVING kicked off in the late sixties on the East Coast, with bands like the Stooges, the American punk wave came to San Francisco late, circa 1976. One of the standouts was a band called CRIME One member, Johnny Strike, relocated for a good spell to Tangier, Morocco, and has distinguished himself as an author with works like *Name of the Stranger*, *Ports of Hell* and *Murder in the Medina*. Bold Venture will be publishing his *The Exploding Memoir* in the spring, a combination of fact & fiction covering the years 1969-1974. A more recent musical effort, Naked Beast, with fellow former Crime members Hank Rank and Joey D'Kaye, still punk as hell, with driving numbers like "Gnostic Wolf" and "Emergency Music Ward" is predicted in this interview, and HoZac will be releasing Vector Command, a two man electro-punk album with D'Kaye Strike describes as sounding like "a combination of Eno and Suicide" as an LP next summer. Mr. Strike did me the favor of answering a few questions about Crime, the punk scene in San Francisco and more.

CRIME's self-produced "Hot Wire My Heart" b/w "Baby, You're so Repulsive," which came out in 1976, was the West Coast's first punk record, but you went on to interview Huncke, Burroughs and even Paul Bowles, indicating prior interest. Did you feel like an emissary from that scene to the punk one?

Maybe the first punk single period unless we count Patti Smith's *Piss Factory*. Or did the Ramones do a single before us? I'm not sure. Not an emissary really since I reverted back to writing full-time which I'd put on hold to do CRIME. I wanted mostly to meet some of the writers who influenced me, Burroughs, Bowles and Huncke and so I thought I might as well conduct interviews as well. I wanted to meet Gysin, Purdy and Ballard too, but I didn't get the opportunity.

CRIME developed a habit of dressing as police officers at Mabuhay Gardens appearances, alarming Herb Caen of "beatnik" infamy and leading up to a gig at San Quentin Prison. What was that like?

Fun, amazing and unnerving, especially when they informed us of the "no hostage" rule. No negotiations would be permitted if we were nabbed by the inmates. But we pulled it off.

I saw Mr. Ferlinghetti's remark on CNN that bags full of cash and no manners are putting the kibosh on San Francisco's DIY character, after which I saw a post that said racist policing was speeding San Francisco's gentrification. Who are SF's current creative underground today and how does it feel?

Being something of a recluse these days I don't know or feel a lot about that, but I did write *San Francisco's Doomed!* From what I've seen and read I'd have to agree with Lawrence. Every new generation feels they are the underground and have their finger on the pulse. We considered ourselves a rock 'n roll band more than anything else. "Underground" was something like "punk" which was invented by the press covering it.

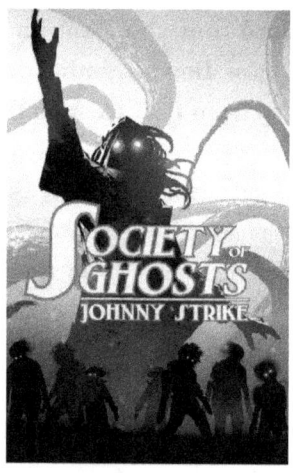

You traveled extensively, including an extended stay in Morocco's "Interzone," Tangier, and Mexico City. Your novel, *Ports of Hell* features an encomium by William S. Burroughs, who was an early advocate of the punk scene in New York. Did he like your music too?

Burroughs was into the music of his day: bebop jazz, old tunes. I understand he was a fan of Viennese waltzes. If you haven't heard his drunken singing of Danny Boy, or Adios Muchachos I recommend digging those up.

CRIME, the Avengers and the Dills were considered the "unholy trinity" of San Francisco punk. The Dead Kennedy's came later, with hardcore. V. Vale provided bridge from past local scenes, having worked at City Lights and played drums in Blue Cheer. How would punks describe their place in San Francisco's counter-cultural lineage?

I thought Vale played piano with a candelabra on top. I believe it was very short-lived. The punks would all have different opinions. I see a definite jump from the Beats to Punks skipping over the hippies ha ha, although we must even give them some credit. I was once a dirty hippy too in the John Waters sense of the word, not the peace and love type.

[EDITOR'S NOTE: Sorry, Val, piano it was.] Your spoken work with backing band Remote Viewer has been described as "lit punk." Have there been performances in San Francisco?

Yes I did a number of readings for Rudos and Rubes when they brought out my short story collection. Mostly fun and it developed into a full-fledged group at first called Doctor D. and finally NAKED BEAST. Our album is in the can and was produced by George S. Rosenthal, Hank's son. I'm very pleased with it and we plan to release it digitally this year. There's some CRIME to it, but also experimental moves including a few short readings I did along with atmospheric background sounds. Rather than a bunch of tunes it's more of a trip, or a listening journey. Joey D'Kaye who filled in for Ripper at times back in the day, has joined us as well, playing a number of instruments including a theremin. Naked Beast has been out for a while now and picking up rave reviews, good airplay and sales. Available in LP, CD and digital.

10 BEYOND WRITING WITH PAUL KRASSNER

RECENTLY DEPARTED INVESTIGATIVE SATIRIST, PROLIFIC AUTHOR AND STANDUP COMEDIAN PAUL KRASSNER WAS A FRIEND OF THE MERRY PRANKSTERS AND THE CHICAGO 8, FOUNDED THE YIPPIES, ONCE TOOK ACID WITH GROUCHO MARX AND WAS MY FRIEND AND LONGTIME PEN-PAL

WHILE Larry Flynt was in the Medical Center in Springfield, 60s activist, investigative satirist and Yippies founder Paul Krassner took over as HUSTLER's publisher. It would be a mistake to stereotype Krassner, author of one of the broadest lives I've heard about so far, as strictly a sixties-based persona, the kind of mistake made far too often in today's pigeonhole-happy media landscape. I see him instead as a timelessly riotous spirit who happened to find himself in the bullseye of change during prime time and opted to participate in that whirlwind rather than objectifying it out of his heart as he grew past it. Krassner says he "first woke up at the age of six," when he scratched one leg with the other during a performance at Carnegie Hall on January 14, 1939, as a violin prodigy rather than interrupt his rendition of the "Vivaldi Concerto in A Minor" and learned his first big lesson from the audience's resulting amusement ("One person's logic is another person's humor"). He was interviewed in 1986 for V. Vale's *Pranks!* and persists into the current age as a standup comic and regular contributor to the Huffington Post and other mags online and off.

Confessions of a Raving Unconfined Nut: Misadventures in the Counterculture, the expanded version of Krassner's autobiography, its title pranksterly co-opted from some procrustean's heartfelt disparagement, will ring especially familiar to fans of his work, but here, for the first time is his concerted effort at a definitive chronicle of his life in toto. *Confessions*, including details of his time as editor of Lenny Bruce's autobiography, as an intimate of Merry Prankster Ken Kesey, as founder of the YIP (Youth international Party or "Yippies"), referencing his relationships with everyone from queen of the conspiracy theorists Mae Brussell to pioneering Black comic Dick Gregory to HUSTLER publisher Larry Flynt to Chicago 7ers Abbie Hoffman and Jerry Rubin to writers Hunter S. Thompson and William S. Burroughs, is important and great. Krassner was conceivably the very first zinester with his infamous The Realist (which explains his gracious and discursive response to some questions I sent him a few years ago as co-editor of a zine called The Gut), for years ran an informal abortion referral service, and as a method journalist in the psychedelic era, turned on with such unlikely subjects as Manson followers Squeaky Fromme and Sandra Good, even once with Groucho Marx (who had this insight into human nature while tripping: "Everybody has their own Laurel and Hardy . . . Your little Oliver Hardy bawls you out— he says, 'Well, this is a fine mess you've gotten us into.' And your little Stan Laurel gets all weepy— 'Oh, Ollie, I couldn't help it. I'm sorry, I did the best I could . . .'"). And those are just bubbles of spit in the ocean of Krassner's magnificent personal history. Shortly after the release of *Confessions* in 2009, I interviewed him.

Q. The just-released expanded version of your autobiography provides a bird's eye view into your interaction at one or another degree of intimacy with literally most notables in late 20th century American culture, from Groucho Marx to Lenny Bruce to Ken Kesey to Robert Anton Wilson. Was it luck or fate, your proximity to all these exceptional people?

> A. It was simply that I had a unique magazine which resonated with the wave-length of such countercultural icons like, and The Realist's circulation increased by their word-of-mouth and gift subscriptions.

Q. You recently left the social networking site Facebook after your account got hacked by some "right-wingers" who used it to mass mail spam of some kind, with no apparent point of purpose beyond malice. You expressed appreciation for the broad range of communications enabled by that site and said you felt conflicted about leaving. Sad but true, the artistry and ethics of popular pranksterism appear to have devolved to this level of immature sadism in modern times, with a few brilliant exceptions like Banksy, the Yes Men, and Alan Abel, who carries on hoaxing the gullible media. Please name your favorite exception to this depressing statistic.

A. I don't know if it was right-wingers; could've been just electronic vandalism. In any case, my decision to quit Facebook was made before the hacker attack. The reason was because, with 5,000+ Facebook friends, it had become a distraction from working on my long awaited (by me) first novel, and so the irony was that at least 95% of them were fans of my writing. My current hero is Julian Assange—WikiLeaks being the ultimate prank, internationally pulling down the pants of arrogant officials who were embarrassed by the truth and whose criminal actions have been exposed.

Paul Krassner

Q. My own interest in weird news began as a child when I heard about the murders supposedly inspired by the Beatles'

White Album, and while not a "conspiracy theorist" per se, I remain convinced that the map is not the territory represented, to quote Korzybski. In your opinion as someone who met with Ms. Fromme and other Family members, however fleetingly, what do you think the politically fired Lynette "Squeaky" Fromme will do now? Abbie Hoffman was able to profoundly shock by wearing an American flag shirt, then the culture grew around this subversion and absorbed it, Larry Flynt had to wear one as a diaper to rouse the same degree of ire. The promotional poster for the recently released biopic American: The Bill Hicks Story pictures that outlaw comic wearing a star-spangled gag. Terrorism has replaced Communism as the prime Bugaboo, and the most obvious enemy is corporate personhood, which seems to have been in the works all along and just now come to fruition. What's next for us vs. them?

> A. I have no idea what Squeaky Fromme is up to. My last contact with her was to send her a note when she was in jail before going on trial for the attempted assassination of then-President Gerald Ford. I teased her about wearing a Little Red Riding Hoodie Outfit in order to fade into the crowd. Abbie Hoffman got busted for wearing an American flag shirt, and now Jon Stewart and Stephen Colbert wore American flag jackets at their televised Sanity/Fear rally. What was once taboo has become a fashion statement. Recently I was at a demonstration against the billionaire Koch brothers, who are the epitome of corporate personhood, galloping toward the marriage of government and corporations, Mussolini's definition of fascism.

Q. Sites like Facebook have empowered human connectivity to the point of becoming instrumental anti-establishment tools and enabling caste-busting interviews and articles with everyone from writers and musicians to metaphysicians to quantum physicists. Conversely, the majority of users are lulled into complacency by junk like Farmville and Mafia Wars. It would be easy to find this especially disheartening, but I find myself wondering if it's ever been any different. Hasn't most of your own life been spent in opposition to the majority mass?

> A: Mel Brooks has said that 95% of everything is crap, which is why Levi Johnston has become a national celebrity only because he didn't use a condom when he fucked Bristol Palin. My tendency has been to seek out the other 5%. Americans have been dumbed down to make them more susceptible to propaganda, whether from TV commercials or politicians. What they have in common is the use of fear to persuade consumers and voters alike. Our national anthem begins "Oh, say can you see?..." and the answer is no, we're blinded by authority figures who reek with hypocrisy. But, in the words of William Bennett —former education czar, drug czar, morality czar, gambling czar— "Hypocrisy is better than having no values at all." Ah, yes words to live by.

Q. Last year I read a book by Adam Gorightly compiling all the theories about the backstory of the Tate-LaBianca slayings, in which he reported that when you became publisher of HUSTLER, pioneering conspiracy theorist Mae Brussell had accused you, Dick Gregory and Larry Flynt as being members of what she called the Power Control Group, a sort of top-down dis-info association. I can't find anything online to corroborate this, and am completely without prejudice, just wondering what you think about that. Robert Anton Wilson defines the word "zetetic" as never fully believing in anyone else's BS(belief system),not even your own. That's the kind of journalist I aim to be, so it's from within this non-prioritized nebula I'm asking.

> A. That's bizarre. Mae Brussell wrote her first articles for The Realist and years later she contributed to Hustler. Like many conspiracy researchers--as brilliant and dedicated as Mae was--she also became suspicious of others who didn't totally agree with her conclusions. I've always wondered whether she would be for or against the 9/11 Truth movement. But, as for the Power Control Group? Here we were busy

misusing our power. In December 1977, when Larry Flynt brought Dick Gregory and me to Nassau Beach in the Bahamas, Gregory taught Flynt how to give himself an enema, and Flynt rubbed sunscreen on my back and said, "I'll bet Hugh Hefner never did this for you." Dangerous control freaks in action.

Q. **Birds falling out of the sky, uprisings in Egypt, Tunisia, London, and countless other recent developments have convinced millions that humanity is rapidly approaching some kind of evolutionary tipping point. Some find evidence for this proposal since one phase of the Mayan calendar ends in 2012, others because of all the expectant energy resulting from this and other phenomena. Meanwhile the same old structures grind on. Are we kidding ourselves? Is it Friendly Fascism time or are we about to be transfigured?**

A. Friendly fascism is here, and I'm hoping that it will be counteracted by a transfiguration, but that may merely be wishful thinking brought about by too many acid trips. There's an old saying, "May you live in interesting times," and it has been described as a curse. It was a curse to the ruling class, but to the rebels who questioned authority and brought about interesting times, it was a blessing.

Q. **After a lifetime spent in journalism, you're working on your first real novel, starring a modernized Lenny Bruce-style monologuist. Immersion in any fictional endeavor can be far more evocative than statistical citation. I'm only guessing here, but presumably this character might be an amalgam of your memories of Lenny and your personal experience as a stand-up, a symbiosis clunkier to render in non-fictional form. What do you think about all that?**

A. When Lenny died, I kept wondering what he would think about this, and what would be his take on that. I realized a novel would serve as an appropriate context to capture such speculation. In the book, those scenes where my protagonist is on stage have been developed in my own performances. I even began to feel that I was channeling Lenny, until one day he reminded me, "Listen, Paul, you know you don't believe in that shit." So instead, I just resent this imaginary character for stealing my material. It's a nice schizophrenic process. I mentioned to my friend Avery Corman--author of Oh, God and Kramer vs. Kramer, both of which became movies--that "Writing fiction is really hard. You have to make up everything." "C'mon, Paul," he said, "you've been making up stuff all your life." "Yeah," I replied, "but that was journalism . . ."

[The expanded edition of "Confessions of a Raving, Unconfined Nut: Misadventures in the Counterculture" by Paul Krassner is available at Amazon and select bookstores, only at www.paulkrassner.com and on Kindle.] Says Paul, "There's a video on my website of my 20-minute reading of Confessions at the Winnipeg Comedy Festival."

11 THE FIGHT OVER CHARLES MANSON'S WILL IN THE MEDIA MARKET

THE AUTHOR'S INVESTIGATION OF MANSON'S LEFTOVERS POST-MORTEM, INCLUDING ONE QUESTION ANSWERED BY MANSON HIMSELF BEFORE DYING AND AN INTERVIEW WITH ONE-TIME MANSON ESTATE CLAIMANT MICHAEL CHANNELS

Pimp Charles Manson's life, which, as an expendable piece of state property, was never protected by libel laws, has been fictionalized again and again and again since he was fingered as a hippie cult leader in 1969. Manson was an outlaw and a pimp who never opposed any murders, whether or not he directed them, and the way his life has been digested by pop culture as a symbol of something deserving ultimate persecution by the media is worth a double-take, regardless of his guilt. Almost as long as the Beatles have served as a signpost of what's compelling in popular culture, Charles Manson's Family and the Tate-LaBianca slayings of August 1969 have stood beside them as their equally revolting darkside. This dichotomy shows the media's role in the anatomy of 20th century Western society. "What do you think's gonna come after me?" Manson asked somewhere in Manson: The Final Words, another recent doc. Perhaps his death will be remembered by historians, alongside Beatle John Lennon's in 1980, as a convenient marker of transition from one era into another.

Many circumstances surrounding the Manson Family and the Tate-LaBianca slayings have never been fully exposed, including the involvement of a secret ring of celebrities trading sex tapes starring themselves, and the fact that aspects of Family protocol, including the use of color-names for female members, were consciously modeled by Manson on the example of a Francis Herman Pencovic or "Krishna Venta," whose Fountain Of The World cult, centered around "Wisdom, Knowledge, Faith and Love" preceded the Family in the same Death Valley location by ten or fifteen years. Makes you wonder what's what.

Manson died a few years ago, assigned a lasting reputation as an evil mass murderer for events that occurred during one of his periods of freedom (roughly 1967 to 1969), and it's rarely noted that this figure so symbolic of the 60s lived an essentially timeless existence as a lifelong son of lots of different prisons. His final years were marked by his near marriage to a woman named Afton Elaine Burton, called by him, "Star ." According to journalist Daniel Simone, Manson may simply have wanted Star and her friend, Craig "Gray Wolf" Hammond, to continue visiting him and bringing him gifts. Burton herself said on her web site at one point that the reason that the marriage did not take place was that Manson was suffering from an infection and had been in a prison medical facility for two months unable to receive visitors. She said she was hopeful that the marriage license would be renewed and the marriage would take place, but it expired on February 5, 2015, without a wedding.

Here's a list of some recent movies made on Manson and the Family, and I've tried to be comprehensive for the purposes of this article, but there are no doubt others, and hundreds more predating them: Reginald Harkema's avant-comedy *Manson, My Name is Evil* (2009),The series *Aquarius*, starring David Duchovny, Brandon Slagle's *House of Manson* (2014)–these produced before Manson's death–followed by the 2018 film *The Haunting of Sharon Tate*, starring Hillary Duff, and Quentin Tarantino's latest film, *Once Upon a Time in Hollywood*. The most recent Manson-related film I've seen is *The Last of the Manson Girls*, adapting late investigative satirist Paul Krassner's encounters with Squeaky (Lynette Fromme). Sandra Good and Brenda (Nancy Pitman), tempered by his connection with conspiracy theorist Mae Brussell, after Manson, Tex, Susan, Nancy and Pat were in prison for the Tate-LaBianca murders. UPDATE: I saw one last week called

Manson Family Vacation where a guy finds out he's his son and sets out for a prison visit. I think that one came out last year (2020).

Freed after years in nut wards after her disruption of an address by Gerald Ford with an unloaded gun in 1975, Family member Lynette "Squeaky" Fromme Manson published her memoir, *Reflexion*, currently available at Amazon.com, offering her personal perspective on what it was like hanging out at Spahn Ranch. Over the past 20 years, *Please Kill Me* editors Legs McNeil and Gillian McCain have interviewed every possible person connected to the Manson Family murders, several of whom have never spoken on record before, for a forthcoming oral history project Legs says will be "explosive."

Charles Manson was accused of sending out brainwashed disciples to commit a series of slayings in the Hollywood hills after listening to the Beatles White Album and deciding it was advocating race war, after which, he was sent back to the "hallways of always" — as he referred to the revolving series of detention facilities that was his lifelong habitat. He died of cardiac arrest resulting from respiratory failure and colon cancer on November 19, 2017, at a hospital in Bakersfield to which he was transported from California State Prison at Corcoran.

The Helter-Skelter Hotline

About ten years before he passed, I found a page on YouTube featuring taped phone calls with Manson himself from as recently as the previous afternoon advertising the chance to ask him a question. This page, the Backporch Tapes, now called Michael's Back-porch, offering near daily conversations about current events with the mad one, was also a chance at direct communication with its imprisoned namesake and topic, a man accused in his time of being everything from a redneck hillbilly to one of the most powerful magicians around. In one of the calls, Charlie gave his opinion on the swine flu then circulating. "That's just a taste of what's coming," he warned, "that's just the beginning."

"What does the swastika on your forehead symbolize?" I typed in. Manson was a confederate sympathizer and reported white supremacist but had also been quoted as saying he received the symbol as a benediction from a Native American fellow inmate named Walks on Top, and that's the story I was looking for. The swastika was a symbol of order and harmony for thousands of years before its association with Nazis and death camps for non-Aryans, and I'd always figured the gesture of branding himself right between the eyes with it probably had more significance than merely racism. That said, I wasn't sure, and I wanted to hear his own answer, nothing filtered through the media lens. Manson replied a few days later in a handwritten note photographed and posted on YouTube. I recognized his signature from Nikolas Shreck's anthology, *The Manson File*. "This means gone in the dream" (or "brain") (probably "dream") "of thy" (or "the") "wars," Manson had written, right under a drawing of a backwards swastika with an arrow pointing at it,then, "I got no reality" and "I'm a servant ." Below the word "servant" was one more doodle which I think was just ornamental. Manson seemed to be saying the swastika on his forehead signified his place in history, as measured by wars on earth, or in the astral realm, as a servant. What did he think about the rumors of Paul McCartney's death and replacement? I forgot to ask.

Michael Channels

Charles Manson and Michael Channels

I decided to send that Helter Skelter hotline page's owner an email requesting an interview. Michael Channels got back to me right away. "I want to first say I am no advocate for ATWA [Manson's acronym for Air, Trees, Water, Animals, the ecological doctrine he champions], the Manson Family or any crime," he began. "I merely got interested in getting Manson's autograph, and after bugging him for so long, he found a liking to me. Then he let me have access he wouldn't others and sat and talked with me. The prison doesn't care about his message getting out as much as people think they do. They just don't want to be shown up or made to look bad, which I also understand. We all meet at a happy medium now on The Backporch Tapes."

Channels has collected autographs and Hollywood memorabilia of all types for about forty years. He's had face to face encounters with some of the biggest names in showbiz since his childhood, lived experiences like visiting Gilda Radner's sickbed before her death from cancer in 1989 and meeting all the astronauts from the Moon landing.

Channels launched the murder-themed website Hollywood 187 (now defunct) — "The 187 in police speak is murder" — well before posting anything on YouTube, and had contact with several of Hollywood's mad killers, including Manson, over the course of its proprietorship. "I am NO ADVOCATE for anything or anyone," he clarifies. "I have collected, and he has told me, lots of information that others may never have seen, and wouldn't if I didn't show them."

Channels's fixation on the Tate-LaBianca case began, as with most people, after reading prosecutor Vincent Bugliosi's account, *Helter Skelter*, and eventually led to a friendship with Charlie himself. "Manson has always given his blessings in anything anyone does, including some of the books put out. He has always been a sharing man, a kind hearted man, really, if you knew him as a person. I have never wanted to join a group or follow another, so [contacting] Manson was just me being me: very curious. Over the years I've heard him say things others never have."

Charles Manson spent most of his life in jails and prisons of various kinds. The Family's killing spree occurred during one of the two or three fleeting intervals of freedom on earth as a son of prison.

"People need to read about Prison," Channels agrees. "His entire life was influenced by the men who came through prison. Old mob men, gangsters, and Vietnam vets. His experiences are all summed up by the stories he sits in prison listening to, of the lives of the men telling them. His life is all about prison and only prison. The thing he did was he brought Prison out into the world with him. The kids and violence of the time took the Prison procedure and applied it to the outside world. They were all confused, that's my opinion."

In one phone call on Channels' page, Manson addressed him as "Soul ." "Manson has called me many things, but I prefer Michael, and he said that was good, because he named all his kids that as well. 'Soul' is like hey, brother, or hey, friend . . . he says that to a lot of people. It's that sixties talk, like, 'you dig.'

ATWA

Charles Manson was preaching the doctrine of Air-Trees-Water-and-Animals or ATWA, a creed still outspokenly advocated by Sandra Good and the recently paroled Fromme ("Blue" and "Red" respectively in the color names given by Manson to his female followers), years before the notorious Tate-LaBianca slayings of August 8th and 9th, 1969 he's accused of having ordered, and decades before human imbalance with nature became the popular topic it is today. Family members were salvaging discarded produce from supermarket dumpsters as early as 1966, as reported in Gilmore's *The Garbage People*. Many circumstances surrounding the Manson Family and the Tate-LaBianca slayings have never been fully exposed, including the involvement of a secret ring of celebrities trading sex tapes starring themselves, and the fact that aspects of Family protocol, including the use of color-names for female members, were mirrored or prefigured in the same Death Valley location by ten or fifteen years by Francis Herman Pencovic or "Krishna Venta's Fountain Of The World cult, centered around "Wisdom, Knowledge, Faith and Love ." When I first learned about

Krishna Venta, it seemed eerie Manson had adopted all the same customs, maybe having to do with the energy of the land or who knows what native energy currents, but I later heard he'd buzzed through the Fountain of the World himself.

Charles Manson was often very theatrical in demeanor when interviewed, at times performing elaborate dances, shaking his head and making strange gestures with his hands in the effort at illuminating some of the more abstract points in his ramble, (which can be seen in a number of videos widely available on sites like YouTube). He had a habit of renaming cohorts, from the color names given to female disciples at Spahn Ranch–in imitation of the Fountain of the World–to "Ansom 13," the one he gave Family member T.J. "the Terrible" Wallerman's wife, Lori. "Ansom 13 was given that because she was a female version of the Manson And Some," explains Channels. "13 is the first cell Manson was in at San Quentin death row. She and his close, close friends back then feel they died in the cell with him, hence the 13." Lori L. Mardesich Wallerman or "Ansom 13" died in October of the year 1998, and when Michael Channels asked Charles Manson the cause of her death in a phone call posted on Backporch Tapes, his question went unanswered. Excerpts from Ansom's diary posted there asserted that the Family's arrest in 1969 was some kind of frame-up by the prosecution's star witness, Linda Kasabian, adding one more wrinkle to the myth surrounding a purported mastermind with extensive connections to the California-based entertainment industry (not just the Beach Boys, as detailed in Nikolas Schreck's *The Manson File*).

Uncertain Fate of the Manson Estate

When Manson died, a number of claimants emerged, among them Channels, who stated that Manson's 2002 will, filed in Kern County in November 2017, names him as the executor of Manson's estate. Channels encouraged DNA testing of another claimant, a 43-year-old

Florida man named Jason Freeman claiming to be Manson's grandson. Freeman's father, Charles Manson, Jr., who changed his name to Jay White, had never been in doubt of his biological link to Charlie, but missed an important hearing, having committed suicide in June 1993. Afton Burton no longer held any claim to Charlie's estate, their pending marriage having been averted by Manson.

"The facts of this case are peculiar since (Manson) was a convicted murderer serving time in prison," state Channels's court papers. "There is not the usual ability of the court to evaluate whether Mr. Freeman would be considered a grandchild, such as visits or family dinners or reunions." Freeman won the rights to Manson's physical remains, allegedly motivated, at least in part, if not entirely, by an interest in preserving his remains and charging for their viewing or exhibition as part of a reality show, despite having failed the blood test.

Manson wrote and signed a will in 2002, naming Channels as his executor, authorizing his body to be released to Channels, and bequeathing all his property to Channels. The will also directed that Channels was to receive all of Manson's music and royalty rights to the songs Manson wrote, as well as his image and publishing rights. It went even farther, preemptively dis-inheriting anyone claiming to be a child of Manson in future, to include all other relatives. Under California law, two disinterested witnesses are required to sign a will, but in this case, there appears only one signature besides those of Manson and Channels. A will is valid if one of the two witnesses was also a beneficiary, and therefore not "disinterested," but that person then carries the burden of proving to the court that the will was not caused by duress, menace, fraud, or undue influence. That may be hard for Channels to do, considering he said on record that the will was sent to him, unexpectedly, after meeting Manson.

This suggests that Channels was not present when Manson signed it, meaning it would be difficult for Channels to prove that the will was valid. Freeman and his attorney dispute the validity of the 2002 will, questioning how it could have been signed in prison by Manson and also apparently signed by Channels. The same goes for another will naming presumptive son Matthew Roberts, which has only one witness and lacks notarization.Complicating matters, someone named Matt Lentz appeared, also claiming to be a biological son of Manson, given up for adoption as a newborn. Lentz said *he* had a will from 2017, (this has not yet been made public) naming him sole beneficiary and a different memorabilia collector, Ben Gurecki, as executor. If deemed valid, that document would supersede the 2002 will favoring Channels and leave Lentz and Gurecki in control of both Manson's body and whatever property, royalty and image rights remain. Matthew Lentz, who claims he was fathered by Manson at a 1967 orgy, Lentz said he would seek a DNA test to prove his biological relationship. arrived late at Los Angeles Superior Court looking disheveled and frazzled after a brief hearing in the probate case of the late cult leader.

Another supposed son, Michael Brunner, filed papers to drop his claims as an alleged heir to the convicted murderer. If these two drop out, it would pit a purported grandson against a pen pal who has filed a will that names him as sole beneficiary to the estate. Until all these claims are sorted out, Manson's body won't be laid to rest. Perhaps this is fitting. As he wrote on the back of the contested 2002 will, "I'm not in the best spot to rest in peace."

The latest update is that the Court has asked Manson's grandson for a DNA test to validate his link to Charlie before passing along any inheritance and Google reports him to be the inheritor as of 11/28/22. Jason Freeman passed this test and had Manson's remains cremated. Highly recommended for those in search of an objective overview of this extremely influential life is Nikolas Schreck's *The Manson File: Myth and Reality of an Outlaw Shaman.*

12 A CONVERSATION WITH GARY LACHMAN ABOUT GRABBING REALITY

GARY LACHMAN PLAYED BASS IN BLONDIE AS GARY VALENTINE, LATER PUBLISHING SEVERAL BOOKS LOOKING INTO HUMAN CONSCIOUSNESS COLIN WILSON-STYLE

IN 1970s New York, the Velvet Underground linked Warhol's scene to the punk scene and Burroughs' presence in the lives of some principals—the *Naked Lunch* author came to CBGBs at least once, was known to receive visits from Patti Smith, and was sought out as an elder by UK pioneers like Joe Strummer when they came to New York —linked it to Beat forebears. I wondered if there was an occult connection to CBGBs, and who better to ask than former Blondie bassist turned metaphysician Gary Lachman? "As far as I know there wasn't anything 'occult' about CBGB, although, as I say in New York Rocker, Chris and Debbie had a kitschy interest in it. In the loft we lived in on the Bowery – a block from CBGB and Burroughs' bunker – they had upside down pentagrams and crosses and voodoo dolls hanging about. I got interested in it from living there when I came across Colin Wilson's *The Occult*. I read it and it changed my life."

Lachman joined Blondie in the spring of 1975 as "Gary Valentine," replacing Fred Smith on bass when he left to join Television, and helping to popularize the band's sixties-style fashion, as recounted in his 2002 memoir, *New York Rocker: My Life in the Blank Generation*. He has enacted a near-complete transformation in the years since into a respected archivist of mysticism and metaphysics. left the band in 1977, to be replaced by Nigel Harrison. Blondie's hit "Heart of Glass" took the charts coincidentally with disco's heyday in 1979, making them the first of the early U.S. punk bands to emerge from Hilly Kristal's CBGBs to crossover to mainstream success.. Despite their association with disco and near disassociation from the CBGBs scene in most people's minds, Blondie frontwoman Deborah Harry has lately gotten her due, and then some, as a female punk pioneer, maybe thanks in part to the oral history *Please Kill Me*.

Lachman has been a full-time writer since 1990. Among his books is *Turn Off Your Mind: The Mystic Sixties and the Dark Side of the Age of Aquarius* and *Dark Star Rising: Magick and Power in the Age of Trump*, examining Trump's connection to Norman Vincent Peale's doctrine of Positive Thinking in relation to his public flexibility with facts, and the influence of occult and esoteric philosophy on the unexpected rise of the "alt-right ." He's written biographies on P.D. Ouspensky and Crowley and the mystical aspects of Jungian philosophy and Steiner and Swedenborg, not unlike the series of biographies of metaphysical figures Colin Wilson published near the end of his life. As it happens, he became closely acquainted with his inspirator. "I met Wilson in 1981 at a talk at the Village Bookshop on Regents Street while I was on holiday in London. In 1983, as part of a 'mini search for the miraculous,' I made a pilgrimage to his home in a remote part of Cornwall. In the early 90s, he stayed with me while he was lecturing in Los Angeles. After moving to London I visited him in Cornwall several times and got to know his wife and children. When he came up to London we met, and I interviewed him a few times. My book about him, *Beyond the Robot*, came out in 2016."

Did Blondie ever hang around with Burroughs? Have the members stayed in touch? "I have to say I never saw him at CBGB, but I did meet him in '96, when I was playing with C&D again. We performed at a tribute to Burroughs in Lawrence, Kansas, along with Patti Smith, Laurie Anderson, Philip Glass, and quite a few other hipsters. There's a funny story about Patti Smith and myself at a news conference about the tribute that I tell in *New York Rocker*. I met Burroughs at this. I read him in my teens but later felt he was something of a fraud – or at least a confidence man. I suspect he would have appreciated this. The only ex-band mate I keep in touch with is Clem; we drop each other a line every now and then. There is a funny story though, about my bit in their reunion in the late 90s. In her book, talking about how I got involved, instead of writing 'Chris spoke with Gary about playing again,' Debbie wrote 'Christ spoke with Gary…'. Her editor missed the typo. I tweeted about it; it was hilarious and strangely apt."

It has been suggested that the slack jawed devotion of Trump's cult mystifying the mainstream media is, in fact, the expected result of psychological conditioning and not a mystery of his weird charisma. Indeed, Trump's studious adherence to/recreation of a list of particulars from past fascist regimes, including recreation of similar photos seems manual and artificial, as opposed to history repeating itself. Is he merely an out-of-control egomaniac or is there a sinister dedication? "There's nothing mystical about Trump," says Lachman, "but he is a serious demagogue, a kind of political guru. Like Putin he is offering a sense of identity in a very chaotic, uncertain time, a return to a kind of "golden age" of a lost America, something from the 1950s. He's clearly interested in establishing an authoritarian state, based on "law and order," stoking up fear in order to present himself as the saviour. He is certainly out for himself but is very good at taking advantage of the epistemological skepticism that has trickled down from the academic heights to the lowlands of media; schools of thought like deconstructionism and postmodernism prepared the ground for "post truth" and "alternative facts." Positive thinking taught him that facts don't matter; your attitude toward the facts is all that counts – this another expression of the idea that "we create reality," that is oddly shared by New Thought, new agers, and postmodernists. And then we have Reality TV, which primed Trump for his position as president when he was on *The Apprentice*. I don't know anything about psy-ops. Trump is giving many people what they want; as I said, he is a very good demagogue, meaning he is good at being one. He is selling a way of life, not a political program. It's not about getting the trains to run on time; it's about feeling part of some grand movement. Reality is up for grabs these days, and Trump has grabbed it."

Gary Lachman lives in London now, avidly pursuing a career as a self-employed freelance intellectual hundreds of miles from the New York City where he cut his teeth as a rocker in a series of punk and new wave bands—Including Blondie and The Know and Iggy Pop post-Stooges— which requires its own round of maintenance. "I get up early, record my dreams, have coffee and toast and read for an hour or so while listening to music (classical). The rest of the morning is devoted to admin: answering emails, posting links to talks, working on my site, and housework. From 12:00 to around 5:00 I'm either reading or writing. I have a 1500–2000-word daily quota. After work I either take a walk or cycle, weather permitting. Dinner at 7:00 while watching the news. Then a film until it's time for the midnight news and sleep."

Gary Lachman

In the forthcoming *The Return of Holy Russia: Apocalyptic History, Mystical Awakening, and the Struggle for the Soul of the World,* Lachman offers commentary about Putin's revival of a national identity rooted in mystic and apocalyptic tradition long before the Bolshevik Revolution. Says he, "In many speeches [Putin] refers to several philosophers and religious thinkers from a period known as the Silver Age, which was from around 1890 to just before the revolution. It was a fantastically creative time, when mysticism, the occult, and spirituality were very influential in the arts and philosophy. If you look at Russian history, you see that it was always profoundly religious, with a deeper sense of the mystical and apocalyptic than the west. Putin is gesturing toward this religious history in the new cold war between the decadent, permissive west and the traditional east."

13 DEAR DR. GONZO

THE AUTHOR'S PERSONAL CONNECTION TO ONE OF THE LAST THINGS HUNTER THOMPSON DID TO SUBVERT SYSTEMIC PROTOCOL IN RESPONSE TO A LETTER HE RECEIVED

GONZO: The Life and Work of Dr. Hunter S. Thompson, directed by Oscar-winner Alex Gibney, is narrated by Johnny Depp, who made a serious study of HST's manner and character before playing him in the movie version of *Fear and Loathing in Las Vegas*, which came out in 1998. I saw it at the Esquire on 5th and Downing. The film intersperses film clips and interviews with post-mortem commentary from loved ones and associates, including Hunter's two wives and Rolling Stone magazine founder and publisher, Jann Wenner.

Thompson was the acknowledged founder of "gonzo journalism," a brand of innovative freestyle reportage appearing in the sixties. *Gonzo* addresses the major touchstones in Thompson's life— his intense and ill-fated relationship with the Hell's Angels, his near-successful bid for sheriff of Aspen in 1970, and the backstory of his best-known book, *Fear and Loathing in Las Vegas*, which details his search for the evanescent American Dream while on assignment for Rolling Stone with a trunkful of mind-altering drugs, in the company of Oscar Zeta Acosta, a fugitive from the Los Angeles Legal Bar at the time. The film also treats of Thompson's deep involvement in Senator George McGovern's 1972 presidential campaign, from which my personal favorite Thompson work, *Fear And Loathing On The Campaign Trail '72* was drawn, and his lifelong intimacy with every twinge of our changing culture.

Dear Dr. Thompson is a work of nonfiction by local author Matthew Moseley about Gonzo journalist Hunter S. Thompson's last act of public theater protesting the wrongful accusation and imprisonment of a young woman who was in the company of racist skinhead Matthaeus Jaehnig when he shot a cop in 1997. I was a hardcore ANTI racist in high school, having actually met Jaehnig once years before this went down and exchanged meaningful looks, which gives this review the feel of a personal retrospective. Lisl Auman, who was handcuffed in a squad car at the time of Officer Bruce VanderJagt's fatal shooting by Jaehnig, should never have been charged with his death let alone imprisoned for it, but I was perplexed at the time by HST's defense of this apparent skinhead sympathizer, and felt a little betrayed by Thompson, who, while never a personal literary hero, had always struck me as constitutionally opposed to Nazism. Like most of the rest of the public, I was in the dark about the true facts of the case.

According to the official story, once cornered by police in a dead-end apartment complex breezeway, Matthaeus Jaehnig shot himself. He was giving Lisl a ride to her abusive ex-boyfriend's house to retrieve some belongings and took it on himself to burglarize the place, which led to a high-speed car chase and the gunning down of the beloved VanderJagt. Lisl was coerced into using incriminating phrases (like "muscle") by bereaved officers when questioned. Two later said they saw her hand Jaehnig the murder weapon and she was sentenced to life without parole.

You've probably heard the word "skinhead" before. Its connotation is muddled. The first English skins, known for their close-cropped haircuts or shaven heads, were primarily influenced by West Indian (specifically Jamaican) "rude boys" and the fashion-conscious "mod" subculture, in terms of dress, music and lifestyle. As the 1970s progressed, racially-motivated skinhead violence in the United Kingdom became more political, and far right groups such as the National Front saw their chance to co-opt the movement before it had spread noticeably to the United States—claiming affiliation with their opponents' arguments being a favored tactic of subversion. By the late 1970s, the general public in the U.S. had largely come to view the skinhead scene as one promoting racism and neo-Nazism, necessitating the formation of groups like S.H.A.R.P. (Skinheads Against Racial Prejudice) in an attempt to settle the score. The whole history is muddy.

I wasn't looking for a fight, so I never claimed S.H.A.R.P. as a teen, instead styling myself as a "rude boy slash mod," one of two or three kids at my high school who attended the weekly Club Rub a Dub nights every Friday from nine to whenever at Sadie's Afro-Caribbean Café in Five Points. When I say, "exchanged meaningful looks," what I mean is I didn't say anything to Matthaeus when we met, but we each sort of knew where the other one stood. I knew he was a racist, which made him my natural opponent, but I wasn't looking to cause any trouble, so I kept my mouth shut. His parents were fervent disciples of Rudolf Steiner's controversial spiritual science anthroposophy, which has faced accusations of racism, despite having been attacked by National Socialist ideologues from the 1930s on. Matthaeus was raised within this doctrine in an overgrown mansion guarded by angry dogs in the Washington Park neighborhood, over the years becoming addicted to crystal meth and drifting deeper into criminality.

While serving a life sentence at Colorado Women's Correctional Facility in Canon City, Lisl Auman wrote a letter to Hunter S.

Thompson to complain that his books were not available in the prison library. She didn't even mention her case at first. Communications strategist Matthew Moseley also wrote Thompson a letter outlining his plan to organize a grassroots campaign to free Lisl Auman from prison and to take on the draconian felony murder law. That's where this fascinating story began. *Dear Dr. Thompson* chronicles Lisl's epic struggles and takes you inside the last and perhaps most heartfelt Gonzo campaign before his death from apparent suicide in 2005, though those details are muddy too.

Thompson died of a self-inflicted gunshot wound on February 20th of 2005, (while sitting at the typer, which reportedly had the word "counselor" at the center of the page). Family members reported to the press at the time their belief that his suicide was a "well-thought-out act resulting from his many painful medical conditions. Says longtime Thompson illustrator Ralph Steadman, "He told me 25 years ago that he would feel real trapped if he didn't know that he could commit suicide at any moment." The deed may also have been in some part a reaction to Bush II's ongoing campaign against privacy and human rights in general; Thompson's novel *Kingdom Of Fear* (2003) showed him to be thoroughly disgusted with the state of affairs politically after the September 2001 attacks. Jann Wenner argues in Gonzo that Hunter's suicide seems contra-indicated in light of the good he might have done opposing such an encroachment. I agree that life beats death. At the same time, I can understand how Thompson might have felt washed up, in light of today's entertainment culture, like his time in the sun had passed. Alive or dead, I'm grateful for the trail he blazed.

Parts of this article have appeared previously in *MileHive* and at the *Examiner*.

14 HIS BROTHER'S KEEPER

JIM MORRISON'S BROTHER-IN-LAW FOR 22 YEARS ALAN GRAHAM FROM LIVERPOOL TAKES OBJECTION TO MY PUBLISHING CLIFF MORRISON'S MANAGER'S REMARKS ABOUT HIM WITHOUT CONSULTING HIM FIRST AND BECOMES A NEW CLIENT OF MINE

ALAN Graham was married to Morrison's sister Ann and has written a memoir about his friendship with Jim, another about his boyhood in Liverpool growing up around the corner from the Cavern Club, and a third about his work as "Captain Pink" with Larry Flynt, so far unpublished. Graham knew all the Beatles as fellow teenage Teddy Boys in his hometown of Liverpool, England, before moving to London, meeting Ann Morrison, the sister of budding rock icon Jim Morrison, and moving to Los Angeles with her. They stayed married for 22 years. Graham became a close friend and drinking companion of Jim Morrison from the time the Doors' first hit, "Light My Fire," was released in January of 1967, until Jim died in Paris under mysterious circumstances in 1971. "I'd spent a couple years around the corner from ground zero of the Beatles' hometown breakout at the Cavern Club on Matthew Street in Liverpool, played witness to the ascension of the Doors and that band's eventual flame-out after the death of my brother-in-law."

Where the child Neal Cassady had been a frontman for sparechanging bums who made it to the top of the counterculture, the child Alan Graham had hijacked food carts for his daily bread in postwar Liverpool, which desperation, he said, coupled with a love of Elmer

Gantry's "intuitive certitude," as replicated by Burt Lancaster in the film version of the novel by Sinclair Lewis, had taught him a lesson in "statesmanship" and got to the same upper deck about ten years later. Since Morrison's death, Graham has worked as a babysitter for the young Sage Moonblood Stallone, the actor and oldest son of Sylvester Stallone, and as "fixer" for porn publisher and free speech billionaire Larry Flynt. He seems to have always found himself in the right place at the right time. "Some people are born with this aptitude," Graham put it in one of his books, "while others have no access to the portal."

James Douglas Morrison (December 8, 1943 – July 3, 1971) was the first scion of a military bloodline not to join any branch of service, going back for centuries to Scottish clan-conflicts. His father, Rear Admiral George Stephen Morrison, USN, fired the first shot in the Vietnam War during the controversial Gulf of Tonkin incident, which led shortly thereafter to the 1964 Gulf of Tonkin Resolution, which essentially gave Pres. Lyndon Johnson carte blanche to wage unlimited war on Southeast Asia. The Morrison clan, bound by a militaristic code of secrecy, had an interest in limiting public knowledge about itself. Hence, popular biographies of Jim are limited in scope, and this is also why a character based on Graham is absent from Oliver Stone's film *The Doors*. "The book *No One Here Gets Out Alive* [by Jerry Hopkins and Danny Sugarman] had been released, to great acclaim, and they wanted to make a movie. [Pamela Courson's] parents wouldn't cooperate with producers [Ed. note – Pamela was Jim Morrison's long-term companion] and the Admiral wouldn't play. A deal was still being considered, lobbied chiefly by Ray Manzarek. I learned that the Admiral could override everyone if he would just step forth and take control of the estate, which was being badly mismanaged. I called Admiral Morrison again, this time to assure him that he could maintain control of the script. Once again, he refused. I wondered why my father-in-law was blocking the deal. Perhaps he knew something no one else did."

MY phone cost $39 bucks, I refilled it periodically with $20- or $30-dollar cards. But Al Graham favored lengthy telephonic remonstrances with the demon of his own past as his way of conveying information to me the ghost writer, and the cheap phone's limited sound quality was getting in the way. Often, we got into shouting matches due to mutual irascibility as personalities. Besides accusing me of "whining" when I tried to explain about my computer crashing, he'd called me "peevish" a couple of times.

Despite all this, I knew it was an extremely important connection and had promised I'd get a new cell phone with better reception. He called one day, and we got into the usual shouting match, which culminated in me shouting, "You can't hear me because you called me on the cheap phone! I got a new phone yesterday, but it has a different number!" in response to his, "I thought you were getting a new phone," whereupon Al, who had a history of heart trouble, went into a series of gasps, which at first sounded just like a heart attack. This would have meant I had shouted to my friend, the old man from the past to death without meaning to.

"Al? Are you all right?" I will be ready for this, if it happens, I thought to myself, an odd sort of detachment. But it turned out the old man had been laughing. "I'll call you back in a couple of hours," he said. I blinked my eyes. My mom had mentioned something about a deal on prepaid cell phones, offering to pay for it, so I emailed and said I was interested. I'd told her something previously about Al's having said he might want me to start doing live stream broadcasting, and Mom invited me to go with her the following day to get a new phone. My mom providing this new cell phone and Al Graham demanding my attention were playing the roles of strange new maternal and paternal icons in the new dynamic, and in the same conversation, Graham told me, "In a way, you might as well be my son."

He had his heart operation, and I found my way to a position at a human resources-oriented call center called the Phone Pit on the outskirts of his neighborhood, working for a company which had cornered the market on improving the equity of employer-employee relations through scientific questionnaires zooming in on job-related problem areas via multiple questions. "Employers come to us when they want to make things better. What we do is called Workplace

Intelligence." I knew this was something I could get behind five hours a day with no trouble.

Captain Pink

When putting together Milos Forman's *People vs. Larry Flynt* film, in Flynt's own words, "I didn't know how to explain Captain Pink." Pink was Graham's superhuman alter-ego, during a time in the 1980s when the outlaw publisher felt especially sensitive. Flynt sought to divert attention from the facts of his own case by turning the tables on all the moralists arrayed against him, which is where Captain Pink came in. For example, when Larry Flynt began a hunger strike for better conditions, his spokesperson, Graham, told the press, "Someone in the kitchen informed him that [the food] was tainted, and he refused it." Flynt's rival brother, Jimmy, filed a conservatorship petition in Los Angeles Superior Court, claiming the *Hustler* publisher suffered from a mental illness "consistent only with an irrational drive to destroy or lose all his holdings, [having] drained the company of millions of dollars in cash for bizarre and imprudent personal expenditures."

Larry Flint - Captain Pink

Alan Graham and Larry Flynt

Among the expenditures that Flynt's brother objected to was the cash required to fund Captain Pink's adventures distracting the press in Springfield, Missouri while his boss was locked up. A gang of pranksters led by Graham served as a contrarian distraction steeped in street theatrics for the stultified townsfolk, exposing town elders and authorities' hypocrisy by successfully tempting these do-rights with cash, pleasure and excess—all the things they claimed most to revile. "Captain Pink is still remembered in Springfield for his toy sword, the pink Christmas lights all over his pink costume, and the satchel full of cash he used to prank his way through town during Flynt's stay in Springfield's Medical Center for Federal Prisoners," says Al. "Springfield, Missouri is one of the most conservative places on the planet, and we turned it upside down."

With Admiral Morrison's death in 2008, the family code of secrecy lost much of its authority, and the time was finally right for Alan Graham to begin relating his unexpurgated adventures. His book, *I Remember Jim Morrison Too*, remains the only Morrison biography so far published to focus at length on portions of Jim's life outside and beyond his seven years of notoriety. Where other biographers are moved to turn Morrison's story into a train wreck and charge admission, Graham's inspiration had been to commemorate the emotional effect of their time together. "Mine is the only one telling the true story of that family. More than forty books would be published about Jim's life after he died, but nobody outside the Morrison family ever really knew him." Writing that testament to his friend and lost brother woke Graham up to the wealth of more stories inside him to tell. In 2010, this reporter helped him edit another three, *Before the Beatles Were Famous*, the revamped *I Remember Jim Morrison Too*, 2022's rerelease of that one in French English and Spanish, and *The Flynt Caper*, detailing Captain Pink upending a town's moral structure as a self-styled superhero while his Mad Hatter of a boss was in the madhouse.

Larry Flynt and Captain Pink

"HERE comes your dream along, are you ready for it? Will you take it?" wrote Graham. "That's the question every person has to answer. Because you're lucky if you dream good, lucky if you dream at all. As a child once I prophesied the winning number in a lottery using information received in a dream. And life is full of dreams, so I always looked at those. Every single time I remembered the dream. Or the essence of the dream."

We were working on *The Flynt Caper* when Al went into the hospital for an unexpected heart operation requiring a special drill that could go in from the side, which sounded pretty drastic, putting our project on an unexpected hiatus. The above paragraph is a snippet from that as-yet-unpublished volume, conveying its metaphorical subtext. This second excerpt, more profane, shows its liver: "The warden saw a pink guy come into his fuckin' prison and sent out his hoods after him. He also told his daughter that if she hung out with him anymore, he'd put him in jail for 20 years legally under the Brown Act for taking his daughter across state lines. Pink ran away with the warden's daughter, took her across state lines to California. Flynt in T.I. (Terminal Island) two weeks for some kind of med checkup. I took his daughter there and the warden was shittin' his pants because his daughter showed up on surveillance with Flynt, so he sent the hoods there. But we took the low road and got back to Springfield, MO while they were in Cali."

Nadia Szold sent an email to me, as Graham's representative, asking whether he might be interested in narrating portions of her documentary detailing Flynt's time in Springfield. "The working title is *Larry Flynt for President,* and it's going quite well. We've got the picture locked and now are on to the finishing elements like music and graphics." I contacted Al, thinking it a perfect fit, but he declined, having tired of going over that old ground full of buried cables, awakening all those sleeping lives. What would happen next with *The Flynt Caper* remained an open question for several months. Graham is currently "off the grid" somewhere outside San Diego and says he's "doing pretty well for an old fucker." He periodically plays with a country rock band that includes former members of the Flying Burrito Brothers, miles away from the perfect end to the life of an honest outlaw in service of following dreams.

For the last sixty plus years, expatriate Englishman Graham, who now lives in the San Diego area, had first-hand experience of a number of pop-cultural hot-points—lucky or fated bystander to multiple noteworthy people and events in the latter portion of the 20th century. After moving to London, where his brother, John, was managing the rock group Johnny Kidd and the Pirates (of "Shakin' All Over" and "I'll Never Get Over You" fame), Graham met his American girlfriend, Anne Morrison, daughter of a career Navy man, Admiral George Stephen Morrison. Graham married Anne in 1967, which was being touted in newspapers as the "summer of love," and shortly after they married, Anne's brother, Jim, became incredibly famous as the vocalist and frontman for a rock group based in Los Angeles called the Doors. Jim was touted in the press as an "erotic politician," well known for his provocative lyrics about breaking through and getting higher.

Contrary to this volatile, dangerous image, the Jim Morrison Alan Graham knew and loved was his friend, his wife's brother, and the son of her family. All his recollections of Jim are colored by this affinity, even those concerning Jim's penchant to upset his own apple cart periodically. "On Thanksgiving morning, 1969, Anne, [Jim's brother] Andy, and I drove from Coronado to Jim's house in the Hollywood hills. We brought a big cooked turkey and spent the day visiting with Jim and his 'girlfriend,' Pam Courson, until a simmering feud from the night before suddenly erupted into a knockdown, drag out fight. In the movie, *The Doors*, Oliver Stone cut and pasted that scene from my manuscript with another piece of mine entitled "*The Japanese Restaurant*."

When Jim died young of apparent heart failure in 1971, after the conclusion of his trial for indecent exposure while onstage in Miami and the completion of what turned out to be the last Doors album, *L.A. Woman*, rumors appeared in the mainstream press that he had faked his death, something he'd reportedly spoken of wanting to do in the past.

Graham agrees this is possible, if unlikely. "In this day and age, I don't know . . . The only person who knows is Pamela Courson (who died of a drug overdose in 1974). Don't forget the body was put on ice overnight. The morgues were closed. It was left on Saturday and Sunday night till Monday morning and his body was really blue. She never saw it. Nobody saw that body till it came from the morgue in the coffin, ready for the funeral. Pamela wouldn't look at it. Nobody looked at it. The likelihood that it could've been somebody else is extremely high and Morrison could've seen it and went into hiding and said this is my chance to get away from . . . his life and the people around him."

Graham's wild years outlived dear lost brother Jim. During Hustler publisher Larry Flynt's fifteen minutes of infamy in the 1980s Graham served as Flynt's assistant, his unspecified job to provide a kind of buffer zone between Flynt and the general public during a time when the outlaw publisher felt especially sensitive. Flynt said he felt his stay at the U.S. Medical Centre For Prisoners for contempt of court and desecration of the U.S. flag was "cruel and unusual punishment," since he was not receiving adequate medication and food (he had refused prison food after reportedly surviving a poisoning attempt and was striking for better conditions).

It was Graham's assignment to make a statement to the press, and he told them, "Someone in the kitchen informed him that [the food] was tainted, and he refused it." Next Flynt stated, in an impromptu jailhouse phone interview with CNN, "I have confessed to putting a contract out on President Reagan's life—I want to kill him," adding, "I have threatened to kill both federal judges who have sentenced me . . . I've threatened to kill at least a half dozen employees at the prison in Butler. I just got 152 days in the hole for hitting a priest between the eyes with an orange." Before Graham could do anything to amend his employer's latest ill-considered utterance, Flynt's brother, Jimmy, filed a conservatorship petition in Los Angeles Superior Court, claiming the publisher suffered from a mental illness "consistent only with an irrational drive to destroy or lose all his holdings," and that he had "drained the company of millions of dollars in cash for bizarre and imprudent personal expenditures." Somewhere in all this uproar, two former security guards of Flynt's told federal authorities they believed Graham was "behind the bombings," presumably referring to the bomb threat against Reagan, which he successfully dismissed as a fantastic story, though it provided a convenient hook for Cliff's former manager Floyd Bocox's statement in an interview years later that Graham was "known for making bomb threats."

Al says he has no patience for things like the "Jim Morrison's baby scam" being perpetrated by Lorraine Widen and her son, soundalike Cliff Morrison who refuses to consent to a DNA test to prove Jim's paternity, supposedly because he'd rather "let people decide for themselves," nor the ongoing exposure of fraudulence conducted by Bocox —but without any feeling of malice or offense, both of these derivative outgrowths are simply beneath his notice. "You know I heard Cliff's actually come to believe the whole fantasy now. To him it's not even a scam anymore, but for her, it's the worst possible form of child abuse." Cliff and his mother, Lorraine Widen, who claims to have had an affair with Jim, are by no means alone in their attempt to assert a connection with Morrison after formal declaration of his death. Every identifiable aspect of a rock star like Jim Morrison is parceled out and marketed as a signature trait for the fans' efficient consumption, and after Jim dies or disappears, anything can happen to the image he left in the world.

Jim's immediate relatives, the likeliest authorities on who he really was, have remained aloof from biographical representations of their deceased loved one because they feel themselves bound by a military code of privacy and decency, and as a result, have generally been excluded from the manipulation of Jim's image since his departure from the public eye. As evidenced by the role he played as consultant in the making of Oliver Stone's film, *The Doors*, Alan Graham has been steadfast in his efforts as the "odd man in" to redeem Jim Morrison's image. In addition to co-producing with Anne a four-phase documentary project about Jim called *Poeté Somnolant* "Sleeping Poet" (Sylvester Stallone and John Travolta both vied unsuccessfully for the starring role), Graham has written a book called *I Remember Jim Morrison Too* intended to include the humanizing element noticeably absent from bestselling portrayals of Jim like the one in Jerry Hopkins and Danny Sugerman's *No One Here gets Out Alive,* and counteract all the attempts to sensationalize the dark side of Jim's image as rock god dead by misadventure.

Alan and Anne were divorced in 1986, but his time as James Douglas Morrison's brother-in-law has obviously left an indelible impression on Graham despite the years he spent as aide and mouthpiece for the erratic, colorful Flynt after Jim's passing. Graham has always been bothered by the grossly inadequate portrait of Jim Morrison that has been growing in the public eye all these years. Says his sister, Norma, "After reading each and every book, I would call Alan and ask him, 'Is this true or fiction?' His reply would always be the same. 'Norma it is lies, all lies. Nobody outside the Morrison family ever knew the real Jim. One day when the time is right, I am going to write my own book and tell it like it really was, who the real Jim Morrison was'. Like a mantra he would repeat, 'One day when the time is right I will tell it like it really was'."

With the Admiral's death in 2008, the time was finally right. Graham's *I Remember Jim Morrison Too* stands forth as the only retrospective on Jim Morrison with a tangible core of emotional obligation to its subject. Where other biographers are moved to turn Jim's story into a train wreck and charge admission, Alan Graham's inspiration is to commemorate the emotional effect of their time together. "More than forty books have been published about him, and each one reveals nothing more than the last. The reason for this is because no one in the Morrison clan has ever revealed the true details (nor will they ever)about Jim's life inside the family. My personal account of these events provides rare glimpses and intimate insights into the other side of Jim Morrison and the people who loved him."

Graham's book is highly recommended, as is the subsequently released, detailing his years around the corner from the Beatles Liverpudlian breakout post-Hamburg. Graham has hosted a podcast called "House of Detention" on the Ghost Radio Network and led the Ghost Radio International Paranormal Investigation Team (GRIPIT) regularly tracking down and investigating opportunists claiming to be the real Jim Morrison or his offspring. "You know I heard Cliff's actually come to believe the whole fantasy now," he told me. "To him it's not even a scam anymore, but for her [Cliff's mother, Lorraine Weiden], it's the worst possible form of child abuse." As to whether his brother-in-law faked his death, Graham says, "I don't know . . . The only person who knows is Pamela Courson (who died of a drug overdose in 1974). Don't forget the body was put on ice overnight. The morgues were closed. It was left on Saturday and Sunday night till Monday morning and his body was really blue. She never saw it. Nobody saw that body till it came from the morgue in the coffin, ready for the funeral. Pamela wouldn't look at it. Nobody looked at it. The likelihood that it could've been somebody else is extremely high and Morrison could've seen it and went into hiding and said this is my chance to get away from my life and the people around me."

15 NEAL CASSADY DENVER YEARS SCREENING SELLS OUT

HEATHER DALTON HAS DIRECTED AND PRODUCED A FILM ON NEAL'S YOUTH IN DENVER. THIS CHAPTER GIVES A SNAPSHOT OF ITS PREMIERE IN THAT CITY

THE debut one night only screening of *Neal Cassady: The Denver Years* at the Sie Film Center on June 26th, 2014, opened with a pre-show reception in the lobby with complimentary drinks and food. Elbow to elbow with other ticket holders in the cordoned buffet-bar area, your reporter was reminded of the line in Gregory Corso's poem, "Marriage," about the grubby, bearded handful of his friends at that piece's imagined wedding, "just waiting to get at the drinks and the food." Co-producer Daniel Crosier, one of the artists whose work is featured in Ms. Dalton's film, presented your reporter with a couple of complimentary prints of wood carvings he'd done of Neal's face. Your reporter gave Mr. Crosier an update on the Beat Guide's progress, and asked him, "Is Karl Christian Krumpholz here?" Mr. Crosier promptly introduced me to the film's other artist, with whom he exchanged business cards. The screening sold out close to showtime, and several people were turned away, including Ed Ward and this reporter's sidekick from the spoken word 90s, Devin Scheimberg. Even Bob Hyatt had to play the "son of Neal" card to get tickets for himself, Vera and Henry. Full disclosure: this reporter's lady friend attempted to subtly convince Bob to try to score one more for Devin, clearly asking too much (though, of course, I don't blame her) and Bob, wisely, avoided that hook. Neal's children with Carolyn, all of whom appear in the film, were in England finalizing the details of her estate or they would have attended.

Neal Cassady and kids

No one had expected such an overwhelming reception, least of all its directors and producers, including Heather Dalton and Colorado Public Television Channel 12. The theater was packed; this reporter and his lady friend found seats in the very front, and he dutifully kept his neck at a 90-degree angle straight up and ahead throughout the excellent, edifying feature, the first film to commemorate Neal's days in Denver before adding his spark to the powder keg of the world at large. A ten years labor of love on the part of director Dalton and all its producers, including Joshua Hasel, this film is full of heart. Its debut screening was a personal landmark for lots of great people in all kinds of ways, and this reporter was glad to join that experience, speaking briefly before the screening by way of promoting his limo tour job and soliciting inside connections for the Beat Guide. He was pleased to note the film's similarity of intention and content to this combined history and localized landmark itinerary and pleased to see his name appear in the credits in acknowledgement of his years of dedication and encouragement. Your reporter found himself standing in the aisle with the three Hyatts after the film's conclusion, slightly choked up with unbidden emotions evoked by the film, and he told them so. Producer Joshua Hasel spoke with him briefly about the roundabout course taken by himself and Ms. Dalton in first contacting Carolyn Cassady, involving travel back and forth to her home in England and a blithe contrariness on her part ultimately giving way to the great and generous sharing of opinions and memories which is the heart of *Neal Cassady: The Denver Years*. "At one point, she didn't even want to talk about the Beat stuff at all," confided Hasel. "She just wanted to talk about herself. She had an interesting life."

Carolyn's personal history as the child of landed gentry who became a devout follower of "sleeping prophet" Edgar Cayce as an adult is rich in lively individuality. This reporter was pleased to learn that the volume, "Love, Always," which he'd assumed was a collection of letters to Cassady, was in fact centered on Carolyn's life as Neal's amanuensis and the legislator of his estate and legacy. This reporter is grateful to the late Mrs. Cassady for all her assistance in fleshing out Beat history, and to Denver media maven Heather Dalton, for providing a forum for Carolyn's voice in this excellent film, which was written, directed and produced in part by her, featuring the talents of several other Denver artists, among them poet Paulie Lipman, artists Crosier and Krumpholz, and the film's other narrator, Rodney Franks. The unexpected and overwhelmingly positive reception of this one night only screening might cause Sie to extend the run time, or in some way lead to further screenings of this opus.

16 NO MORE BEATLEMANIA: THE MONKS MEET ROCK & ROLL

CONVERSATION WITH MULTI-INSTRUMENTAL MUSICIAN EDDIE SHAW ABOUT HIS TIME PLAYING BASS WITH THE MONKS IN GERMANY

AN unconventional musical act composed of former U.S. GIs in Germany, the Monks were active for a few years in the sixties before Polydor records spoiled the party by demanding a more traditional sound. Bassist Eddie Shaw exchanged emails with Zack Kopp recently regarding the band's bizarro twinship with their incongruous contemporaries the Beatles. Originally called The Torquays, whose lineup included most future Monks, plus a vocalist named Zack something and a German guy named Hans on drums, the gang of mostly-expatriate friends had a fun-loving spirit amid the military starkness. "We played a club called the Maxim Bar in Gelnhausen. It was where GIs went off base to drink and find females. We called those nights the 'Saturday Night Fights' because before the night was over, someone would get into a fist fight over some girl and then the military police would come in and throw a tear gas grenade to clear the place out. Larry always bought his gas mask with him and put it on while the rest of us were rushing to get out the door. He would sit on stage and play *Green Onions,* until the MPs made him get out. That way he could claim we played the required time. Therefore, the bar owner owed us the full sum of our contract. Hans always watched us with a slight smile on his face, as if asking, 'What are they doing?' I think he worked for the post office."

The Monks are underrated, little-known, and hard to find the truth about, unless you consult bassist Eddie Shaw's website or the books he's written on this one-of-a-kind band's exceptional story. For a long time, they didn't even have a Wikipedia entry, and now that they do, some of the facts are blurred or incorrect. "I have never read Wikipedia about the Monks," says Shaw. "I don't want to. Everyone has their own conception of who we were. Some claim we were born in a petri-dish. My favorite is the one by the girl group Pussy Galore who told People Magazine that they had heard a recording of a band from Germany named the Monks. The Monks were GIs and were AWOL from the army. While the Military was looking for them, they showed up on TV singing, *I Hate You but Call Me*. And then they disappeared to never be seen again. Each one of us was influenced by his own musical heroes. Mine were people like Miles Davis or Moondog. Larry's was the guy who played *Green Onions*. Gary's influencers were north-woods folk artists. Dave's was of course, Elvis Presley. And Roger's was? He never talked about music. He beat the drums without using cymbals and that's all I knew about him. He didn't talk about himself much. As it turned out, we became the owners of our sound. It was a sound no other band had. You can identify the Monks as soon as you hear them - just like the Beatles. It's ironic that the members of the Beatles claim they got their professional chops playing in Hamburg. The Monks did too."

The Monks in St. Pauli district, Hamburg

The Monks are one of the more notable sixties acts, in terms of uniqueness. I found out about them when I learned what I thought was the Fall's "Black Monk Theme" was a cover as a teenager. My subsequent research was briefly complicated by the existence of an English punk band by the same name, but the first Monks don't sound like anybody else. "Every person in the Monks came from a different musical background," Shaw explains, "Gary Burger was a country player. Dave Day played Elvis ('My life started the day I heard Elvis') Roger Johnston was a Texas swing drummer. Larry was a classically trained piano player (mostly played in his living room) and I was a multi-instrument jazz player. In order for us all to get along, we had to deliberately forget our influences and preferences. To play together we had to adapt to a much simpler (yet complex) form of music known as Uber-beat, which we invented. We worked to find the tension points of a song, and this sometimes required 13 or 15 bars instead of the normal 8 or 12 bar compositions. The music sounds easy to play but it is more complex than that. Our managers first heard us and picked us up in Stuttgart where we played for a couple of months. Because of boredom) we experimented with the audiences there. According to our managers, if the audience was not paying attention to the band, then it was a failure. If they loved you, it was also a failure. The best response was to have them arguing about the band on stage. 'Make them watch you as if in shock.' We were getting our haircuts when Roger decided to have a tonsure. That's when we all decided to do it. Our manager Karl said, "That's it!"'

The Monks shaved their hair in Monk's tonsures, a ring of hair around a bald crown, and wore dark cassocks onstage at the same Hamburg joints rocked by fame-bound Liverpool acts with slicked back pompadours a few years prior as they sweated through the same kinds of grueling shifts as entertainment for the various clubs in Germany. They never thought of themselves as forerunners of anything, and dressing like Monks without acting like Monks in the heavily Catholic Old World of the 1960s may not be connected to Crime playing San Quentin dressed as cops in the late seventies but is perhaps the first emergence of the shock-rock credo. "There were many, many accusations of blasphemy from many sources. Old women loved us when they saw us on the street, but when they saw us flirting, drinking alcohol and using profanity. They were shocked. The further south in Germany (the more Catholic) we went, the more anger we would raise with some people. We were even attacked onstage during a concert in Munich."

Hamburg's Reeperbahn district, referred to as the "Grosse Freiheit" ("great freedom") by addled patrons, where they often found themselves playing places like the Top Ten Club, has long served as a destination for English acts from the Beatles to the young Billy Childish, and acts from elsewhere in Europe, but the Monks were unlike others in this crowd as disaffected Americans kitted out with robes and weird haircuts. "One thing we noticed was the type of girls we attracted. They were not the innocent young baby face types screaming for Beatles. Our fans were young, and they had experience. We liked that. We experimented and lo & behold! The Monks were born. All of a sudden - a rainbow-colored life. From there we went to Hamburg and found ourselves in the middle of many well-known Beatle-ites. People like Tony Sheridan (*My Bonnie Lies Over The Ocean)* hated us, but we managed to get our own fan base there and after a while - when we sarcastically would play the Beatles tune, *I Want to Hold Your Hand*,

The audience would sing along with *I want to fuck your hand*. Hamburg was a place of wild rowdy people and we fit in well there. The newspapers began to call us the anti-Beatles."

Eddie Shaw is one of two surviving members of this cluster-busting act, along with keyboardist Larry Clark, who lives in Murfreesboro TN, retired after some years as a computer technician, and who Eddie says has stopped giving interviews as far as he knows. The Monks never had a mop-top phase, but the presence of German visionaries as advisors at a crucial formative moment is another bizarro parallel between the two disparate acts. Where the Silver Beetles had Klaus Voormann and Astrid Kirchherr, the Monks had a brace of post-modern consumerists. "Our managers were well-known in their business as advertising people," he says. "There were four of them: Karl Remy was the 'idea' man. He kept referring to us as playing the music of the future. He won a prize for his TV ad of the year, featuring Volkswagen. Walther Niemann was the 'managing' manager who found compromises for all the arguments we got into. Gunther & Kiki were our graphic artists & publicists. And we had one more manager, Wolfgang Gluszewski, who managed our tours. I believe they are all deceased now. I heard Kiki committed suicide." Monks frontman, lead guitar player and vocalist Gary Burger passed in 2014, after a brief stint as mayor of Turtle River, Minnesota— "When Gary died, it felt strange. I had no clue because the news was not shared. I got the info from a person I did not know. Turtle River, MN had a population of about 70 people, I think"—as did drummer Roger Johnston—"he was the first to pass. He was living in Bemidji, MN and played one reunion tour in NYC (1999). I think he died the next year," and rhythm guitarist Dave Day, who Shaw says, "played all the reunion tours with us until he passed in 2006. He is buried about 50 yards away from Jimi Hendrix in Renton, WA."

Besides having written a memoir of his time in the Monks, the authoritative text on that outfit's formation and heyday, *Black Monk Time* (1995) Shaw authored a sequel to that volume called *Black Monk Time Too* a journal of the band's late nineties reunion tours in the U.S. and Europe— "After years of not speaking about the Monks, I was awakened by two people at the front door of my house, in Carson City, asking if I was Eddie Shaw of the Monks. From that day on things changed for all of us. I was surprised to learn that many Monk songs are being covered by many groups, including movie soundtracks like *Big Lebowski*. Our music was earning us money, something I had never expected. That's when we (The Monks) were asked and decided, as a group, to get together and play a number of reunion tours, starting in NYC and Las Vegas in 1999, ending in London, Berlin, and Frankfurt in 2006." Shaw has written several more books, including a collection of short stories titled, A Cowboy Like Me—Vol. 2 "all names have been changed to protect the guilty," and a historical volume on Giacomo Beltrami's discovery of the source of the Mississippi River. The latest and greatest is one called *Passing Through Minnesoda and Other Altered States* to be published in August 2021, which is a fictionalized memoir of Eddie Shaw's musical experience in the 1970s. An accomplished musician, he also has some non-Monks recordings available, *Minnesoda/Copperhead* 1970's - songs recorded in three different studios -Minneapolis, Chicago, Nashville (from the memoir, *Passing Through Minnesoda), and Jass in Six Pieces* - Eddie Shaw and the Hydraulic Pigeons, experimental jazz tracks with Eddie Shaw on Trumpet.

Taken in front of the Top Ten Club. The Beatles also played here.

Wikipedia makes reference to the band's innovative managers advising them to tour Vietnam and cement their anti-war reputation, but it fell through at the last minute. "The day we were supposed to leave was after a two-week vacation. When three of us showed up, in Frankfurt, to depart - it was the same day we received the message from Gary saying he went home to Minnesota . . . and Roger went home to Texas. They didn't think it was a good idea to go to Vietnam, especially after one member of Tony Sheridan's group was killed by a Viet Cong terrorist who threw a grenade at the stage as they were playing in Saigon. When I read Gary's message, I gave a sigh of relief. I was tired - as we all were. After working six months in Germany to get money to buy my way home, I and Larry caught a tramp steamer. On the boat I read a newspaper article stating the Monks had broken up and Larry was suing Gary and Roger for breach of contract. When I asked Larry about it, he denied it."

When asked who, if any of the bands' contemporaries had an influence on their sound, and how he would describe the Monks influence or effect on the musical scene to follow, Shaw says, "The Fall was one of the first groups to play some of our songs. Mark E Smith was a good friend and sang with us in a reunion concert in Berlin. He also almost knocked the onstage photographer off the stage when the song was finished, and he was walking off stage. He liked to shock the audience. It was great fun. People liked us and they even knew the words to the songs. That's in *"Black Monk Time Too - The Resurrection of The Monks."* (A word to the buyer: Shaw's books are available far more affordably via carsonstreetpublishing.com than Amazon.com but are available at both outlets). "Monks' tunes don't compete with the human messages of, *"You're nothing but a hound dog,"* or *"I want to hold your hand."* But consider this; as it is with humans, there may be only six degrees, or less, of separation in the musical outcome. If the vibrations of thousands of compositions can be reduced to just one of six total existing songs worldwide, then how it is played creates the unique DNA of its existence. This DNA explains how The Monks are identified. Recently, I heard of a new group calling themselves the Monks. After a friend introduced me to them, I asked one of them, 'Why are you using the Monks name? Wouldn't you be more successful if you called yourselves the Beatles.' He had no response. I thought it was funny. Okay, you got it, Zack. That's my piece of information."

RARE BUT SERIOUS 97

Left to right - Monks managers - Kiki, Gunther, Walther, & Karl

17 THE CENTRAL JOKE: MY DINNER WITH FANTE

DAN FANTE'S FIRST APPEARANCE IN DENVER AT MUTINY NOW! BOOKS BEFORE ITS TRANSFORMATION TO MUTINY INFORMATION CAFÉ, FOLLOWED BY A DINNER WITH OTHER AUTHORS IN ATTENDANCE AND BACON IN THE BROWNIES

I was at the Mutiny counter paying Jack Jensen's pale-skinned flossy haired partner Jean for a copy of *FANTE* when a plump, pretty woman with glasses and short brown hair in a light purple dress came up to me and said, "You wrote the article, right? And I saw you guys talking, you're friends with him. Please come to dinner at our house tonight. My name is Susan."

Susan and her husband, Stan, with close cropped black hair in a short sleeved blue button up shirt, were friends of Jack Jensen's—his paintings were hanging all over their house a few blocks away—lurid, sneering, smiling graphics with captions like WHO MADE THE RULES and WHICH END IS UP. The couple had a huge antique cabinet in their dining room stuffed with 20th century gas station kitsch, hand-painted figurines and trinkets and action figures and other bric-a-brac. I stood staring at appreciatively for a while, but no one ventured to say anything, and he couldn't think of a comment either, so he turned back around.

Over dinner Dan Fante talked about the new detective thriller he was writing. I fumbled conversation: "Did you ever end up reading *The Killer Inside* when I recommended it to you?"

"Who wrote that?"

"Oh, Jim Thompson. I haven't read much Thompson but felt like recommending that one because of its central joke."

"No, I didn't," smiled Fante.

"What was its 'central joke'?" asked Piccirilli, suddenly keen.

"Oh, you know, the way he always speaks in aphorisms. Like how everything he says is a cliché. Because he's supposed to be this good guy sheriff for all the townspeople, but he's secretly this crazy— "

"You'd have to be crazy to think of that as 'the central joke'," said Tom, author of multiple suspense narratives.

Well, goddammit, I thought. That's the central fucking joke. That's the central joke, buddy. Bur Dan Fante hadn't read it either. There was no one to defend me. I sat there. "Yes."

Nobody mentioned the Occupy protests, which were spreading all over the world just then, signifying rebirth or heralding the onset of a defensive crackdown by the state. I didn't bring it up. Dan Fante mentioned how he'd been through pretty much every self-help program known to man in his efforts to beat the raging demon on his back, "I went through EST, I even tried Scientology."

"They'll do anything to turn a profit," proclaimed Tom.

"Well," I interposed, "My friend Marvel was a Scientologist for something like 13 years, in the Celebrity Centre, until she escaped with her husband, and it's actually a really hardcore mind control trip they put on everybody who joins . . . they make people believe everybody who's *not* a Scientologist is actually in the service of an evil alien god . . . you see, so they're the only good guys. So, profit is a factor, but there's a lot more going on than simple greed."

"I'd say that's pretty much common to all cults," said Fante, who seemed impeccably on his guard.

"That's textbook cult thinking."

Well, maybe it was. "I guess so."

Susan had made brownies with chunks of bacon in them using bacon grease to cook them. I ate one. It was good. I'd brought a copy of my own self-published first book, *Undamned!* "Here you go, Dan. Might make for good reading on the plane."

"You say that's your *first* novel?" observed Tom.

"Yeah, that's my first."

Tom had upwards of twenty-five novels on action, adventure, horror and death. "Good luck on the road," he proclaimed, barely smiling, his giant, heavy face.

"Good luck to us all."

It felt good knowing Dan might read a book I'd written inspired by his father John's writing. The copy I'd brought had arrived from the automated self-publisher without its copyright imprint, even though I'd entered it online, so I had to handwrite one into the "much respect" inscription barely showing on the flyleaf, the ballpoint having run plumb dry of ink.

Tom Piccirilli died of something brain-tumor-related in summer of 2015 after writing a noir called *The Last Whisper in the Dark* while working on something else called *Blue Autumn*. Daniel Smart Fante also died in 2015.

18 USED BOOKS
PROMOTING EVENTS FOR ALAN GRAHAM AFTER FINDING A PUBLISHER FOR NEAL'S SON BOB HYATT'S BOOK BEAT BASTARD, DENVER USED BOOKSTORE CULTURE AS BACKDROP

WHILE writing the first edition of that Denver and the Beats book, I moved from the Capitol Hill neighborhood to southeast Denver and into an apartment where I broke up with my girlfriend before I finished it, which means that edition was written "on the road" in a heightened state (I'm moving again in a couple of weeks, so this addendum was also composed in transit). The move southeast put me right next to the highway—which meant I heard the sounds of streaming humanity in both directions every day, all day, even in sleep —beside the Colorado Station light rail hub.

The light rail is a comparatively recent modernization of Denver transit I hadn't used much since it lay outside the bounds of my chosen trajectory. But I'd moved southeast, into a little district of apartments, rehabs and care centers, near the same neighborhood as the house I'd spent my teen years in, and now it was going my way. I still liked Cap Hill and LoDo, and now I needed the light rail to get back to the open mics I'd started hosting at Mutiny Information Cafe. The newly discovered mode of conveyance was so convenient, felt so streamlined and fast, it opened up a new perception of the civic grid.

Muralist Tommy Kaui Nahulu ("Will Work For Peace") has painted Jack and Neal on the East facing wall of The Fork and Spoon Café on the northwest intersection of Colfax and Logan (in the same building which formerly housed Taki's Golden Tempura Bowl, long a favorite source of healthy, cheap Japanese fast food for writers and artists in Denver, including myself, and you would've liked it, too, and before that, for years, it was the Metropolis. I mean the place has history). We almost held a *Denver Beat Scene* Book Release at Fork and Spoon, on the 58th anniversary of *On the Road*'s publication, but the owners backed out for some reason, and we had to relocate to City Grille on short notice. Don't get me wrong, no hard feelings. That event was well attended, and the one at Kilgore Books unexpectedly even attracted some descendants of Neal's contentious half-brothers, the Dalys. All of whom were very well-mannered, might I add— one even offered to share a vegan sandwich, while another produced black and white family photos of young Neal shirtless and crewcut on hot Denver sidewalks I had never seen in any book, like a pocket miracle. [By the way, EDITOR'S NOTE Neal's illegitimate granddaughter Vera Hyatt is only interested in broadening familial connections previously unknown, if anyone is listening.]

I always took the light rail, running alongside I-25 Eastbound, in the northwest direction, stopping first at Denver University—where Neal Cassady's future spouse, Carolyn Robinson, came in 1946 to study theater arts and set design—and always said a little affirmation for all the Cassadys, Hansens and Hyatts, all descendants of Neal, both legitimate and otherwise, by name as the bell rang and we pulled in. A series of tiles decorated with abstract carvings running along the length of the whole thing, like a series of streams or vines or snakes, with one central vein through the mural's center—like the World Snake hallowed in Kerouac's Dr. Sax, and presumably inspired by the same indigenous legend that inspired Jack—but whoever put the tiles in sometimes got the order wrong, particularly at the D.U. stop, so that sections of that Snake are not contiguous, and liable to appear anywhere.

Next I proceeded to the Louisiana/Pearl hub, where I wished the best on those two streets – then further faster northwest along the highway up over the rise, past the remains of Gates Rubber Co. at left, future site of apartments, I guess, where Neal had a job recapping tires as a youth, and hallowed his name one more time, before curving rightward to the Broadway stop, where, if going to the bank, say, I disembarked and caught a northbound O bus.

Passing under the overpass just north of Broadway Station on the O down Lincoln Ave. the other day, I saw a bunch of homeless people clustered there with shopping carts full of belongings, catching shade on the 102 degrees day, and maybe sleeping there at night—so crazy rents have gotten, and so crowded homeless shelters have become in this Queen City recent years.

I remember when my family moved to Denver from St. Louis back in 1983, there were homeless people under the same bridge, then not for many years, now here they were again, from the legalized pot drawing tourists, for one thing, and all the eager speculators finding ways to further market Denver, and who knows what else. There had been the same talk about all the Californians coming here and spoiling things back then, too, then for many years it stopped. Now here it was again. Denver has always been a waystation. A place where things were always changing, in a way that was reliable—there is mention of the brown cloud in ancient Native legends, only it wasn't so full of toxic waste back then—and the same xenophobia may have been present in some form when Neal Sr. and Maude Scheuer first came here with newborn Neal prospecting for a future back in 1926. They certainly had street cars in those days. On Colfax Avenue, even. There are pictures.

New things have happened in the Beat Scene relating to Denver since that first edition was published, all of which bear reporting far more urgently than did my prose fiction fabrication formerly placed in this noble, final space, and only once I've told them to you will I feel I have justified this portion of literary and cultural history by my treatment as an amateur historian (a word to you ardent collectors, the inferior first edition with "All About Angles" appended is sure to be a collector's item—snap 'em up.)

Of all Neal's known offspring—his daughters and son with Carolyn, Cathleen Joanne (b. 1948), Jami Cassady Ratto (1949) and

John Allen Cassady (b. 1951); his son with Connecticut socialite Diana Hansen, radio host Curtis Hansen (b. 1950); and Robert Hyatt, who is 70 years old in 2016— the first to write an autobiography was John Allen, dual namesake of Neal's Beat friends, J. Kerouac and A. Ginsberg. His unpublished *Visions of Neal* is an account of his and sisters Jami and Cathy's upbringing in Los Gatos, CA by Carolyn and the peripatetic but seemingly mostly-present-somehow-anyway Neal. Without question, this excellent book deserves a wider audience, and much respect to him.

Robert Hyatt

Since publication of the first edition of *The Denver Beat Scene*, Neal's eldest known living son, Robert Hyatt, has become a close friend, entrusting me with a copy of his memoir, written as a legacy for his own children long before he found out Neal was his own father. Bob bought me lunch several times, came with me to my mom's house for Thanksgiving dinner, and did me the honor of inviting me to his late granddaughter, Olivia's funeral. After minimal editing and an enjoyable search, I'm proud to say *Beat Bastard: An Adoptee's Portfolio* by Robert Hyatt was published by Robin Stratton's Big Table Publishing sometime in 2016, providing unembellished accounting of the author's coming to maturity without known biological origin in some of the most turbulent decades in recent Western history (40s-

70s), (though the last two and the current are surely in there, too). Ms. Stratton had interviewed this author for her Boston Literary Magazine a few years before I got the Beat Book offer and spontaneously asked a lot of questions about Beat lit, so it seemed the perfect fit, having been named for Irv Rosenthal's Chicago mag and occasional performance space that was an early Beat venue.

19 SELF-MADE: ARAM SAROYAN ON INVENTING HIS OWN TRADITION
A SELF-DESCRIPTION OF AUTHOR ARAM SAROYAN'S APPROACH ASSEMBLED FROM PUBLISHED PASSAGES AND QUOTES AND APPROVED BY HIM

POET, novelist, biographer, memoirist and playwright Aram Saroyan's career bespeaks lifelong intimacy with a rich vein of experience. Saroyan declined to be interviewed for this piece, having already written extensively of the authors and topics covered. He sent me a copy of one of his books to reference. All Saroyan quotes are from his *Door to the River: Essays and Reviews from the 1960s into the Digital Age*, Black Sparrow Books, Second Printing, 2010.

He was present when the nation at large got its first shot of Jack Kerouac's conservative side, having accompanied poets Ted Berrigan and Duncan McNaughton to the home in Lowell, Massachusetts, the landed Beat King shared with his mother and wife for an impromptu interview. "I was most surprised by the figure we saw on the other side of the screen door. There was a short, stout guy with a potbelly in a T-shirt—a guy who looked like a construction worker who'd let himself go. His voice was a bellow . . . and the next thing we knew there was a scuffle going on with another body of the same approximate size and bulk that turned out to be Kerouac's Greek wife, Stella." (The Driver: Reflections on Jack Kerouac, 110) Kerouac made statements in the ensuing interview—such as, "And here comes a whole bunch of rabbis walking arm in arm . . . tee-dah tee-dah . . . and they wouldn't part for this Christian man and his wife. So my father went POOM! And he knocked a rabbi right in the gutter. Then he took my mother and walked on through," and "Goy means joy" (111)—which, coupled with his 1972 appearance alongside Ed Sanders on the William Buckley Show, effectively disestablished for most his reputation as countercultural Wildman and made him seem more the drunken spokesman for convention.

"Publishing per se never easier for me than in the sixties," Saroyan says on page 74 of *Door to the River: Essays and Reviews from the 1960s into the Digital Age*, in *Occupation: Writer*, "but the honeymoon was over quickly, and I stood as bemused as my father had been when he saw the effect of his tv appearances on his book sales. What, or where, exactly, was the culture in all this? . . . such a great boost of confidence seemed to come forward to us . . . We felt special—that we mattered, that we might have an impact on the way things were—and I believe all young people deserve to feel that way and know that more often than not they don't."

Aram Saroyan selfie

Aram's father, William Saroyan, author of the classics *The Human*

Comedy, My Name is Aram, and other works of enduring genius, including the play *The Time of Your Life,* was one of the greatest literary sensations of the 1930s, possessed of a voice so in demand he could leap atop a publisher's desk, after being offered an advance of thousands, demand, "Double or nothing, you son of a bitch!" and get what he wanted, no questions asked, according to a speech Dan Fante gave once. At first preferring to downplay his heritage, giving characters based on himself names like Wesley Jackson, in time, the elder Saroyan became known as outspokenly Armenian, making a reliable literary hook of his cultural heritage, as did Dan's father, John Fante (true life inspiration for the pinball maniac Willie in Saroyan's The Time of Your Life, 1939) in an era of devastation and reconstitution when America's sense of itself as a nation-of-immigrants seemed crucial to the reinstatement of prosperity. Along with Hemingway, Fitzgerald, and the elder Fante, William Saroyan was a leading light during a time when writers were equivalent to rock stars in public estimation. While not nearly as well-known today, he was among the more widely read and respected writers of his time.

By comparison with his father's loose, exuberant, style, Aram's voice is more clinical than emotive. As one who came of age in the sixties, Aram never qualified as a Beat poet himself, though his minimalist poetry is known and revered worldwide, and he was on intimate terms with most of that movement's flowers, including *Gunslinger* author Ed Dorn, who, he said, "is among his contemporaries perhaps closest in temper and out look to [Amiri Baraka]," Michael McClure, "an unabashed visionary who takes all the risks of that stance to make his statement" and "fast speaking woman" Anne Waldman, late of Boulder's Jack Kerouac School of Disembodied Poetics at Naropa University, of whom he writes, "Of all the poets of my generation, none has done more to bring poetry before the public at large . . . She has made a genuine contribution to poetry today; perhaps now is the time for her to give more thought to her resources and direction." (Performing Poet, p. 134)

Besides Kerouac, Aram Saroyan had connections with multiple other Beats, including Amiri Baraka, Ed Dorn, Anne Waldman, and

Lew Welch, who disappeared into the foothills of the Sierra Nevada with his gun in 1971—he is believed to have committed suicide, but his body was never found—about whom Saroyan wrote *Genesis Angels: The Saga of Lew Welch and the Beat Generation*, and the solo performance piece, *A Tender Mind: The Life and Times of Lew Welch, Beat Poet*, though the two never met.

Several notable Beats embraced Libertarianism after the heyday. Kerouac hero Neal Cassady's fellow Denverite Hal Chase took the disconnection from convention even farther by removing himself from the grid as completely as possible, retreating to a private farm, raising crops sufficient to his family's needs and home schooling his children. Wherever the body ended up, Lew Welch took this game the farthest, removing himself entirely. Says Saroyan, "Welch, who struggled with alcoholism, seemingly spent his life alternating mountain hermitages with urban life, writing about each with the humility that is perhaps his primary hallmark. He doesn't separate himself from his environment, whatever its nature, by any sense of superiority, but rather he perceives its dynamics by giving himself without restraint to its reality . . . Lew Welch [has] yet to be celebrated as he [deserves] to be."(Reedies, 150, 152) And he never came back. "His body was never found." (149)

Of Baraka, formerly LeRoi Jones, he says, "when I first knew him, he was *the* hipster, a kind of literary Miles Davis, and while surrounded by admiring literary colleagues, most of them white, was also a pivotal social figure in bringing together the black and white artistic communities." (Amiri Baraka, 15) This in advance of his leaving the downtown scene, changing his name to Imamu Amiri Baraka, whereby "uniquely among his peers, in a few short years he had realized a creative efflorescence comparable to what Allen Ginsberg achieved with the recent publication of "Howl," and a few years later, "Kaddish"(16). . .the situation is far worse for many in the African-American community . . . Baraka speaks to that difference, [addressing] a well-nigh lifelong sociopolitical emergency. And so Allen Ginsberg also seemed to see it, although he wouldn't demonize his opposition." (20)

He's not a fan of Charles Bukowski, who he nevertheless admits, "has given writing and reading to a large public who might otherwise shine it, as they used to say," (The Bukowski Crown, 26) by "keeping the dark side of the picture in view" (25). "Bukowski is fine, I want to say, but can he really be a model of the first-rank artist? Or isn't he, rather, an easy interlude—and thank God for them—before you move on to something actually great." (28)

Aram's experience as an interviewer, reviewer and commentator extends beyond strictly literary circles. "In August of 1966 in New York City, Gerard Malanga, the twenty-three-year-old poet and assistant to Andy Warhol, is also becoming known for the dance he does, dressed in leather and wielding a whip, in front of the Velvet Underground, the rock band led by Lou Reed and sponsored by Warhol . . . Malanga doesn't have a place of his own to live at the same time he is frequenting famous night spots and attending big parties of the period . . . [his] *The Secret Diaries,* along with Jim Carroll's *The Basketball Diaries* and William S. Burroughs, Jr.'s *Speed,* seems to me a major prose testament of the sixties. Centered like the other two books in Manhattan, it achieves a gathering pitch of intensity uniquely its own." (The Secret Diaries, 119-121) Saroyan wrote and narrated the documentary film *The Moment*, directed by George Sandoval, 2001. His poetry and prose has appeared in *The New York Times Magazine, New York Times Book Review, Village Voice, The Nation,* and elsewhere, and he taught for 15 years in the University of Southern California's Master of Professional Writing Program. He built his career, in part, on informed perception of the timeline of influence. Understanding how there couldn't have been a Kerouac without a Thomas Wolfe, an Allen Ginsberg without a William Carlos Williams, or an Aram Saroyan without a William Saroyan, however distinct one from another, gave him a privileged insight. "I grew up in the shadow of a famous writer," he says, "grew up in his shadow in a general sense," which circumstance encouraged him to make his own incomparable way, it still being the case, in America, that "writers often invent their own literary traditions—not necessarily a bad thing, given a responsive practitioner at large among the models and monuments literature offers." (Inventing a Tradition, 3)

RARE BUT SERIOUS 111

Sculpture by Aram Saropyan

20 MIKE MCQUATE AND JAMI CASSADY ON THE JOAN ANDERSON LETTER
MCQUATE WHO FOUND IT, CASSADY WHOSE LATE FATHER NEAL WROTE IT

NEAL'S fabled 1950 "Joan Anderson Letter" to Jack—the missive which inspired the Beat Generation into existence from the ashes of the "New Vision" founded by Kerouac, Ginsberg and Lucien Carr at Columbia—with its spontaneous fluidity of manner and quality of all-inclusiveness minus slavish attention to form—was discovered in 2012, and various claimants entered litigation toward its ownership. As detailed in Nicosia's book, the Sampases attempted a claim on this artifact, too, its recipient having been Jack, after all, but were unsuccessful in their gambit. According to Nicosia, the Sampases attempted a claim on this letter, too, but were unsuccessful in their gambit.

JAMI CASSADY RATTO: "Jim Sampas and Simon Ward had sent a proposal, but the family didn't like it. Besides getting 50%, they had 4 "editors" that would get nine percent EACH! Jim said they wanted to make it a book of Neal and Jack's correspondence, but we figured if all they were really after was the letter, we should get more and maybe a separate contract. So that was that."

Minus the portion published posthumously in Neal's *The First Third*, the bulk of this letter, long thought lost overboard innocent Gerd

Stern's houseboat, but had been in the possession of a record producer Jack Spinosa, in whose house it was discovered by Mike McQuate when cleaning it, with Spinosa's daughter Jean, after her father's death in 2012. McQuate's knowledge of Ginsberg, Cassady & Kerouac caused him to look twice at the document that otherwise might have been tossed away forever.

Michael McQuate with Gerd Stern

MIKE McQUATE: "Somehow Jack Spinosa got this lot of stuff from the Golden Goose Press, a small publishing company, and Jean Spinosa (Jack's daughter) had no idea how her dad had gotten this particular lot of papers and publications. At the moment of discovery of the Letter it was just a few pages in an envelope amongst piles of other papers that Jean Spinosa didn't seem to care about too much and only knew that something needed to be done with all this stuff that had been sitting on a sagging bookshelf for decades. I agreed to haul it all away, go through it all later, and see if it might have any value to anyone. She agreed to give it all to me and I was in the process of packing it all up when I came across the letter. Jean took it back from me that night and I let her do it because neither one of us knew how valuable it might be at that moment. Sometime soon after Carolyn

Cassady died, Jean took the Letter to Profiles in History, and together, they tried to ram the auction through before anyone could mount a legal challenge, but it didn't work. After the auction was blocked by an injunction from the Cassady family, Jean sued Profiles in History, me, the Cassidys, et al."

Neal has several known offspring—his daughters and son with Carolyn, Cathleen Joanne (b. 1948), Jami Cassady Ratto (b. 1950) and John Allen Cassady (b. 1951); his son with late Connecticut socialite Diana Hansen, radio host Curtis Hansen (1950-2014); and his son with Denver's Maxine Beam, Robert Hyatt, who is 73 as I write this. John Allen's unpublished *Visions of Neal* is a collection of childhood memories of his father in Los Gatos, where Neal and Carolyn settled in the 50s while Neal was working as a brakeman on the Southern Pacific Railroad, which remains officially unpublished. Robert Hyatt's book, *Beat Bastard: An Adoptee's Portfolio*, published by Big Table Publishing in 2016, details its author's growing up as an adopted orphan to discover, as a senior citizen, his biological father's identity. Neal's daughters Cathy and Jami have edited and published a book by the late Carolyn Cassady, entitled *Travel Tips for the Timid; or, What Guidebooks Leave Out*, and City Lights will be publishing the Joan Anderson Letter that started the Beat Generation.

JAMI CASSADY RATTO: "We agreed the letter should be presented as a scholarly book by itself with Gerry doing a forward and maybe Dave Moore or Bill Morgan doing an afterward. He even had two publishers lined up. When they found out City Lights had rights from *The First Third*, they backed out. Now it stands that the letter will be published, in its entirety, along with a big push by City Lights for the 50th anniversary of *The First Third* in 2021."

[EDITOR'S NOTE: *The Joan Anderson letter*, by Neal Cassady was published, on August 31, 2020, by Eyewear Publishing, and is available at Amazon and some bookstores.)

21 THE INVENTION OF D.I.Y.
PROMOTING AL GRAHAM'S BOOKS IN THE DENVER UNDERGROUND

I was recommended by old friend and Denver Slam Empress Suzi Q. Smith to read Beat poetry at the Clyfford Still Museum one night. It went very well, with me shouting cut up sheets of poetry from all the Beat Generation writers—male, female, black, Jewish, Christian, Atheist, gay, straight—flinging pages around for effect, and surprising myself by choking up in the strangest of places—as when relating Gregory Corso's comment in an interview that the reason women are underrepresented in the Beat lit canon was because at that time in U.S. history female rebellion was countered with the threat of incarceration in mental asylums. That made me cry.

I started walking around the room I was in very slowly, at one point attracting a small crowd of rapt listeners on and around a bench between myself and a big red painting by Clyfford Still, where I held place a while before walking another few steps. After I did that for two fifteen- or twenty-minute sets, a couple of poets from the DU scene came up and said I should have just kept walking around through all the rooms instead of staying in that single big one, but it was too late. Then the sleek female museum liaison gave me a check for $200, and I walked outside to where a band was playing and lay down in the grass with my friend Felicia from New Mexico for a few minutes, patrons walking around, before walking back to her car and driving back to Colorado Blvd., where the motels near my place where.

The first one we tried, a La Quinta, seemed too expensive to me, and I asked would she mind if we tried another. The next one, in Glendale, was equally expensive, which surprised me. "I used to come here with my girlfriend sometimes, and I think it cost something like 35 bucks . . . but that was a long time ago."

Felicia shook her head. We ended up driving back to La Quinta, where she angrily refused my repeated attempts to pay. The next morning, she sent me a text: "Do you need me to pick you up?"

"No need," I answered, feeling headstrong, and started across the pedestrian bridge outside my building to meet her at La Quinta.

"I'll be in the lobby," she had texted, and I assumed she meant the Perkins right there, where we'd be getting breakfast, but in fact she meant the lobby of La Quinta, so it took a little longer getting started than intended.

"Did you see that guy? she asked, as we approached the restaurant. "Some weird guy was walking around in the parking lot putting his feet on people's cars. Like if he saw a nice-looking Mercedes, he'd go up and put his foot on it. I got the impression he was making some kind of a statement."

I hadn't seen it, but the story gave me the sense of the characteristic lifeways there must be of a La Quinta Inn just off the highway with a Perkins appended. We drove around going to garage sales and a couple of thrift stores, then, after lunch at Senor Burrito's, where she told me the phrase "D.I.Y." sounded like something was making up, adding, What the? "Were you ever in the Portland punk scene in the 90s?" she demanded. "No, I've never been to Portland. The 90s? What?" None of it seemed to make sense, but I could hardly blame her after getting stuck with the motel cost. Felicia stormed off back to Santa Fe, and I walked over to Fahrenheit Books, proprietor Bill Montague, long my favorite of Denver's used bookstores, where I ran into the venerable Dave Lachmann unloading some signed first edition antiques. Dave used to be one of two bookstore clerks in the basement of Joe DeRose's bygone Denver coffeehouse, Muddy's, which has had a few locations over the years, the one I frequented having been 22nd and Champa, across from a big, dedicated parking lot (or was it?), though both spaces have long since been occupied by other utilities and structures.

Himself an original Denver Beat, Dave knew me in the Henry Alarmclock days, played witness to my development as an author over my years in this great city and has always been extremely supportive. Bill Montague wasn't in Fahrenheit's on that day, co-owner Hillel in his place, who Dave Lachmann greeted as "Hill!" upon entering—upon hearing Dave's voice, I emerged from the stacks where I was browsing and greeted him incorrectly as "Bill!" (to his credit, instead of pointing out my error, Dave Lachmann never mentioned it, and may even have greeted me as "Henry" in return*).

Dave and I were talking, and the subject of Gary Reilly came up. Even THIS name took a minute to remember before it all washed over me. Gary Reilly is the name of the deceased Denver author, never published widely in his own lifetime, who had impressed me as being easily the greatest John Fante impressionist I'd ever come across, and not in strictly an imitative way, rather, in Reilly's resourceful provision of a credibly distinct voice clearly having evolved from that template of hospitality (insofar as regards Reilly's Asphalt Warrior series, a fictionalized account of the years he spent earning dough as a cabbie in Denver while writing his art, though several other volumes show not a trace of that influence). After he died, all of Gary Reilly's works have been slated for publication by Denver's Running Meter Press (and many have already seen print, including of the Asphalt Warrior series), Editor in Chief Mark Stevens having been among his best friends during his life and, though cognizant of Reilly's literary ambitions, not having realized his extreme talent and prolific output during his life.

So Gary Reilly comes up, and Dave Lachmann says, "That's what you need, a loving press who understands how good you are, and dedicated to bringing your books out."

"Yes, that would be nice, wouldn't it. I'll try to fill that slot."

"Because you've probably got something on hold right now, don't you, or something in the works?"

"I've got this book called *Overgrown*. Needs a few months to finish, but I've got one out looking called *Camp Elasticity*, too. Think I just found an agent. Possibly."

"Boy, you've always got something going!" marveled Dave Lachman from the depths of his beard

"That's true." It was always something.

"What else are you doing?"

"Well, I'm doing this, too." I reached into my bag and pulled out a red poster emblazoned with two red book covers and text and handed it to him. "Editing books for Jim Morrison's ex-brother-in-law, Alan Graham." For all our occasional telephonic clashes, largely rooted in syntax and misunderstanding, I had decided to use my association with the garrulous Graham to teach myself the skill of statesmanship, or maybe learn it by osmosis, and those first two "free range" bookstores were the proving ground. And why not, as Jack Kerouac once asked Steve Allen.

"And you wrote that Beats and Denver book."

"That's right."

"There never would've been a Doors without the Beats," observed Dave.

"Nor a Beatles. This guy is 72 years old, from Liverpool, knew all the Beatles as teenagers, married Morrison's sister and moved to L.A. He also worked for Larry Flynt. And he's written a book of Beat poetry himself. Oh, here's a flyer, too."

Dave let the poster collapse back into its rolled-up shape and accepted the black and white flyer. "And what's this for?"

"It's a book release party at Kilgore Books next to Wax Trax. It's coming right up. And we're selling a line of sunglasses soon. Are you a Jim Morrison fan?"

"I am."

"Perfect. You hear that, Hillel?"

Hillel was behind the desk, studying Dave's books and figuring a price to offer him. "What's that?" He looked up from toting amounts.

Dave handed back the flyer and I handed it to him. "Been working with Jim Morrison's brother-in-law, have this poster, these flyers, some books. Gonna try that place next door now."

"What's his wife's name, Pamela something?"

"Pamela Courson, but this guy was married to Jim's sister, Anne."

I walked into the shop on the corner, where a gray-haired man and woman sat behind a huge desk piled with books. "I'm a local author, and I know you specialize in first editions!" I announced. That's what I'd thought, because they had refused to buy used books from him several times over the years and typically given that excuse, as if they only wanted the newer copies.

Alan Graham's books

"No," said the woman, nonplussed.

"Oh, I'm sorry." They took a poster, promising to hang it, and refer all the askers to the place next door or Mutiny or Kilgore's. "Excellent, thanks." I gave them a complimentary copy of Graham's chapbook, another introduction to the Ministry of Rock (as a Catholic minister, Graham boasted decades of experience as a grief counselor and employer of the indigent and loss prevention specialist). Neither of those bookstore owners knew it, but I'd be back soon with more books and another pleasant enquiry about something else more science-fiction-like.

I hadn't talked to Al in a few days. Things were moving forward with the Dead Rockers Society sunglasses deal, in which we planned to market signature shades to all the impersonators of bygone rock acts on a certain company's roster. Graham was also working on some way to capitalize on the Pokemon Go craze that was sweeping the nation at that time by coming up with an alternate version called Mojo-Risin-Mon or something along those lines.

The day after my first date with Sibyl, I received an alarmed email from Bob Hyatt. He had discovered several errors with the names of different characters in his memoir. A whole rewrite would be necessary. I'd lampooned his Luddite tendencies regarding cell phone technology but it seemed I'd been too trusting of Word's "replace all" feature. I ended up having to make all those changes myself and resend them to the publisher line by line. Then came an email from local journalist Gregory Daurer asking if Hyatt's book was a self-publishing venture. This pissed me off, that status having once been held as a badge of inferiority among the writers of my generation when who cares after all, really. "The publisher normally subjects clients to a thorough vetting process. She deferred in this case out of respect," I snapped back. At least, my mood was snappish. I kept thinking Al Graham would call at any minute, but he didn't. He'd sent another box of books and I noticed they didn't have ISBNs, which meant they might miss going down in posterity.

"Now we need some ISBNs," I thought.

Reverend Al Graham

I went to a couple of shows by local Doors cover bands to sell off the contents from the box of books Graham had sent, the first in Lowry Town center, accompanied by Christine Mc Manus, where he was greeted by the band's Morrison and Manzarek, and the joint's owners had me stand in a little glassed-in case at the back of the room, where I sold nothing, and once in Colorado Springs, with Hillary Leftwich, following dinner with her family.

I saw my second Doors tribute show that evening, slipped out just before it ended to set up my table in the concert hall lobby, and after standing there for about half an hour, periodically shouting "Books for sale by Jim Morrison's brother!" "The most authentic biography of Jim Morrison you'll ever read!" and so on for about half an hour, succeeding in selling a single copy, which sale had also included a few strange moments of conversation. "I'm sorry if I'm coming off aggressive," had said my interlocutor, a Mr. Greywolf, with a silver beard, who also wore a fringed leather jacket and a red bandana on his head. "I just fixate on things, and I can't stop talking. I have some form of traumatic brain injury."

"No, you don't seem aggressive, at all," I reassured him. "I have some form of traumatic brain injury too."

"Sucks, doesn't it?"

"Well, I've been able to manage it so far."

"What?"

"I say, it seems to be manageable. Might have healed by now."

Greywolf urged me to sign the book he had edited and made me promise to call him regarding turning something into a script, asserting that he was in demand on the Internet Movie Data base, whatever that meant. "Okay," I said, "I have a couple of novels that could stand being turned into scripts."

"No way. Can't do it. No novels. Won't work. But if you ever need a script made, look me up."

"Thanks."

Hillary Leftwich drove me back to my new apartment, gave me a hug goodnight in her I STAND WITH STANDING ROCK T-shirt, and drove away back to her own place in Capitol Hill. I sent Al an email about my second Doors tribute show and received this in response:

Hi Zack,

I am still having difficulty with leg circulation issues, having a new procedure on the 16th of November, hopefully it will be resolved then.

Bummer to see the new generation NOT buying books, sorry to say we live in a world of short-burst conversations in an abbreviated language worthy of imbeciles only. The written word is edging toward extinction.

Al

22 8TH ANNUAL NEAL CASSADY BIRTHDAY BASH, 2/10/2017, DENVER

UNTIL A FEW YEARS AGO, DENVER'S MERCURY CAFÉ HAD A TRADITION OF HONORING NEAL'S BIRTHDAY WITH ANNUAL LITERARY-MUSICAL SHOWCASES

THE 8th annual Neal Cassady Birthday Bash went off with a bang at Denver's Mercury Cafe on February 10th of 2017, with a variety of Bohemian attendees and presenters. I was pleased and surprised when Bash founder band guru Mark Bliesener asked me to read something this year. My friend Becca Mhalek (Jane Doe, ex-Nightshark, others) agreed to accompany me on her saxophone, and Mark had us open the show. I read something cobbled together from my proposed 2nd edition of *The Denver Beat Scene,* my recently published novel, *Overgrown,* and some other writing of mine. Becca's intuitive expertise enabled the combination of our forces in what poet Jerry Smaldone (*Fatto a Mano, All Flesh Shall See it Together,* and others) called "the best pairing of words and voice I've heard." That's him saying that.

The next presenter was Neal Cassady's eldest living known son, Robert Hyatt, star of the 2017 Birthday Bash, giving the first of two readings including excerpts from his newly published *Beat Bastard: An Adoptee's Portfolio* (2017), where he displayed his pragmatically empathetic intent in the first by answering the questions he felt the audience would likely want the answers to more than anything else—questions like how are he and Neal different? How are they similar? In his second reading later in the show, Hyatt detailed the protracted process of discovering his biological parents' identities (Hyatt never learned his biological father's name until he was himself 66 years old). Creds to Robin Stratton of Boston's Big Table Publishing for bringing Bob's memoir to the public arena, and creds to him for writing it.

Other performers that night included *Gunslinger* author Ed Dorn's widow, poet Jennifer Dunbar Dorn (*Manchester Square*, others), poet Nick Haberman, Chicano noir fiction author Manuel Ramos (*My Bad: A Mile-High Noir*, *The Skull of Pancho Villa*, others), Denver poetry scene stalwart Ed Ward, who read a story called "All Shook Up" accompanied by Dean Roquentin on guitar and voice, City Park Advisory Committee. Spokesman Andy Sense, who announced the plans for rain-activated Cassady quotes in City Park–what a great idea —(contact him here with your favorites: andrewsense@gmail.com), and singer-songwriter Marty Jones, who brought down the house with three or four rousing numbers to close. The lineup changes every time. None of Neal's other children and their families made it to Denver this year, but are sure to return for the next one, or send a representative. Best to them always.

I'm glad to see Denver finally honoring its influential son, as manifested in recent practical occurrences like those rain-activated Cassady quotes throughout the City Park landscape and plans for a Platte-side luxury hotel in Neal's name, despite uneasy juxtaposition with Neal's own flophouse childhood. My reading ended with my idea for establishment of a self-sustaining local creative scene in the coming year involving civic recognition and appreciation. I'm thankful for the homegrown tradition of the Neal Cassady Birthday Bash, paying tribute first, and most organically, by far. Thank you, Mark Bliesener. Thank you, everyone who performed this year. Thanks to all who attended. Thank you, Marilyn Megenity, for providing a home for the Bash at your worthy establishment, the Mercury Café, all these years, and indefinitely into the future. Until next time.

23 REPRINTED

PROMOTING THE REPRINTS OF AL GRAHAM'S BOOKS ABOUT GROWING UP WITH THE BEATLES IN LIVERPOOL, AND HIS FRIENDSHIP WITH HIS WIFE'S BROTHER JIM MORRISON

YEARS later, I reprinted those Morrison articles online at a site called Marijuana Free Press. When I got to the one about Al, titled "His Brother's Keeper," I remembered Graham getting upset the first time I'd gone to press without contact, and quickly looked him up on Facebook. There he was, surrounded by a pack of rescue dogs. Before long, I was back in the exact relationship to this remarkable character, helping him edit and ghost write the same books we'd talked about when they first met.

Al has bailed Cliff Morrison out of jail in the past and looked after him as a sort of errant nephew. This may or may not have anything to do with a potential blood relationship to the late Jim Morrison. Cliff has petitioned that a DNA test be conducted to verify his claim, but that option has been formally forbidden by the Morrison Estate. Some have chosen to interpret their refusal as some form of admission. In fact, the Morrison family is given to a code of hermetic secrecy, as indeed is more common than not among military bloodlines, preventing access from without. Many aspects of Jim's life are hidden in plain sight and lacking mention in most of the bios due to the strict code of military reticence adhered to by the Morrison Estate.

What makes Alan Graham's book about Jim Morison a cut above the rest is that it's the account of a family member, Jim's brother-in-law, his sister's husband for more than ten years, who knew the family dynamic, who knew Jim more thoroughly as a full person than anyone stunned by his fame or impressed by the Doors to distortion.

Said Al Graham by phone that afternoon: "You know, Jim had a little Fagin period just before he met the other Doors. When he was living on that rooftop, and writing poems every night? Commanded a whole gang of street kids." Usually, Al quoted Shakespeare. This time, it was Dickens. It is to be noted that Morrison's own creative flavor was a direct product of the Beat Generation's influence (as is the third volume by Graham, entitled *Poet Rain*).

Conspiracy theorists have pointed out ties to military intelligence families in most of the rock stars to emerge from the Laurel Canyon scene, which included Jefferson Airplane, the Mamas and the Papas, Crosby, Stills, Nash, and Young, and for a time, the Doors. Compelling speculation of a secret government connection aside, few realize that Jim Morrison was the very first scion (meaning elder son) of a military bloodline dating back before the Revolutionary War— presumably unto Scottish clan conflicts—not to have chosen a military career. In this sense, he may have been, himself, a soldier in a different sort of war, giving him a definite social and cultural placement, making his a significantly American story, and his family's the legacy of an Eternal American Family—Colonially speaking, that is. Indeed, when it came to most Western celebrities and news items about the Western Lands in general, "the truth was always moving," which was a phrase of mine to encapsulate the sense of constant uncertainty and selective omni-science native to speciation of today's media cloud, anything could be "proven," yet literally "nothing" was "meant to be," or incontrovertible over time—and especially so in the case of Jim Morrison.

The next release event for Al Graham's books would be held at Mutiny. I reached out to my friend Claudzilla in the Denver art rock scene, who was extremely helpful. I respected her very much as a hard-working promoter of the ideal of Weirdness in Denver's music scene.

The first band she set me up with, Gabriel Albelo's Silver Face, ended up bailing because of one member having to work. Claudzilla suggested I contact another one of her friends named Jeff Josh Barr, and his outfit, Klaus Dafoe, agreed to play a very tight instrumental set of electric guitars and a stripped-down drum kit to great effect.

Mutiny logo

24 PAUL WILLIAMS: REMEMBERED

WILLIAMS INVENTED ROCK CRITICISM WITH HIS CRAWDADDY! MAGAZINE

PAUL Williams was among the first writers to take rock 'n' roll seriously as an art form. He preached that gospel in *Crawdaddy!* a magazine he co-founded as a college student, and in *Outlaw Blues* (1969) and other books about Bob Dylan, Neil Young and the Beach Boys. And yet, he had other chapters in his life, some light, some dark, including being friends and literary executor to Philip K. Dick. Zack Kopp offers a career-spanning look for PKM.

> *"A person's vitality – and I appreciate the humor of myself, a dead man, speaking of such things – is difficult to capture in words. Our friends race through our lives like shooting stars, and when, of an evening's conversation, we manage to enclose their fire and our own within a few hours and the space of a room, it is a taste of eternity, the true meaning of friendship."* -Paul Williams (1948-2013), quoted in the blog created by his family.

Paul Williams, the founder of the pioneering rock 'n' roll magazine *Crawddady!*, died at age 64 on March 27, 2013, from complications related to a 1995 bicycle accident. Blindsided by the early onset

Alzheimer's that was partly the result of his injuries, his wife and son took donations for his care. The generosity of friends and fans allowed Williams as gentle a passage as possible.

Cindy Lee Berryhill, Williams' widow and antifolk co-founder, said, "Starting in 2009, I kept an online journal, a blog called Beloved Stranger, about caring for my ailing post-brain-injured spouse. Honestly, it kept me sane. I wasn't able to get out much for years. I had a very young son and then took care of my husband who was descending into early onset of dementia. It was a very difficult time, so I wrote about it. It was cathartic and I was able to connect with new and old friends via the writings."

Williams's life was dedicated to self-determination and evolution, included intimacy with multiple interesting people and musical and social scenes, and was full of interesting associations with outsiders, some later revered as pioneers of various things, others roundly vilified.

He created *Crawdaddy!* (named after the first English club to host a show by the Rolling Stones) in 1966, during a brief enrollment at Swarthmore College in Pennsylvania. As rock music matured, Williams felt the form deserved a critical organ. Said *Rolling Stone* when it appeared, "[Crawdaddy! is] the first serious publication devoted to rock & roll news and criticism." Williams went on to write more than two dozen books ranging from rock critique to metaphysics, then resuscitated *Crawdaddy!* for a latter-day run from 1993 to 2003, at which point he called a halt to production due to financial difficulties (perhaps a prescient move, whatever those difficulties may have been, considering the unexpected expenses occasioned by his hospitalization and care following the aforementioned accident).

As a cultural artifact from the age of print media, you'd think this pioneering venture might have been lost with the advent of stored data, but archivists, impressed by the quality of *Crawdaddy!* have been at work to preserve most or all of the catalog. I was able to locate several sales notices for complete archives of *Crawdaddy!* online, all of which had already been sold, and an archive covering issues spanning the period from 1975 to 1979, linked here (archive.org). The closest I was able to come to anything satisfactory in the public domain was that compiled by *Paste Magazine*, with the option to purchase back issues (pastemagazine.com), or the one curated by Rock's Back Pages going from 1966 to 2000, and there's a page on Instagram called Crawdaddytv celebrating Williams' legacy.

As editor in chief, Williams had everything to do with everything one-of-a-kind about *Crawdaddy!* His recurring column "What Goes On" was the first voice on several landmark rock 'n' roll issues. He was probably the first journalist to recognize Jim Morrison as deliberately aiming for godhood with rock theater—"The first show was the unexpected by way of the familiar, anti-climaxing nicely with 'Light My Fire.' . . . the second show, opening with "When the Music's Over," made the first an introduction. If 'Horse Latitudes' had shaken us stem to stern, still we didn't know how lost we were till Jim spoke, without accompaniment, the Sophocles section of 'The End.' And then fell, worshiping some young lady knelt before the stage. And suddenly flew into the air, a leap to make Nureyev proud. And finally swung his microphone on its cord, around his head, toward the audience, more and more violent, prepared to release—everything; and we knew he'd do it. One of us would die. 'This is the end,' he sang into the now-frustrated, un-violent microphone, 'my only friend,' and Jim was wonderful, shrugging his shoulders and letting the boys carry on in 'Light My Fire.'." (Williams, *Crawdaddy!* Sept. 1967)

His recurring column "What Goes On" was the first voice on several landmark rock 'n' roll issues. He was probably the first journalist to recognize Jim Morrison as deliberately aiming for godhood with rock theater. He wrote a piece entitled "Record Business '68" that highlighted the three-way disconnect between bands, their promoters, and fans, calling attention to problem which was only to metastasize: the insidious over-mastering of creativity and fun by marketing and sales imperatives —"There is is confusion afoot in the rock music world, a familiar confusion that arises from lack of understanding, lack of communication, and lack of common effort in a common cause. It is not surprising that rock musicians, record company executives, appreciators of the music, and radio station powers-that-be should each hold separate views of what rock music should be. It is not surprising that they have widely different opinions as to what rock music is now. What is perhaps a trifle unnerving is their curious refusal to even so much as consider the fact that they are all in the same boat together; each one clutches the elephant as though he were the only blind man in the world."

Williams also had the prescience to detect the Beatles impending breakup three years before it became official, at a time later cited by all members as the end of their time as a collective of personalities: "So, after months of contradictions, rumor becomes fact: the Beatles have broken up—they aren't a group anymore. Each has his separate plans, and they don't seem to include group recordings. John and Ringo are involved in films, George in the sitar, and Paul seems very much the American college student, taking a year off to find himself: 'I'm spending a lot of time alone in the house, just doing things or thinking. I've a year to find out what I want to do. It's very self-indulgent.' Meanwhile, the Beatles are committed to one more group movie, and at least one album plus the movie soundtrack. And I think we can expect a few surprises.' (Williams, *Crawdaddy!* Feb. 1967). Indeed, the Beatles surprised us with a few more arguably great albums after *Sgt. Pepper's*, but the unity of form was notably absent, which is good or bad, depending on your viewpoint. Williams can be seen in photos of the circle of journalists invited to John and Yoko's Bed-in for Peace at Montreal's Queen Elizabeth Hotel, and his voice can be heard in the chorus of "Give Peace a Chance ." Williams also had the prescience to detect the Beatles impending breakup three years before it became official (with perfect timing, according to quotes from the fab-tops), and arranged for *Naked Lunch* author and occultist William S. Burroughs to write a regular column for *Crawdaddy!*, touching on such things as time travel, the nature of beauty, and the fall of art (In June 1975, Burroughs interviewed Led Zeppelin guitar wizard Jimmy Page, then living in Aleister Crowley's former residence on the shores of Loch Ness, scene of an untold number of magical rituals and since razed). (*Crawdaddy!* June 1975, reprinted at endofthegame.net).

Outlaw Blues

Near the beginning of his *Outlaw Blues* (1969), Williams wrote, "Very few people have the balls to talk about 'rock and roll' anymore. *Revolver* made it difficult. *Between the Buttons, Smile* and the Doors lp are making it impossible. 'Pop music' can only be defined by pointing at a current chart . . . rock has achieved the high standards of mainstream music, but conversely . . . rock has *absorbed* mainstream music, has become the leader, the arbiter of quality, the music of today. The Doors, Brian Wilson, the Stones are modern music and contemporary 'jazz', and 'classical' composers must try to measure up."

Williams can be seen in photos of the circle of journalists invited to John and Yoko's Bed-in for Peace at Montreal's Queen Elizabeth Hotel, and his voice can be heard in the chorus of "Give Peace a Chance ."

Paul Williams at Bed-in for Peace

Outlaw Blues was published in 1969 containing artistic investigation of many acts of the time, prefiguring Lester Bangs's *Psychotic Reactions and Carburetor Dung* by a few decades. The two journalists were in print contemporaneously, but Williams's style was always more expansive in spirit than Bangs's comparative regression to power chords, not that there's anything wrong with that. *Outlaw Blues* was potentially the first serious book on rock music, including lines like "The Beatles say they'd 'love to take you home with us'; the Stones aren't polite but they'll 'get you safely to your door.' What more could you ask?" and "Two words are really significant to Jefferson Airplane's sound and appeal: complexity and kinetics."

In the spring of 1967, Williams' then-girlfriend Trina Robbins, assisted by Bhob Stewart and Art Spiegelman, introduced Williams to the speculative fiction of Philip K. Dick. The two writers met in August 1968 at the 26th World Science Fiction Convention. Their friendship lasted through the rest of Dick's life, including the period where he felt a pink laser beam had been fired into his eye revealing the true nature of existence (see the VALIS Trilogy by Philip K. Dick). Williams began working on a profile of Dick for *Rolling Stone* in 1974 and it appeared in the Nov. 6, 1975, issue headlined, "The True Stories of Philip K. Dick ." The article covered a number of subjects, including the aforementioned pink laser epiphany, and Dick's drug use (amphetamine addiction and infrequent LSD experimentation) as a factor in his writing, and an influence on his outlook on the nature of reality. For several years after Dick's death, Williams was his literary executor and used that position to get several of the author's previously unpublished novels into print. From 1983 to 1992, Williams ran the Philip K. Dick Society, which boasted thousands of members internationally. The society's range was a significant influence on promotion of Dick's work internationally

Philip K. Dick and Paul Williams

In 1986, Williams published *Only Apparently Real: The World of Philip K. Dick*, one of the first biographies of Dick, and is a featured interviewee in three documentaries about Dick: a biographical documentary BBC2 released in 1994 as part of its *Arena* arts series called *Philip K Dick: A Day in the Afterlife*, *The Gospel According to*

Philip K. Dick, produced in 2001, and *The Penultimate Truth About Philip K. Dick*, another biographical documentary film produced in 2007.

The 1960s was a great decade for people who were manipulators of the vulnerable and weak minded. The notion of Divinity's availability to anyone who claimed it fostered a rise in communes and cults, from the Manson family to Mel Lyman's Fort Hill Community in Boston. Lyman, described as "casual and real and unresponsive" by one member in this video compilation, was one who claimed to be a manifestation of God's spirit on Earth, and Williams, who knew Lyman from his years in Boston, stayed at Fort Hill for a few months in 1971. The community set up in Boston's predominantly Black Roxbury neighborhood by white intellectuals from the Cambridge area moved into several empty apartment houses bordering the park. Relations with the Black neighborhood immediately deteriorated as armed members of the new Fort Hill Community were witnessed patrolling its grounds. Williams was one of these armed guards during the few months he spent on Fort Hill.

He later told *Rolling Stone*'s David Fenton that he'd had to escape under cover of darkness after being told he would not be allowed to leave, having become convinced they were a dangerous cult who would kill anyone who threatened them. "I said I was leaving the day before and they said I wouldn't be allowed to. They said they'd be watching me 24 hours a day."

"The Lyman Family's Holy Siege of America" by David Fenton appeared in Rolling Stone in Dec. 1971.

Author of 25 books and editor of 17 more, Williams assumed a new role after writing one called *Das Energi* in 1973, but he was following the same evolutionary directive. As Western society at large began to consider things unseen, he turned his own mind to its reviewing. Guerrilla journalist types might consider him to have gone New Age or be flakey for having written books like *Das Energi, Coming,* or *Energy and Essence,* but as Williams summed it up in these lines from poem of his I found online called "Common Sense," there seemed an imperative to evolve.

> Let us serve as models.
>
> And let us vow
> to enjoy our work so much
> that the hesitant and the fearful will grow jealous
> and drop their chains
> and run to join the fun.
>
> How to prevent world catastrophe:
>
> 1) Admit that it could happen.
> 2) Decide that it will not happen.
> 3) Commit your vision and energy to number two without ever forgetting number one.
>
> To choose to build a bridge
> is the essential act of love.

. . . and a favorite chorus in most outlaw blues I can think of, from the Rolling Stones' "Midnight Rambler" to Bob Dylan's "Like a Rolling Stone ." Williams was a lifelong Bob Dylan fan, and Dylan's having won the Nobel Prize for Literature in 2016 for his lyrics makes an appropriate parallel to his own attempts at making rock 'n' roll an art deserving of intelligent consideration and review. As he said in *Outlaw Blues*, "A dream is a portrait. Moving target for the mind. Waking is the shift from one level to another; here to there but not in space or time. This stuff is all important. And the hell of it is, rock really does communicate. It discusses this stuff in its own peculiar ways, and many an idea comes and goes without a conscious thought. Shifting, moving, existing, gone . . . How rock communicates is a mystery to me. Some days I stand in the shower till evening, pushing at songs in my mind."

Williams married the Japanese pop singer Sachiko Kanenobu in 1972, raising two sons, Kenta and Taiyo. One summer, Philip K. Dick suggested the couple move up to Sonoma, where he was living at the time, and they drove out to visit him. According to Kanenobu, the car they were driving happened to break down right in front of a real estate office, Williams leapt out, ran inside and purchased a house right down the street, where Kanenobu still lives, though the marriage ran its course, and Williams met Berryhill (*The Adventurist, Garage Orchestra*, others) met in 1992 and married in 1997.

Paul Williams on right, courtesy of Cindy Lee Berryhill

Anti-folk, Berryhill's banner, is among the new breed of authentic, organic countercultures that included Hamell On Trial, Kimya Dawson and Berryhill in its roster. Some people call it acoustic punk. Paul and Cindy Lee had one son, Alexander Berryhill Williams, and Paul lived with his last family in Encinitas California for several years before catching a traumatic brain injury in a bicycle accident, after which he succumbed to early onset dementia and a steady decline to the point where he required full-time care. A trust fund was set up for Williams's care, and it lasted as long as he lasted. Says the multi-talented adventurist Berryhill, who is also an author, currently revising her latest cluster buster while giving guitar lessons online, "Paul's oldest son, Kenta, was with his father when he passed away. Remarkably an hour before he was gone Kenta got us on FaceTime together and Alexander and I told Paul how much we loved him. I told him how beautiful his books and writings look at the gallery, with the admiring eyes reading his words. I also told him I would help his books and papers and writings find a home."

25 HOW I MET ANTIFOLK
A BRIEF OVERVIEW OF THE MUSICAL SUBGENRE

Antifolk is among the new breed of authentic, organic countercultures. Some people call it acoustic punk. I heard about it as an updated form of folk music whose name was coined after somebody got ousted from an ivied folk club for allegedly playing a punk song at open mic night.

When asked how she remembers it, co-founder Cindy Lee Berryhill, whose exemplary latest CD, The Adventurist, was released on Omnivore Recordings, says, "I was taking a trip around the US on a Greyhound Bus . . . landed in NYC and fell in love with the city at first sight. I found my way that first week, to the Folk City open mic night, a contentious exercise in rubbing the old guard of folkies (mostly songwriters from the 70s) up against this new generation of souls that were sprouted on punk rock and 60s folk rebellion. I met Kirk and Lach, then called the Folk Brothers. A month later I was still in town and hanging out with them and the other disgruntled up and comers . . . One day Kirk and Lach and I met at a cafe and talked about, even made a sort of to-do list of things we could do to get our burgeoning scene of music friends more sort of gelled into a cool scene. I tossed in the name Antifolk, which was a take on an LA club called the Anti Club. Lach had another name but Kirk and I rallied for Antifolk and we didn't even find out that Lach agreed until it showed up on one of his fliers that month."

My first connection to the genre was through Michelle Shocked, though I hadn't heard the phrase yet, when I saw her refuse to play along with David Letterman's showbiz smarm when appearing on his show to promote her first big hit, "Anchored Down in Anchorage" in 1983. Shocked went on to disgrace herself years later by making homophobic comments during a show, or possibly some 2nd or 3rd person comments misinterpreted as having been homophobic—there's some controversy regarding this; look up the article by investigative satirist Paul Krassner for more of the dirt. I'm hoping she's innocent, who knows.

Cindy Lee Berryhill was approximately my second connection to the genre, via Teletunes, the bygone alternative-slanted weekly video program that formerly appeared on Denver's PBS Channel 12, one of the first bricks in my staircase to musical identity, and my introduction to punk rock, with her first blockbuster, "Damn, I Wish I Was a Man."

Considered retroactively, Antifolk can also be said to include decades of precursors like lo-fi pioneers The Roches, and Jonathan Richman, whose assumption of a staunch anti-fame stance following early success with the Modern Lovers—including a preference for more intimate audience-performer relations and lowered volume—may be seen as a precursor to the same contrariness which gave birth to punk rock and its latest offshoot Antifolk. A lot of Antifolk artists I won't go into here due to a lack of familiarity, but here are some names: Diane Cluck is great, Loudon Wainwright and Suzzy Roche's daughter, Lucy Wainwright Roche is great—I don't know what she's calling herself, is it Antifolk?—and let me take this opportunity to say: a bygone Denver band called Pee Pee is one of the best I've ever seen (Doo Crowder's one to watch for sure, good music lovers). Antifolk might be seen as the cousin of cowpunk, a genre blending punk sensibilities with old school outlaw country nuts and bolts, a genre including Arizona's Meat Puppets, Giant Sand, Tex and the Horseheads, and, at times, Los Angeles stalwarts X (founding member DJ Bonebrake plays drums on Berryhill's *Adventurist*), which perhaps found its fullest expression as a blend in the works of Chicago's Waco Brothers, itself an offshoot of London's Mekons collective, most of whose members were heavies when punk hit UK in the late 1970s, and which genre has been tweaked still further by Albuquerque, New Mexico based "Southern Gothic" duo, late of Chicago, The Handsome Family.

Kimya Dawson—formerly one half of the Moldy Peaches, possessed of a hauntingly clear, sweet voice and sharp, insightful lyrical mind. Dawson's "My Mom" is about the most heartrendingly devoted and tenderly powerful song I've ever heard, while her seemingly extemporaneous but surely not entirely free ramble "The Beer" is among the most joyfully inventive ones. Dawson is also known for her extensive collaborations with children and one mainstream moment was having a song or two featured in *Juno*. The last album of hers I've heard was 2011's *Thunder Thighs*, featuring the masterpiece, "Same Shit (Complicated)."

One man band Ed Hamell, or Hamell on Trial, plays a battered acoustic guitar from 1938, I think he said it was, whose repertoire spans from the acoustic punk edge of "Disconnected" to the epic Nat King Cole tribute "Big As Life" to more recent "Happiest Man in the World" and his very latest, a collection of spoken word a la Lenny Bruce and Bill Hicks combined with his musical soul-punching called, "Rant and Roll." A dedicated father, Ed's got a tattoo of the word "Detroit" across his chest. That's his son's name. Detroit Hamell is a frequent poster on YouTube. He needs your likes.

Ed Hammel's caught a skull fracture due to a car crash some years ago and is well past recovery into a strengthy revival.

Jeffrey Lewis, another Antifolk exponent, reminded me very much of the early Jonathan Richman when I first heard him, more because of his manner than any commonality of sound exactly. The resemblance was strong. 2014's *A Turn in the Dream: Songs* was one of the greatest albums of that year, and his latest with the Junkyard, Manhattan, which came out in 2016, is also a great one. Besides being a musician, Lewis is a graphic artist, amateur historian and social commentator—check his lessons on YouTube. There was another guy who came to the v shows at Mutiny named Andy something who said he knew Jeffrey Lewis (who I tried to get a show at Mutiny Info. Café last November or so, but he ended up playing across Broadway at the Sputnik, which performance I missed).

David-Ivar' Herman-Dune's twenty-year career has been marked by record releases; touring the world with the likes of Arcade Fire, Of Montreal, Kimya Dawson, Wanda Jackson and Sleater-Kinney; showing at Art Basel and the Milan Trienniale; double-digit Peel Sessions and high-profile festival appearances; a comic strip and limited-edition toys; film soundtracking; and even producing and curating his own festival in Paris. In 2015 he settled in San Pedro with his partner, Mayon, and launched his own imprint, Santa Cruz Records, home to both his own music as well as multiple film soundtracks. He quickly found his place in the Pedro community, gifting peach jam to his neighbors from his backyard harvests (dubbed Yaya's Yum Yum Jam), contributing comics to the legendary local newspaper *Random Lengths,* and picking up a standing Saturday night gig at The Alhambra, a still-rough-and-tumble dive that dates back to 1904, officially designated as the oldest continually operating bar in Los Angeles. "I was lucky enough to have renewed my visa in 2019, because now they are all canceled, which means I would have been in a horrible position, not being able to stay here, and being kicked out of my home. So at least that went OK, even if neither I nor my girlfriend can leave the country, because it would cancel our visas! So, with my mother sick back home, it feels weird to be stuck. But San Pedro is the best place to be stuck at I feel. I ended up being able to write and record this album, and to keep doing my comics, so I'm alright really."

So the one about Antifolk having been founded in reaction to some kind of prohibition by the straights turned out to be fake. It's folk music grown into negating its ossified nature and name to get back to the freshness and freedom that started it. Which is the same thing punk was in the first place anyway—Clash frontman Joe Strummer's own first greatest influence having been Woody Guthrie, of "This Land is Your land" and "This Machine Kills Fascists" written on his guitar.

26 DIVINE MADNESS WITH PHILIP K. DICK

PHILIP K. DICK'S 2/3/74 EXPERIENCES AND HIS INHERENT TOLERANCE FOR AMPHETAMINES

Philip K. Dick (1928-1982) enjoyed a run of moderate popularity and commercial success as a science fiction author of weird personal circumstance lasting from the 1960s until his death in 1982, by which time, his multivalent conversation with God had given SF a new form to follow, much like re-breaking then casting a bone to alter the direction of its growth. Considered collectively, his writings embody one remarkable recent attempt to unite the disparate fields of theology and creativity in literature. He produced a countless number of sci-fi/spec-fic novels and a series of non-SF novels in the '50s, only one of which, the (in my opinion) excellent *Confessions of a Crap Artist*, was published before his death. Aspects of the author's deliberate speculation on the God concept are prominent throughout his catalog along with a preoccupation with the realness of things commonly taken for granted.

The title of Dick's 1978 novel *VALIS* is an acronym for Vast Active Living Information System[1]. This prescient characterization of the internet was conceived by Dick as his gnostic vision of God. Bishop Pike disappeared without a trace during a spiritual expedition to the Dead Sea in 1969 in search of the Biblical "burning bush." *VALIS* chronicles a series of mystical experiences gone through by Horselover

Fat (a German translation of his name) through February and March of 1974. As his series of visions increased in length and frequency, Fat believed he was living a double life, one as himself, and one as a Christian persecuted by Romans in the 1st century A.D. named "Thomas." Unwilling to accept this self-diagnosis unquestioningly, he sought other rationalist and religious explanations for these experiences, as chronicled in the semi-autobiographical novels *VALIS* and *Radio Free Albemuth* (1976), each another manifestation of his lifelong interview with God.

Philip K. Dick books

Late *Crawdaddy!* magazine founder Paul Williams was named executor of Phil's literary estate. Their conversations recorded in Williams' *Only Apparently Real* (1986) cover all the weirdest parts of Dick's legacy in unrehearsed-ly frank detail. Readers receive the most authentic portrayal of the visionary eccentric Dick in his own words in conversation with the intelligent, perceptive Paul Williams, who knows him well enough to respond in ways that further the conversation and clarify points in an efficient manner. Almost all of Phil's books were written on speed (except A Scanner Darkly and maybe some after) but according to doctors (according to Dick) there was something about his metabolism that prevented the drug from EVER contacting his neural tissue! In other words, it was like he was taking a placebo the whole time, and he came to think of it as a protective camouflage while researching the habits of the drug fiends he was hanging around with in the persona of one of his characters, undercover narc Bob Arctor from *A Scanner Darkly*.

Dick's widow Tessa served as his amanuensis during the events of 2/3/74, during which he experienced a beam of pink light being fired into his head and felt the true nature of reality had been revealed to him. She has written and published *The Owl in Daylight*, and several other excellent books about their transformative experience, copies of which are available on Amazon. Author of several other works of fiction and nonfiction, Tessa says, "The Owl needs more exposure. I consider it my best work so far." Pay heed. Her late husband never came to any firm conclusion about exactly what had occurred during his experience of ekphrasis or "unforgetting" as he referred to it—Had he gone mad? Was he being visited by aliens? Was the government after him? Had it, indeed, been an encounter with the Divine?—and spent the remainder of his life writing book after chart after list after book in a dedicated effort to understand it perfectly. These notes (all past/present/future editions of the VALIS Trilogy excepted), which he referred to collectively as his Exegesis, were published by Houghton Mifflin Harcourt after a delay of more than twenty-five years in. Dick died of a stroke in 1982, and has made a number of post-mortem appearances, notably in Michael Bishop's *Philip K. Dick Is Dead, Alas*, first published as *The Secret Ascension* in 1987, set in a Gnostic alternative universe where his mainstream work is published but his science fiction is banned by a totalitarian USA in thrall to a demonically possessed Richard Nixon.

All the political tensions in Dick's life and work were influenced by the dominant political tone in the U.S. when most of these books were written (upheaval of the sixties, the counterculture, Vietnam, the CIA, Nixon, etc). But they're the opposite of period pieces, more precisely they are the tropes at play in Dick's ongoing dialogue with God or the system epitomizing God. Dick was at least as exhaustive in his efforts at categorizing said entity as he was open minded in his efforts to explain the events of 2/3/74. He often used German as a tool of transliteration, and sometimes a historic motif, as in *The Man in the High Castle* trilogy (first volume 1961), where he spends a few books reimagining the aftermath of WWII if the Nazis had won. Frequently accused of being paranoid that the government was meddling with his life, his effort here seems to have been an equation of repressive policies in effect at the time in the United States with Nazi suppression. The title of another book, *Galactic Pot Healer*, might make you think of marijuana and space-mysticism holding hands, but is actually a reference to ceramics. Jones's world and other of Dick's fictional landscapes also feature ceramic references, maybe because of the pottery craze going on in the 60s and 70s when they were written, but that's just a guess. A pot healer is a craftsman who repairs broken pots and a gigantic being known as the Glimmung has enlisted the services of the pot healer protagonist in what the Glimmung apparently knows is a failed mission to raise Heldscalla from the bottom of its planet's ocean floor. What could go wrong?

27 JOHNNY STRIKE'S LAST WISH

JOHNNY STRIKE OF SF PUNK BAND CRIME SENT ME AN EMAIL A FEW DAYS BEFORE HE DIED

BORN Gary John Bassett, formerly of "San Francisco's only rock and roll band," Crime, later member of Naked Beast, with much the same lineup, Johnny Strike passed away a couple of weeks ago at the age of 70 following a protracted bout with cancer, per his publisher Michael Lucas. I got the feeling from some things he said in emails that Strike craved greater recognition as a writer.

Fans of good writing will want to read Johnny Strike's last book, *The Exploding Memoir,* published just before he died. The adventures of a proto-punk-mod-turning-glam in post-hippie San Francisco with an underground band called WolfSnake, the first to wear all black in that multicolored scene. Strike's book is presumably based, in some part, on its author's own adventures as a young man in the same wild land between eras, considering its title. Not entirely, though, since it also has an over-arching motif of intrigue centered around a part-Tibetan mystic named Dr. Kublar, and the main guy's name is Eddie, not Gary or Johnny. That might be what he means by the word "exploding." Read his other books too if you're after good writing. *Ports of Hell, Murder in the Medina, A Loud Humming Sound Came from Above, Eyes of the Stranger.*

As a freelance writer with a fondness for punk, I interviewed

Johnny for the first time several years ago. Last year he offered to help promote a book I'd written satirizing political polarization in the wake of the 2016 election. "Do you bash Trump?" he asked, and I tried to describe how instead it was a book I'd written "about a guy who tries to do the opposite of opposing or agreeing with anyone else, and what his life looks like that way, once he's doing his own thing instead, with everyone else's opposition or agreement as the case may be in the background." Johnny seemed to understand, but now he's gone, I wish I'd explained it more clearly. I'm glad I let him know I thought Crime had made the ultimate punk gesture by playing San Quentin dressed as police officers, like a William Burroughs novel come alive onstage, offending everyone who cared to take offense. This radical extension of the street theatre prevalent in San Francisco was common drag for that band at Mabuhay Gardens but wearing it in prison took steel legs. Johnny described it as, "Fun," (with a capital F), "amazing and unnerving, especially when they informed us of the 'no hostage' rule. That meant no negotiations would be permitted if we were nabbed by the inmates. But we pulled it off."

Crime described themselves as "the crime wave band with the deadliest sound in town," providing a West Coast counterpoint to East Coast bands like the Stooges and the Ramones who are still better known today. Call it crime wave, rock and roll, or punk, their music was probably the first San Francisco-based iteration of the raw, real sound taking hold in the middle 1970s.

Johnny Strike once said he wanted his music to "stick pins in people" rather than make them feel comfortable. Presumably, he had a similar ambition when it came to his writing. I promised him an article on that I never got around to writing in his lifetime. Which makes this it. The attention paid to grammar and presentation in his *Murders in the Medina* is impeccable. The book is typo-free, and never less than impressive in word choice. Readers will never doubt they are reading the work of a true master. *The Exploding Memoir*, while its delivery is less high-tone, is a different type of narrative, and as such, perfectly suited to itself.

Strike was never shy about citing a strong connection to, and conscious furthering of, multiple previous influences.

His interview of hobo and Times Square hustler Herbert Huncke, who, along with Neal Cassady, inspired *On the Road* author Jack Kerouac's adoption of spontaneous prose, is documented in *The Huncke Connection*. He spent a brief stretch as an expatriate in Tangier, where fellow American Paul Bowles, whom he met and interviewed while he was there, relocated permanently in 1947. Strike also met with and interviewed Moroccan author Mohammed Choukri during his relatively brief stay in that country.

Johnny took issue when I overstated the duration of his stay in Morocco when I reprinted our first interview on my blog some years later, saying, "You say I was there for several years. It was only seven months. I have a thing about sloppy work."

He volunteered a blurb for my last book, requesting a synopsis and all the other blurbs I'd received so far, to weigh his own against, before backing out unexpectedly, due to unexpected medical issues, saying, "Sorry man but you couldn't ask at a worse time. I'm finding it difficult keeping my own publisher and editor happy. If that's not enough I'm involved with a music deal and some unexpected medical issues. Really no time in the day for anything else and I don't see it easing up anytime soon. I do hope to read your book at some point, and I wish you nothing but success."

Strike reacted with elation to his receipt of a free copy of *Market Man* when it came out, saying, "GOT THE BOOK! MANY THANKS! It looks terrific. It now goes on the stack of books friends wrote, and that I must read, but looking it over I think it will go on top."

I knew he was sick, but I didn't expect him to die when he did. I hope he got a chance to read it.

Besides expanding the bounds of possibility in rock and roll as co-founder and frontman/vocalist of Crime, Johnny did the same thing with later musical outfits, among them Naked Beast, which reportedly began as a literary vehicle and included fellow former Crime members Hank Rank on drums and percussion and Joey D'Kaye on guitars, synthesizer and theremin providing a backdrop for his own nasal vocal incision on songs like "Doctor D is Dead" and narrations like "Crazy Carl's Thing ."

Having heard that departed spirits were likeliest available to the living in the first few days after death, on the day Gregory Ego sent me the news Johnny had died, I tried checking in briefly. "I don't know if you'd bother to check on me, Johnny, seeing as we never met in the flesh, but I'm doing all right, if you're listening," I said into the air, taking stock of myself, "By the laws of orthogenesis. That's a school of thought holding that all things are evolving in a definite direction, also known as teleology. How the hippies evolved from the beats. And the punks evolved from the hippies. How Johnny Strike interviewed Huncke before that man died, and I interviewed Johnny Strike before he did. How Johnny and I were both probably just as surprised when the guy they interviewed died. Which means whatever's coming next will be here soon, whatever form it takes, if it hasn't already begun to emerge. And it probably has if we know it yet or not.

I haven't read *Ports of Hell* yet, but it's probably great. Tells the story of an expatriate in Tangier who becomes associated with someone named Elias who claims to be from the fabled lost continent predating Atlantis known as Lemuria. This was the first of his books to receive good press from William S. Burroughs, who was possessed of the necessary discernment to rate Strike's descriptions of otherworldly or supernatural phenomena as those of a man who'd witnessed what he described. "This is what marks the artist, he has been there and brought it back." *A Loud Humming Sound Came From Above*, Strike's collaboration with illustrator Richard Sala, is a collection of twelve short stories including one set in a profiteering methadone clinic, one in a hotel "where the suicidal find terrible reasons to live," plus ten more similarly canted, each with an accompanying illustration by Sala, author of *Black Cat Crossing* and *Hypnotic Tales*. I haven't read that one yet either, but the title is great and it's first on my own list of books my friends wrote I must read.

Strike's *Name of the Stranger,* set in Tangier and San Francisco, has been described by one reviewer on Amazon as "[taking] the reader on a shrink's quick descent into his client's maddening hell where he finds there is no exit." Another commentator on the same site described it as "a suspenseful read bringing to mind such greats as Raymond Chandler, Jim Thompson and Charles Willeford, [having] moments of high comedy and witty dialogue, qualities that easily give [it] a place among the classics." The last email he sent me was a link to "Make a Suggestion at the Berkeley Public Library." I haven't been able to find an expiration date yet, but the next thing I heard, he was dead.

I don't know about you, but I'll be sending the Berkeley Public Library a friendly email suggesting they stock some of the books described above, in case that was Johnny's last wish.

Johnny Strike

28 PRETTY TUNES WITH SOUR, DISASSOCIATED LYRICS: A CONVERSATION WITH JAZZ BUTCHER AND GENTLEMAN ADVENTURER PAT FISH

MY INTERVIEW WITH THE JAZZ BUTCHER PRECEDED HIS DEATH BY ABOUT ONE YEAR

Photo by Philip Dufour, Paris 2019

First let me say I've been a fan since *Bloody Nonsense* came to my attention as a teenager in 1986. "Caroline Wheeler's Birthday Present," in particular, made a huge impression. An album called *Big Questions* ended up becoming my favorite, and your latest, *Last of the Gentleman Adventurers* was a real work of art and greatly appreciated by this listener. I don't know how it did in any charts, but I hope you made millions or broke even.

"It's funny that *Big Questions* should mean so much to someone. It was very much a final scrape of the barrel in terms of the stuff that we recorded for Glass. I can't even remember being involved in the track selection. Yet Glass Supremo D. Elvis Barker, with his impeccable taste, managed to turn this grab-bag of out-takes, contributions to one-off compilations and ill-advised cover versions into something really rather listenable.

"I'm glad you like *Last of the Gents*. I'm quite proud of that one myself. We made it to mark the band's thirtieth anniversary and we were incredibly lucky to have our friends Richard Formby, Tim Harries and Jonny Mattock for that session. They are all busy men and I could not believe our good fortune when we found a window to work with all three of them. We raised the money for that project with a crowdfunding campaign. People were incredibly generous and before we even entered the studio there was enough money to cover recording, travel, accommodation, mastering and manufacturing. When we did the deal with Fire Records for the re-release of our catalogue we made it conditional upon their doing CD and vinyl versions of *Last of the Gents*, so it continues to sell.

"For a small band like ours, there's not much money to be made from record sales. The money, such as it is, is in the writing and publishing. That said, I'm proud to be able to say that none of our albums ever made a loss.

You've played in David J.'s band(s), and he in yours, and I heard you met at art school, is that right? How's it been working with him and being friends through the years of changing music trends? What were your teenage roots, musically speaking?

"David was at art college here in Northampton, whereas I went to university in Oxford. Although I had seen Bauhaus a few times as a paying punter, I didn't know David at the time I met his brother

(Bauhaus drummer) Kevin first, just socially, when I moved to Northampton and we got on well. I finally got to meet David at Kevin's birthday party on a canal barge in the summer of 1983, just after Bauhaus had split up for the first time. The night was remarkable for one of the very few live appearances by the Sinister Ducks, David's more than partially demented collaboration with Northampton's own Alan Moore.

"I have never actually played in a David J. band as such, though we have played together on stage a few times as guests at each other's solo shows. Both Max Eider and Owen P. Jones have toured with him, however, and we all crop up here and there on his recordings. He's been known to turn up and join in at Jazz Butcher shows too."

Jazz Butcher Conspiracy in the corridor, Northeast London Polytechnic, 1985 by unknown photographer.

Is this the Watchmen guy or a completely other Alan Moore? That's an interesting connection.

"First off, yes, it's *that* Alan Moore. He's good friends with David J and has done a number of interesting collaborations with him over the years, including an EP based on Alan's *V For Vendetta,* which has recently been re-released by Glass Modern in a luxurious new expanded format. The Ducks were Alan, David and Alex Green on sax, with artwork by Edwin Pouncey aka Savage Pencil. They released one 45 on Situation Two Records, probably in that very summer of 1983.

"Alan has lived all his life in Northampton and doesn't much care to travel anywhere else. He has written two books (not comics) about the town: *Voice of the Fire* and the enormous, mind-boggling *Jerusalem*. He's far from being the grumpy recluse that he is sometimes said to be. As his sleeve notes on *Last of the Gents* demonstrate, he's always willing to help out a pal, but if anybody is struggling, Alan will be there for them. He is, in his own way, a proper pillar of the community. I love him.

"At the end of 1982 a very, very early manifestation of the Jazz Butcher had opened for Bauhaus at the Hammersmith Palais in London. After the show I thanked Kevin for the opportunity, only for him to deny all knowledge of how we had come to be there. It turned out that David had been observing us from afar, and it was he who had us added to the bill.

"Over the autumn of 1983, Max and I opened a run of shows for David in his capacity as a solo artist and we got on well. There was talk of his producing our second album. Things became complicated and by March 1984 David was our bass player. He stayed for two albums and a European tour before going off to start Love & Rockets with his old compadres. His studio experience with Bauhaus was invaluable; he taught us loads of useful things; not least how to get concert promoters to give you free drinks."

"At the time we met, David and I were into some very similar stuff. Obviously, we shared things like the Velvet Underground, Bowie and Eno, but there was also a shared enthusiasm for simpler, more classic singer-songwriters like Dylan, Peter Perrett, Nick Drake, Roddy Frame and Martin Stephenson. We used to trade cassettes all the time. I recall the wonderful moment where I sent him a ropey home recording of the Velvets' *Stephanie Says*. It was only available on some grungy bootleg in those days and David hadn't heard the song before, which led, delightfully, to his thinking that I had written it! A similar thing had happened when he brought John Cale's *Rosegarden Funeral of Sores* to a Bauhaus rehearsal. All the other guys in the band thought David had written it; and for the longest time, he let them continue to believe that.

"I think, deep inside, that we both just wanted to be Cale."

Can you say more about your appreciation of John Cale—what did you like about him especially?

"I think I probably came to Cale when I was about sixteen, through the fact that Eno produced his album *Fear*. Of course, I loved that record and I've followed Cale for the rest of my life. I was enjoying his solo stuff long before I "got" the Velvet Underground.

"I've never really taken a moment to ask myself why I like his work so much. I guess that it has something to do with the fact that although he loves to experiment and 'push the envelope', as they say, there always seems to be a strong, beautiful musical base to the work. His Music is a fine example: the performances are deconstructed, fragmented even, as though blown to pieces by a cluster bomb flung casually through the studio window, but deep underneath, buried in the wreckage, are really strong, beautiful songs. Somehow, the fact that this beauty is poking up from a heap of smoldering rubble seems to amplify the emotional impact of the tunes.

"Cale has a very nice take on a sort of dignified, world-weary resignation: 'Back in Berlin they're all well-fed...but I don't care. People always bored me anyway,' he sings on *Paris 1919's* "Half Past France" over a stately, disassociated drone of strings. Not bad for a young man still in his twenties. He even wears a white suit in the cover photographs. Impeccable!

"Another thing that I enjoy about Cale is that his songs are so good that they can be presented in even the simplest acoustic format and still have the impact that they might have had with a live band or an elaborate studio production. Obviously, I've seen him perform live on many occasions and with many different musicians, but the shows that have really reached me are the ones where he has performed alone with a guitar or a piano. As things turned out, I was lucky enough to open for him at one such show at the Forum in London in 1993.

"Great songwriting, beautiful music and paranoia teetering on the very brink of overt hostility: what's not to like?

"Tale out of school: one evening in September 1983, not long after Bauhaus had split up, I wandered into my local dive bar to find David J doing an unadvertised solo performance in the back room. It was the first time that I had heard my new pal playing solo and I watched, fascinated, as he worked through tunes from his first solo album *The Etiquette of Violence*. After a few numbers I remarked to a friend "Well, it looks as though Dave's going for the 'John Cale of the Group' ticket." With that. I headed out to the lavatory. On my return, I walked into the room to find David halfway through a cover version of *Fear is a Man's Best Friend*. Oh, how we laughed!"

Photo by Pierre Guillaume, Paris 2019.

Where are you these days, creatively? What impression would you most like to be making these days, as a creative exponent (to include social commentator, musician, and any other chosen themes)?

"Oddly enough, having just written that stuff about Cale, I fell to thinking about this question and realized that I do rather seem to be trying to follow in his footsteps to some degree. Even in the days when our stuff was considered borderline comical (and there was the occasional joke, I have to admit!) a lot of the songs were about disassociation, rejection and 'walking away'. More recently, the lyrics have become more overtly 'dark' while the tunes have become simpler and more melodic. I'm on record as saying. 'What I do is not entertainment.' People can take that as they will.

"Because there is very little work out there for an act like mine, and therefore very little money, I can't currently afford to keep a full-time band, so the vast majority of my live performances are solo affairs. One ends up with a single elderly, not very photogenic gent with a guitar, playing pretty tunes with sour, disassociated lyrics. Top ten material it is not.

"The Cale influence, then, is still very much in effect, as is the lingering influence of his old band mate Lou. I love classic soul music (as did they) and that is becoming more and more of an influence on my songwriting too. My guitar sound owes much to both John Martyn and Syd Barrett. The attitude that I hope to convey owes much to the languid insouciance of Kevin Ayers, whose appearance on children's tv singing Marlene Dietrich's "Falling in Love Again" with a bottle of Champagne and an exploding piano blew my teenage mind.

"Grace under pressure? A warm heart in a cold world? Or the sound of an enormous steel door in Hell clanging shut forever?* It's really not for me to say."

I understand this lockdown is making people who live in part by public appearances rethink their next steps. I don't really dig the virtual thing as a substitute for live stuff, but I'm about to shoot some vids of me reading shorts and link to a Patreon page to see what happens. What are you gonna do next as a performer?

"Just as the 'lockdown' started, I saw some bloke with a guitar advertising his 'live' gig on Facebook. There was a photo of this unprepossessing geezer with an acoustic guitar and, behind him, a large, homemade poster screaming 'PAYPAL ME!!!' I shuddered at the grasping vulgarity of it.

"So I'm having trouble going down the route of 'virtual' shows. I have, however, been very taken with Max's way of doing things, which is simply to record a number at home, then park it on the YouTubes and let people watch it for free. I intend to do something along similar lines over the next few days. Not that it will be in any way liable to cheer people up in their time of isolation. That's just not where I'm at these days. (Insert evil cackle here.)

"It's pretty frightening to think about the immediate future. To be honest, I have already depended much on the kindness of friends and strangers over the past year or so, but one cannot decently rely on that being an endless resource. I've no idea as to when it will be safe to go back to work (I think that live arts events are likely to be the very last things to come back), but when I do emerge, I think that I shall probably head straight back into the recording studio. I'm lucky enough to have people still interested in releasing my shit, so that would seem to be the best plan. And yes, there are songs."

The Brian Wilson references in the beautiful song, "Shakey," on last of the Gentlemen Adventurers caught my attention, as a fan of his—what inspired them, if anything in particular?

"'Shakey' was one of those songs that came really quickly. I think the lyric was pretty much a question of free association. I was, I think, trying to explore a landscape of personal devastation. Brian's horrible childhood and the resultant misery and paranoia of his later years seemed a good fit. His wife really did find him chopping out powders with his two school-age daughters one Christmas morning. It don't get much more devastated than that. Of course, the trick then is to point out in the chorus that for us mere mortal types, even this desperate nadir is way beyond our pay grade. 'Let it go, boy. You can't afford it.' Bleak.

"I never really identified with the 'social commentator' thing, any more than I did with the asinine 'Monty Python of rock' label with which some deaf people tried to saddle us back in the eighties. I do like songs about real things that are expressed in simple, colloquial language, stuff like the *Waiting* album by the Fun Boy Three, or, of course, Dylan. I suppose that this does mean that an element of 'social commentary' is inevitable much of the time and, obviously, I do have my own opinions about things, but the social commentary thing is not what drives my songwriting. I'm not Billy Bragg, even though (fact fans!) he and I were born in the same city on the very same day.

"As I have watched my musical and (counter) cultural heroes die off over the last decade, I have come to feel that there is a certain responsibility upon those of us left behind, however mediocre we might be in comparison. It's simply not good enough anymore to have a laugh and a knees-up while the adults take care of the serious shit; like it or not, we (that is to say: our generation of writers and artists) *are* the adults now. I feel that if one's not prepared to take on a little of that responsibility, then there's not much point in trying to make art. I suppose what I'm trying to say is this: if you're not doing shit that moves people and means something, sit down and be quiet.

"A quick shout out to some of my other favourite artists who are still out there doing it right: Bob Dylan; Peter Perrett; Dave Kusworth; Patti Smith; Chuck D.; Tom Waits; Sonic Boom; Tinariwen; Vic Godard; Phil Parfitt; Rolo McGinty; Steve Savale and the Asian Dub Foundation; Tim Keegan; Robert del Naja and the Massive Attack collective; Micky Greaney; Mavis Staples . . . and, of course, John Cale and David J. Haskins."

*: Thanks, Harlan Ellison! x

Photo by Philippe Dufour, Paris 2019.

AUTHOR'S NOTE; I heard the Jazz Butcher's Bloody Nonsense when I was 15, and "Caroline Wheeler's Birthday present" and "Drink" and "Partytime" became life anthems automatically. I remember being struck by his friendship with David, Kevin, Daniel, every one of them round the bend, and wondering how he wasn't better known, being such a talent. Decades later, we became friends on Facebook and I interviewed Pat by email for my website and it felt like a conversation between old friends and was a testament to his good nature. I tuned into Live from Fishy Mansions for the first time on the night he cancelled and was struck by his good grace in apologizing that night's show for cancelling on account of feeling like he was about to choke every time he started to drift off the night before. I remember he made a point of how scary a feeling that was, and said it's not the Covid, very sorry, be back soon, etc. Then in the morning (Oct. 5th, 2021) he was dead. It might have been two days, but I think it was only one. Thanks, Pat.

Pat Fish in the dark, Frejus, south of France '87 by Franck Yeznikian.

29 JUAN F. THOMPSON AT MUTINY

SON OF HUNTER S. THOMPSON APPEARS

Juan Thompson

I'D been hosting a variety show at Mutiny, and it had its moments of greatness, but ASCAP had begun cracking down on open mics likely to feature artists playing covers, so I was repurposed to literary liaison based on my past success with Dan Fante, who'd come visiting a couple of times. Arranging lit events instead felt better, that Henry Alarmclock suit didn't fit anymore, and I wasn't the only one doing that for Mutiny. Juan Thompson, Hunter's son, invited there by owner Matt Megyesi, assented that he continues to discover nuances of his late father's character in answering a question from the audience during his own recent appearance there. Such is this reporter's relationship to the Beat Generation—before Heather Dalton pulled my coat to write a book about the Beats and Denver, I considered myself to have bypassed or somehow outgrown them. Thompson was intelligent, thoughtful, well-spoken, and courteous. In person, his resemblance to video I've seen of his father as a young man was undeniable, I mean to say there was no mistaking him upon first sight, though his manner of conveyance seemed far more sensitive and effective, and his voice pitched less grumbly and low. His rendition, in a public appearance no longer than an hour, of his and Hunter's complicated relationship, fraught with discord and anger and only redeemed at the very last minute, was flawless in terms of composure and impactive effect. On the Facebook event page, the physical appearance hadn't been as apparent, and seems incidental as hell, not worth mentioning now, but as Thompson himself reminded the audience last night, "Our fathers are always with us." In the last few years, Colorado became one of the first U.S. states to legalize marijuana for medical, then recreational use, resulting, predictably, in an influx of tourists and, eventually, transplants to Denver, drawn by sensational and/or entrepreneurial prospects. I was hosting a variety show in the Baker Neighborhood at the time, where bumper stickers reading, "Keep LoDo off South Broadway," were the currency, but we knew it was simply a matter of time before the contagion spread that far. Seeing their chance, the majority of lessors raised the rents, as a result of which, whole areas of the city traditionally considered enclaves for Denver's creative community –artists, writers, musicians, comedians, actors – Capitol

Hill, the Baker Neighborhood, most of Central Denver are some – were promptly priced beyond range. In my particular case, I am now paying a hundred dollars more for a space half the size of one I've been paying a hundred dollars less for, and it's located far outside my preferred district. I count myself lucky. But how long will it last?

30 PAUL KRASSNER GOES BEYOND WORDS
MY TRIBUTE IN THE FORM OF A EULOGY

PAUL Krassner, who died in August of 2019, was the first writer from the prior generation to lend a helping hand when I started soliciting interviews as a zinester. Paul's informal journal, The Realist, was the first modern zine. I read an interview with him in V. Vale's *Pranks!* anthology, found his email address somewhere, and sent him one. We did an interview and became regular correspondents with each other for about fifteen years, as I went on to interview more and more people and develop more and more connections with forebears and peers and upcomers. When he died, I wanted to write a tribute right away. I had a conversation with Lee Quarnstrom to do something with in connection with that, but my paying contact wasn't biting, and I had a few other ideas on the burner. I got sidetracked. A few days ago I was in the books section at Goodwill and thought of Paul Krassner a few minutes before happening on one of his books. I didn't purchase the copy of *Pot Stories For The Soul* I came across that day since I thought I probably already had a copy, if I hadn't sold it by now, but I knew he was saying hello. I'm about to write it, Paul, I thought. I know it's been a while, but it's gonna be great.

Paul Krassner was the Lenny Bruce of journalism. He first came to my attention in Tom Wolfe's *Electric Kool Aid Acid Test* as an associate of the Merry Pranksters who never rode the bus anywhere but was active in organization and promotion of the LSD experience, including Kesey's Acid Tests, once tripping with Groucho Marx, as recounted in his *Ravings of an Unconfirmed Nut*, published in 2012 (and there's probably another recounting somewhere else). Paul was the child violin prodigy who grew into angel or coauthor of transgressive comedy founding Father Lenny Bruce's autobiography, *How to Talk Dirty and Influence People*. He was a freelance journalist on multiple sensational topics throughout his life—a film called *The Last of the Manson Girls* burlesques the early years, and *Patty Hearst and the Twinkie Murders: A Tale of two Trials* is a great compilation including more recent work. He invented the awesome self-descriptor "investigative satirist," and, in his later years, he was a standup comedian (videos of his performances as such can be turned up easily on YouTube). He was also an insider in the founding of the Yippies, meaning something like outspoken hippies, whose conclave included Abie Hoffman and other members of the Chicago 8 or 9 or however many there were, but Paul's friendship with Lenny was a lifelong pillar of his character. In his last several emails to me, he spoke of being at work on a pseudo-autobiographical fiction about a modern-day Lenny Bruce-type comic. These emails included summations of the action and even brief excerpts as attachments. My email to Paul's daughter expressing my condolences was replied to most graciously, but my follow-up inquiry about the unpublished Bruce-type manuscript went unresponded. As a hungry fan, I hope someone empowered to do so looks through Paul's files and renders that work to fair completion because I want to read it. As a mortal, I'm struck by the bittersweet perfection that there should be so many undiscovered manuscripts. Keep writing, folks.

It makes sense this manuscript has perhaps been lost to the sands of time; carelessness having been a central altar in the Pranksters' thesis. For years, Kesey published a journal called *Spit in the Ocean*. A film called *The Magic Trip* released in 2011 was cobbled together from the hours and hours of footage recorded by the Pranksters of their psychedelic bus trip to the Chicago World's Fair in 1964. That's a few hours edited down from many thousands. This stuff was filmed without any plan to eventually delete incidental or non-optimal footage or edit it into a cohesive form easily digestible by the squares, or maybe one or two of them did have such plans but it was never the point. Kesey declared he had gone beyond writing, considered himself to have done everything possible for him to do in that form and graduated to affecting reality itself, perhaps every fantasist's true aspiration—to imagine things into existence like a god. "The novel is a jealous mistress. She requires more attention than I'm willing to give." He didn't have the urge to engage or go farther.

Ken Kesey and his Merry Pranksters did a lot to popularize taking acid for fun as opposed to spiritual development. Not to say they lacked soul, but it was more about activities than contemplation for the Pranksters—like when they drove their bus backward down a main street festooned with ironic Barry Goldwater promotion— "A Vote For Barry Is A Vote For Fun"— making waves in the real world. This kind of attitude led, in part, to a lot of people thinking it was the Age of Aquarius when it wasn't really yet, but who can blame them, when no one was wearing a clock. It's not me. In a scientific sense based entirely on likelihood, without any soul, it makes sense Paul's last book's still unpublished and "Intrepid Traveler" Ken Babbs' excellent memoir of the Prankster years, *Cronies*, is still awaiting publication— he sent me an email: "I'm tired of waiting for a book publishers to publish Cronies, my big book about the adventures with Ken Kesey, Neal Cassady, the Merry Prankster and the Grateful Dead, so I'm initiating an online petition to encourage a publisher by showing publishers through this petition how many people want to read this book and will buy it. To sign the petition, click here." That link's not active anymore, so I think he found somebody. That's good news.

Paul Krassner was more than a Merry Prankster, of course. In my judgement, his most essential self-had more to do with the Lenny Bruce Archetype. He was a natural ally of their transcendentally transgressive ethos, though, having instinctively scratched one leg with the other while playing violin at Carnegie Hall as a child without interrupting the melody, making the audience laugh—which became a touchstone of his style. And his friendships with the other Pranksters were true, good, lifelong ones, at least the ones I know about. I know I made at least one and probably two attempts to arrange a panel in Denver with Paul and Ken Babbs and George Walker, which came very close to happening but never did, I can't remember why at this late date. I did an interview with Babbs, reviewed another one of his books, and pre-ordered *Cronies*—which everyone might want to do if you've got a few bucks, let me now recommend—then one day, and I can't remember exact details, but I came upon Lee Quarnstrom's email.

Besides his own affiliation with the Pranksters, Lee also had dealings with Larry Flynt's Hustler magazine, as did Krassner. Lee was that magazine's former Executive Editor during Flynt's mental breakdown, and I think Paul was, too, for a while, or maybe he just wrote for them sometimes. That magazine seems to have become a safe haven for all manner of creative outlaws in the seventies, and you know that can't be bad. Among the many connections I made following in Paul Krassner's footsteps as a freelance writer drawn to the unconventional was someone who played Flynt's *agent provocateur* on the outside while he was locked up in a mental hospital in Springfield, MO. I asked Quarnstrom if they knew each other, but they hadn't met, being on opposite sides of the same patron. I remember trying to use the right words in saying how much I liked the Pranksters' slogan "Stay In Your Movie" and ended up saying something weird.

"That's just saying I'm the star of my movie," Lee Quarnstrom simplified. "I'm the center of my universe." Then he told me a story I haven't got good notes for, but I think it was something about how there were kids in the neighborhood who came around when he was sitting there tripping and rotated around him as though he were the center of the universe, not really playing but rotating like planets. Something like that. And I may be misremembering it.

"That's right. Don't be an extra," I think I said. And that's all it was, really, but how incredibly eloquent and accessible a metaphor for we millions raised by the movies all these decades, to think of existence itself as a film, with directors, and extras, and stars, and I'm doing my best to keep it current—only maybe now it's stay in your own meme.

"Did Cassady think of that one? I've always wondered." Stay In Your Own Movie sounded to me like just the kind of phrase the Neal Cassady known for successfully bluffing the cops despite being high on speed and acid and who knows what else might have coined.

"No, I think it was Babbs. He was the foreman. A lot of people think of Kesey as the leader, but he was not so much the leader as a guy with higher consciousness who could explain it well. That was always the point, lifting the wool over people's eyes, and not politics, but this was all happening against the backdrop of the Vietnam War, so they think of it as a political deal. I started as an activist, but the thinking was so militaristic. My consciousness at the time was, 'How can these people be so angry? How can you end violence with violent thinking? That's when I found the Pranksters, where it was more about personal dynamics between a group of special people."

This conversation took place sometime in the fall, I think September or early October, when Paul had just died, and before Lee Quarnstrom, and I rang off, I mentioned that whatever I wrote about our conversation, wherever it ended up, might be part of a tribute to his memory. "A great man," Lee responded. "No question about it."

31 A CONVERSATION WITH GARY WILSON ABOUT LUCKY BREAKS, ENDICOTT, AND PET DUCKS

MAD POP GENIUS TALKS ABOUT HIS INFLUENCES AND INSIGHTS

Gary Wilson started writing *avant garde* classical music at 13 years old in his hometown of Endicott, New York, which he says he'll always have in his heart and soul. "I was playing cello and string bass in the local school ensembles. This led me to the music of Composer John Cage and the avant garde. Mr. Cage had a big influence on me." This was perhaps the first great stroke of luck in Wilson's long career as a self-made artist of unconventional music, in the course of which, he's covered new wave, rock funk, free jazz, lounge, and experimental styles. His 1970s concert performances "included cellophane, duct tape, bed sheets, fake blood, flour, and milk." Often these early performances would have their electricity cut to encourage Wilson off the stage. After moving west to California in 1978, encouraged to seek a record deal after receiving a small amount of radio play in Endicott, Wilson recorded three singles, *In the Midnight Hour/When I Spoke of Love* (1978), the *Forgotten Lovers* E.P. (1979) and *Invasion of Privacy* (1980). The Residents sent fan mail, but mainstream commercial success eluded him.

Young Wilson's early interest in the paragon of musical abstraction was to be rewarded by an influential audience with the master as a teen. Wilson received the important advisement from Cage during this visit that you always want to irritate your audience in some way. He also confided that he himself had never succeeded economically until age fifty, which Wilson says always stuck with him for some reason in Michael Wolk's film *You Think You Really Know Me: The Gary Wilson Story* (2005).

"I was already playing cello and string bass with the school orchestra / chamber ensemble. Also one year with the New York State Youth Orchestra. My cello teacher Mrs. Schaffer and her students would occasionally perform my avant-garde music for after school shows in the school auditorium. She was familiar with my music, and in 1969, when I was 15 years old, she suggested I reach out to John Cage, who was already my hero. I went to our local post office and searched through a Manhattan telephone book for Cage's telephone number. There were a lot of people named John Cage in Manhattan. I finally got the right John Cage phone number and he gave me an address to send my musical scores to. Two weeks later I called Mr. Cage and he invited me to his house in Haverstraw, New York."

Gary Wilson went to Albert Grossman's Bearsville Studios in Woodstock, NY in 1976, well-known host to sessions by Bob Dylan, R.E.M., Patti Smith, The Rolling Stones and other notables, to record versions of "6.4 = Make Out," "Chromium Bitch," "Groovy Girls," and "I Want To Lose Control." In a gesture symbolic of his love for his super-hometown of Endicott, which remains central in his pop landscape despite his relocation to San Diego, California in 1978, Wilson finished recording, *You Think You Really Know Me,* his first album, in his parents' basement, sometimes solo and at other times accompanied by a backing band called The Blind Dates—"I'm good friends with like-minded musicians. We have a good time. He pressed, distributed, funded and released the album himself, pressing 300 copies in 1977 and a further 300 in 1979, two of which he still has.

Wilson's last show before falling out of public currency for a number of years took place at CBGBs circa 1980. In 1991, Cry Baby Records re-released the album, pressing about 1000 copies. Beck gave him a shout out in 1997 on his record "Where It's At," but Wilson's wild years seemed over. Formerly singled out as the guy you wanted at your party to do the thing no one else would, and for walking pet ducks around Endicott of a morning—"When I was in grammar school the local department stores sold baby ducks and chickens for Easter. Not to eat but as pets. I had a few pet ducks growing up. Some passed away. Some were given away to neighbors that had more land. Ducks remind me of little dinosaurs."—and began settling into distinguished mediocrity, when fortune took another turn.

"Many wonderful things have happened to me since 2002. I call 2002 the year of my resurrection. I was working a late night, minimum wage job when my good friend from Endicott Vince Rossi called me at work. He mentioned a New York label (Motel Records) wanted to reissue my 1977 self-released album "You Think You Really Know Me." I said sure, not thinking much would come of it. Then everything changed in my life. That's when writer Neil Strauss wrote the article about me in The New York Times. Next thing all the big city newspapers started writing articles about me and my album. A real magical time. Questlove inviting me to come on the Jimmy Fallon show. Michael Wolk's documentary premiering at Lincoln Center. Being included in the MET's annual fashion gala (Chaos: Punk To Couture). Earl Sweatshirt inviting me to appear with him on the Jimmy Kimmel show. Peanut Butter Wolf and Stones Throw Records signing me to their label and including me in the Stones Throw Records documentary

Our Vinyl Weighs A Ton. And I was recently included in the *Other Music* documentary."

The music on *You Think You Really Know Me* has a quality of unaffected sincerity that reminds me partly-almost of the early Modern Lovers, but the sound is nothing like, incorporating elements of smoothness and soul and self-congratulatory excited barks a la Michael Jackson (I'm thinking of "You Keep on Looking") but nothing at all like him either, in fact far more like Alan Vega during and post Suicide with a seemlier voice shouting, "Hey!" and rhapsodizing, "Whoooo!" between the verses. When asked to name the three or four biggest influences on his sui generis style, and what makes them top ranking, Wilson answers like this: "Had a chance to audition (playing guitar) for Jonathan Richman at one of his shows in the early 1980s. My father was a musician so I was brought up in that world. Dion. At 10 years old, I wanted to be like Dion ("Runaround Sue"). When I was 10 years old (1963) and in grammar school my mother would curl my hair similar to the teen idols at that time (Dion, Fabian, Bobby Rydell, etc."

Wilson released an album called *Tormented* in 2020, featuring instant classics like "The Sin-Eater," "Gary Lives in the Twilight Zone" and "You Looked Cool in Outer Space," plus a few referencing Endicott memories. The way Wilson romanticizes and mythologizes Endicott in songs like "The King of Endicott," "Electric Endicott," and "She Makes me Think of Endicott" is a beautiful testament in rock and roll language to the way a teenager's hometown personifies life itself and everything in it as life's first playing field. "I moved to San Diego in 1978," he says. "Winters here are pleasant. I hadn't been back to my hometown of Endicott for over 25 years. When the Motel Records reissue was coming out in 2002, director Michael Wolk was making his Gary Wilson documentary. He brought me back to my hometown of Endicott in 2002 for two concerts at the local theater turned performing arts center. Michael Wolk threw a big party for me in the basement of the theater after the show. A lot of people from my past showed up for the party. It was fantastic. Put my band The Blind Dates together and played shows around San Diego. At that time most of the local cool bands and press didn't like my band. This was before my resurrection and 2002 reissue of *You Think You Really Know Me*. Now things have changed for the better. Winters here are pleasant. I always remind myself that what I am doing now (with records and concerts) is what I dreamed of doing when I was a young teenager. And the best part of this musical adventure and resurrection is that the audience and critics like my music. What more could I ask for?"

The story of Wilson's misplacement and relocation in the musical ranking may have been foretold in the preamble to his meeting with John Cage. "My mother drove me from Endicott, New York to Haverstraw, New York to meet with Cage. When my mother and I arrived in Haverstraw we became lost in the wooded area. We stopped at a local general store and I called Cage and told him we were lost and couldn't find his house. Mr. Cage drove down in his car to the small store and picked me up and drove me to his house. My mother waited at the store. As we drove to John Cage's home we talked of different things and music. I was 19 years old when my mother passed away. I was close to my mother. I read a few books about the afterlife and I bought the book *Seth Speaks*, which brought some comfort to me during my mother's passing. I didn't contact my mother but I hope I see her again when it's my time. When we arrived at Cages home I noticed how sparse the furnishings were. For the next several hours John Cage and I went over my scores with Cage correcting some of my notation. Twenty something years later John Cage came to UCSD for a series of shows at the San Diego college. At that time my girlfriend Bernadette Allen was a grad student at UCSD. I managed to meet up with John Cage at the college and asked if he remembered me from twenty-something years ago. He said he did and I gave him a copy of *You Think You Really Know Me* and told him he inspired me to record this album. Here's a photo of me as a teenager in our local high school chamber ensemble."

32 DEATH TO DR. MADD VIBE: A TALE OF TWO MOVIES
THE FIRST ALL BLACK PUNK BAND AND POSSIBLY THE FIRST PUNK BAND, DEATH, A MOVIE ABOUT THEM, AND A MOVIE ABOUT ONE OF THEIR INHERITORS, THE BAND FISHBONE

BEFORE THE PHRASE "punk" became well-known, a Beatles and Alice Cooper-inspired black band in Detroit called Death consisting of three brothers was bashing out songs just as rocky and strong as those of their white counterparts the Stooges and the Ramones. Death was among the better proto-punk bands during a period when the US rock music scene was severely segregated in terms of what types of performances were expected from blacks. Death fell short of mainstream success for much the same reason as their stylistic heirs Fishbone years later: they were too black for the white kids and too white for the black ones. Presumably, Death had it worse, being from Motown, arguably the Capital City of 60s and 70s African American musical style. The band's atypical nature delayed its mainstream acceptance by more than thirty years, during which time the Hackney bros.' unreleased demo tapes languished in the attic of a house in Detroit until their eventual release by Drag City Records in 2009 under the title, "For All the World to Hear," and the subsequent release of a DVD called "A Band Called Death," a rock documentary and family history the bulk of which follows the brothers as they attempt to navigate the intricacies of the music business as a band, and which has made Death increasingly popular among indie music enthusiasts since its release. My personal favorite album by Death is Spiritual Mental Physical, a collection of demos and rough cuts from 1975 that was released in 2011. This collection is infused with a manic punk rock joy grounded in seventies cool and to my ears seemingly predictive of Fishbone. The band was composed of a trio of brothers, the eldest of whom, David Hackney, experienced some kind of disconnection from reality. Hackney became convinced Death was the best name, the right name, the perfect name for the band, the name no one else had. He also designed T-shirts featuring the word DEATH in gold capital letters and four circles in the pattern of an arch. Hackney died in 2000 of lung cancer, but not before leaving the band. His brothers Dennis and Bobby Hackney released two albums of gospel rock in the early 1980s as the 4th Movement, and currently lead a reggae band called Lambsbread. Death was the first all-black punk band (preceding Philadelphia's Pure Hell by a couple of years) and possibly the first punk band.

My first exposure to Fishbone came in middle school, via a girl in my study hall who mimed the several faces frontman Angelo Moore took on throughout "These Are The Voices (of Modern Industry)" the band's prescient lament of the corporate takeover of radio fare, which was in constant rotation on bygone Denver video show Teletunes. That radio-friendly song only showcases one aspect of Fishbone's multi-genre uber-democratic approach to musical art, having gone all the way from ska to heavy metal to funk to soul and back to ska in the course of its nearly 51 year career. Formed in South Central Los Angeles in 1979, in the days of forced busing of students to white neighborhoods, when the members were in junior high, they are perhaps best considered a punk band, with that word interpreted to mean freestyle, unbound by habitual conventions like genre. There are certainly moments, such as 1988's "Subliminal Fascism," or 2007's "Faceplant Scorpion Backpinch," when they more than earn that title stylistically as well.

The last few years have borne witness to a revival of Fishbone's career, beginning with the release in 2010 of a retrospective documentary named after one of their songs called "Everyday Sunshine," bearing witness to the ups and downs of the band's career, followed by the release of their first new collection in years, "Crazy Glue" in 2011, representing a confident demonstration of its enduring ability with songs like the title track or "Deep Shit Backstroke ." September of 2012 saw the release of Angelo Moore's latest solo project as Dr. Madd Vibe, "The Angelo Show, the Olegna Phenomenon," featuring vibrant, electrified tracks like "Optimistic Yes" and "Revolutionary Girl." Current tour information and updates are posted regularly at the band's Facebook page and their official profile at MySpace.

The band's lineup has changed over the years. As recounted in Everyday Sunshine, founding guitarist Kendall Jones's deserted father was apparently some kind of Christian extremist. Other members were surprised, after Kendall's mother's death in the late eighties, to hear this villain quoted and praised by their brother. During the recording of 1991's The Reality of my Surroundings, Kendall, probably the most responsible for Fishbone's tendency toward heavy metal sound on albums like 1996's Chim Chim's Badass Revenge, started coming apart at the seams. Kendall was obviously down about a lost relationship and his fondness for alcohol was making it worse. Discussions with his father convinced Kendall Fishbone was doing "the devil's work," calling the band and everything it stood for "demonic." His father's influence was to grow over the next few years, ultimately leading to Kendall's departure from the group to join his father's organization in Novato, California in 1993.

John Bigham stepped into the lead guitarist role for the band's slot on Lollapalooza in the summer of 1993, notably the only time this author was fortunate enough to see the crew live, at Fiddler's Green I think it was, or maybe Red Rocks. In time, the conflicted Kendall's reconnection with his good/evil father took on elements of cultish abuse – there are stories of the wayward son trying to baptize their instruments and forcibly attempting baptism on his own girlfriend, causing her to join forces with other members of Jones' family, and founding Fishbone bassist John Norwood Fisher to attempt to an intervention. All they wanted was to return their childhood friend "Special K" to his former wise cracking self and were charged with kidnapping for their trouble. The ensuing trial almost destroyed the band and their love for each other. All charges were eventually dropped, but Kendall never officially rejoined the familyhood. A variety of members came and went over the years. With the departure of longtime trumpet player / backing vocalist Dirty Walt in 2005, rumors of the band's decline began, but in light of their resurgence to quality productivity, such are easily dispelled. Jones himself appears near the end of Everyday Sunshine, performing with the current lineup in a small club show. This reunion spurs talk among the participants of a reunion tour, which is quickly dismissed by Moore, but all tempers seem healed, at least for Everyday Sunshine happy ending purposes. "Never quit a band for Jesus," reflected Jones at the Mill Valley Film Festival.

Fishbone is notably one of the most deliberately democratic of modern musical acts, giving every member a stake in its eventual success or failure, featuring multiple lead vocals and styles, as well as multi-instrumentalism among its members. This mutable quality makes them hard to classify in marketing schemes and has led to a perversion of their viability in both the white and black cultures. In line with this mood of extreme tolerance, Moore has adopted the pseudonym Dr. Madd Vibe for his solo output, including spoken word and experimental musical expressions, most recently exemplified by this summer's excellent "The Angelo Show, the Olegna Phenomenon ." The latest Dr. Madd Vibe release, by name "Sacrifice," is forthcoming this year. Moore has grown enamored of what is perhaps the most untechnical of musical props – the theremin, which creates eerie wavering sounds via users' disruption of the electronic force field it emanates. Talk about freestyle. This unfettered direction is often at odds with super-humanly technical bassist Fisher's vision of the band, this being far more concerned with composition and delivery of groove oriented, conservative (not to say "right wing") funk. Says Norwood,

"I wanted to be in a band with Angelo, not Dr. Madd Vibe!" Not to worry, the reliable incongruity of Moore's eccentric, free-form stylistics experiments and Fisher's sober determination to provide solid funk for the band's eclectic audience has been a central theme of this outfit's enduring sound over time, and can be counted on to give us all a friction strange as fiction to the ear.

(A non-identical version of this was published at www.itspsychedelicbabymag.com)

33 BEYOND TWO TONE WITH ANGELO MOORE
AN EMAIL INTERVIEW WITH FISHBONE'S ANGELO MOORE

Angelo Moore

Ska-punk-soul-funk-jazz-metal powerhouse Fishbone started as an all-black Los Angeles band in 1979, and became known in the 80s as populists of a Jamaican style called ska, among other helpings in a musical gumbo perhaps more eclectic than has ever been seen. Ska music preceded reggae in its land of origin, sharing the characteristics of emphasis on the offbeat and use of the guitar as a rhythmic instrument, but at a faster pace.

Angelo Moore, also known as Dr. Madd Vibe, vocalist, saxophonist, theremin player, and frontman of Fishbone, Dr. MaddVibe and the Missing Links (name recently changed to Angelo Moore and the Dr. MaddVibes), Angelo Moore and the Brand New Step, and others, typically stays active touring and recording 24 hours a day, 7 days a week, and 365 days a year with all his outfits. "My introduction to ska and reggae was the Specials, the Selecter, Bad Manners and the English ska explosion," reports. "Afterward, I discovered Jamaican ska culture . . . Prince Buster, Alton Ellis, the Skatalites, Ska Cubano, Toots and the Maytals, et cetera. I don't have too much of an opinion on the Jamaican rub a dub scene other than the fact that I enjoyed it thoroughly in the LA and behind Orange County areas."

Fishbone's exposure to the punk sound came through its black founders' being bused to a white high school as preteens and teens, as seen in Chris Metzler's partly-animated 2010 Fishbone biopic, *Everyday Sunshine*. Fishbone's anti racist stance was shown in their lyrics, in songs like "Fight the Youth (With Poisoned Minds)" and a series of band T shirts with slogans like RACISM SUCKS and FUCK RACISM surrounding their logo, "and fuck you if you don't like it . . . with love."

English ska bands like The Specials and Bad Manners, with songs like "Concrete Jungle" and "Lorraine," opened the door to black participation in punk disaffection. Accordingly, the members of Fishbone were making the most of integration in Los Angeles in the late 1970s and 80s as they familiarized themselves with the other culture's ethos —"The Bad Brains where one of the first bands to spark my awareness [of punk], then the Sex Pistols, the Anti-Nowhere League, the Damned, Black Flag and the Circle Jerks, the Dead Kennedys, and the list goes on. Fishbone had a chance to play CBGBs back in the day a couple of times in the late 80's and early 90's as far as the punk scene."

They also played there on the club's final week open in 2007, as part of a tribute to founder Hilly Krystal, bassist Norwood Fisher proclaiming, before the band launched into "Subliminal Fascism": "Without CBGBs that fostered a small scene and turned it into a worldwide event—punk rock—it wouldn't be no Fishbone, it woudn't be no Lollapalooza, no motherfucking Warped Tour, NOT SHIT . . . CBGBs represents freedom. I'm glad to be here."

Fishbone decided at its outset to give each member—some of them multi-instrumentalists—an equal stake in its success or failure, incorporating several distinct styles over the years. This multifarious quality makes them hard to classify in marketing schemes. To demonstrate the range of their appeal, Eugene Hütz (*Gogol Bordello*), Perry Farrell (Jane's Addiction, Porno for Pyros), and Keith Morris (Black Flag, Circle Jerks, Off!) appear alongside George Clinton, Ice-T and Branford Marsalis in *Everyday Sunshine* as fans. Why no hip hop in the gumbo? "Fishbone doesn't need hip hop because we play the musical styles that hip hop is made up of, like funk, R&B, and jazz. But I love hip hop, the Sugar Hill Gang, Eric B and Rakim, N.M.A. and the long list goes on."

To be fair, there's something pretty close incorporated in a Brand New Step song called "Brand New Pendulum," wherein Angelo acknowledges that the fascism in this joint has gone from being subliminal to "the real deal dough now."

"In regards to Dr.MaddVibe, I'm still here and making the magic happen. At present, because of the coronavirus, all of my shows got cancelled, so to get around that, I'm putting together the online Angelo Show, where I will be performing some of my solo material, including 'The Brand New Step' and Dr.Madd Vibe and some spoken word, with organ, piano and sax."

What's next for these stalwarts of the punk soul cycle, these inheritors of 2 Tone tough love? "New releases with original members. It's gonna be good."

On YouTube currently are a collaboration between Angelo and legendary animator extraordinaire, Joe Horne, touching on racism and bigotry in the corporate industry, is entitled "Doin' the Monkey for the Honkey"; another new song—"Homefree"—"about the saga of robbin' from the rich and giving to the poor"; and videos for Brand New Step numbers on Ropeadope Records "Karma Cash Back," "Centuries of Heat" and "Dream Crusher ." "And, soon to come, 'Los Angeles'."

34 LARRY FLYNT FOR PRESIDENT: NADIA SZOLD INTERVIEWED
A CONVERSATION WITH DIRECTOR NADIA SZOLD

NADIA Szold's documentary *Larry Flynt for President* was scheduled to have its premiere in 2019. But COVID put the kibosh on that. In the interim, the subject of the film, free speech crusader and *Hustler Magazine* founder Larry Flynt, died on Feb. 10 of this year. The film will now be shown on June 12 at the Tribeca Festival. Zack Kopp spoke last year with Nadia Szold about the film, the hypocrisies of Reagan's America and the debacle of Trump, which Larry Flynt may have prophesied.

Larry Claxton Flynt founded *Hustler Magazine* in 1974. As an unabashed pornographer who didn't have to worry about offending advertisers, he used his soapbox to reinvent media. The epitome of pulling oneself up from the dregs to the heights, he came of age in an area of trenches near a coal mine in Kentucky.

By 1984, with his media enterprises a resounding success, Flynt felt he was perfectly positioned to run for office on the Republican Party ticket as an act of satire and rebellion against Ronald Reagan's America. He also felt that he had to run, because, as he told an interviewer, "I will be the first man elected president of the United States from prison."

Accordingly, in an effort to boost his chances, Flynt zeroed in on a member of Pres. Reagan's foreign relations advisory board, Alfred Bloomingdale. Bloomingdale's mistress, Vicki Morgan, allegedly hosted sex parties for prominent White House officials, and Flynt hired investigators to film her. This surveillance resulted in an apparent video recording of Reagan getting doggied by a woman wearing a strap-on, which tape has since disappeared. "There's gonna be some checkbook journalism like you've never seen," said Flynt at the time, promising further tapes implicating the whole crew. This phrase refers to the practice of paying large amounts of money for exclusive rights to material for newspaper stories, especially personal ones.

Reassembled from hitherto unseen footage from his campaign, plus other footage of Flynt and associates, the archival documentary *Larry Flynt for President* is currently in post-production and will premiere at the Tribeca Film Festival in June. Like most public gatherings, this annual platform for surfacing talent was recently postponed on account of the coronavirus but should be coming soon or going virtual.

Director, producer and writer Nadia Szold began working in theater in her teens in New England. In 2001, she founded a company called Cinema Imperfecta out of her apartment in Red Hook, Brooklyn. Her *Hope & Anchor*, *Thievery*, *The Persian Love Cake* and *Some Kinda Fuckery* were the first short films produced and directed under this banner in Paris and New York. Szold earned a degree from Werner Herzog's Rogue Film School. This institution specializes in the "Art of Guerrilla Filmmaking and Lock-Picking," its curriculum covering the "athletic," some might say opportunistic, tactics required by self-funded, independent filmmakers, investigative and otherwise, tricks like creating one's own shooting permits to neutralize bureaucracy, for example. Szold's second feature, *Mariah*, starring Dakota Goldhor and Evan Luison Louison, filmed in Mexico during the rise of vigilante groups reclaiming cartel-controlled regions, made extensive use of these resourceful techniques.

"There's nothing more encouraging than a raucous audience of college students laughing and hollering at a test screening," Szold says. "We screened a rough cut for around 70 students, the majority having never heard of Larry Flynt. If the film entertains and provokes intelligent questions from kids, you're gonna be OK. In terms of opposition? I like to live by the motto *illegitimi non carborundum*, Latin for 'Don't let the bastards get you down.' There are always battles, and the marathon nature of making an archival documentary can be exhausting. It's a labor of love. I often thought while making it that if Larry and Althea [Larry Flynt's wife] didn't have soul, then what would've been the point? I could never have spent that much time thinking about people I didn't respect or wasn't fascinated by."

A snippet of the Reagan speech about making America great again appears. The technique of using a rolling screen to switch scenes is masterful. A clip of Reagan dancing with his wife, the screen rolls, and it's Flynt with water-weights in a pool after the shooting, with his voice, "I think it was the FBI or the CIA got me, one. In terms of opposition? I like to live by the motto *illegitimi non carborundum*, Latin for 'Don't let the bastards get you down.'

Larry's late fourth wife, Althea Flynt (née Leasure; November 6, 1953 – June 27, 1987) took charge after Larry's subsequent near-fatal crippling shooting in Georgia in 1978 and the multiple bouts with bipolar disorder which led to his campaign for President of the United States in 1984. "If you dissent too loudly, they will kill you," he said later. "There's a lot of truth to that. Well,

they tried. I'm still here." Althea died on June 27, 1987, at age 33 after drowning in the bathtub at the couple's Bel-Air mansion. She is buried in the Flynt family cemetery plot, located on Lakeville in Salyersville, Kentucky. In pain after the shooting, Flynt consented to having those nerves in his back carrying pain from his legs cut, sacrificing his dream of ever walking again for a pain-free existence. Flynt's heavy dependence on painkillers before this operation coincided with his wife's eventually fatal slide into opiate addiction. "I'm responsible for my wife's death, and that's a heavy burden to carry," he said.

Althea was *Hustler's* first life-size centerfold. She married Flynt in 1976. After being made Publisher/Editor of *Hustler* shortly thereafter, she kept the magazine afloat during Larry's "born again" experience. During this time of personal tumult, the magazine's contents reflected the change in its publisher's character, featuring nude women strapped to glass crosses and scripture and verse.

It was around this time that Flynt had a psychotic bipolar manic episode in 1977, which he described to Rudy Maxa of the *Washington Post* in 1978:

> *"I promised to give up my wife for Him. I promised to see myself castrated, too look down and see myself with no sexual organs and look up and say, 'Yes, God, it's okay, if that's Your will, that's fine.' I spoke in tongues. There were animals eating at my neck, like baboons and monkeys, gnawing at me. He told me my calling: to bring peace on earth. And He told me there had been a distortion of His Word, which confirmed my thing on religions but only one God. Then I had to pray for my wife, Althea – He was taking Althea away from me, a natural death or an accident – oh, how I had to pray. Then I asked Him about Lenny Bruce, and I got the feeling Lenny was in hell so I prayed and prayed and prayed for Lenny. But it seemed like He only reached down and picked up half of Lenny. I remember saying something like 'Did you get him, did you get all?' and then I looked very close up at Jesus and He was holding Lenny in His arms . . ."*

From Snidely Whiplash to Larry Flynt to Donald Trump, from cartoons to porn to game shows, the billionaire bully archetype is a recurring theme in modern American socio political history, and the timing is optimal for a film documenting the overlapping of that type into the realm of politics. In this case, however, it happened by accident.

Larry Flynt

Says Szold, "I was literally inside Flynt's archives on 8484 Wilshire when Trump announced his run for presidency. I thought the timing couldn't have been better and that we had an urgency to get the film out before the 2016 election, when, inevitably, Trump would lose and drift back into oblivion. Clearly, that didn't happen, and I actually didn't get any serious offers for funding until after Trump won and it sunk in that this would be the new normal."

At first glance, the two archetypes would seem to have a lot in common. *Screw Magazine* publisher Al Goldstein said, "Larry Flynt only knows he's alive when he sees himself in the media." Goldstein also compared Larry Flynt to Humpty Dumpty, a comparison also frequently used on Trump.

Both Larry Flynt and Donald Trump battered their way into the political arena by sheer market share as opinionated billionaires from beyond the inner circle, Flynt with his skin mags as a bona fide and Trump his reality show(s).

"Both are bombastic, take-no-prisoners loud-mouths who epitomize a kind of '80s porno-capitalism," says Szold. "Shock-jocks of politics who use their savvy of the press to get attention and keep it on them. But they couldn't be further apart. First of all, Larry Flynt came from extreme poverty and is an actual self-made man. His first memory is that of his father shooting a shotgun at him and his Ma as they ran over a grassy hill in the holler of rural Kentucky. His parents split and he was raised by his hard-working mother. Another time he was shot was in 1978 at 36 years old by a white supremacist offended by an interracial spread in *Hustler*. That time he was hit, and it left him paralyzed from the waist down. This is all very different from someone who claims he could shoot someone dead on 5th Avenue and his constituents would still love him."

Despite having run for President as a Republican, Flynt was staunchly opposed to current political trends, having famously offered $10M for incriminating video or pics of Donald Trump, apparently without success (so far). "You'll have to ask him if anything came of that," Szold said before Flynt's death in February. "Larry Flynt is a progressive, who, in 1983, when he launched his campaign for president, was using his voice as a citizen to protest the direction that Reagan was taking the country in. He saw that Reagan was gutting social programs . . . grossly favoring the rich, purporting the myth of trickle-down economics (a theory, which, ironically originated as satire at the turn of the century). Now we are premiering in the midst of another general election, and the parallels have shifted. Incumbent Trump is much more similar to then-incumbent Ronald Reagan. Can Larry then be compared to Bernie Sanders? I don't think so. Sanders is earnest. Larry's a rascal."

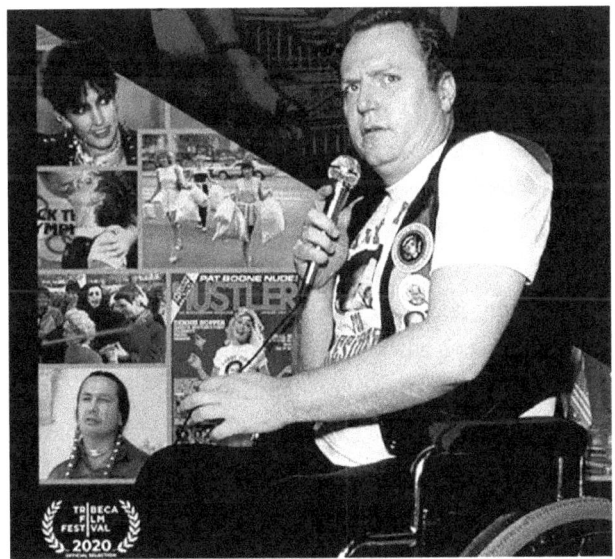

In 1983, he was imprisoned. "The Springfield Medical Center exists for one reason and one reason only: to get rid of people they don't want in society," said Szold. Flynt arranged a series of scandalous events in the small Missouri town where he was imprisoned to draw the attention of the press away from himself. In one loud public caper, conducted by outside agents, he successfully inverted the town's moral valence by offering drugs and sex and cash to the all the most ostensibly high-minded citizens.

"Flynt always dangled the carrot which everyone, including myself, saw as the key to whatever the next step was," remembers Alan Graham, an assistant to Larry Flynt. "like the character Guy Grand in Terry Southern's satirical novel *The Magic Christian*."

Southern was one of the hangers-out at Flynt's mansion, along with Dennis Hopper—with whom he was reportedly collaborating on a screenplay about the Doors in an upstairs room—American Indian Movement activist Russell Means, Tim Leary, Norman Mailer, G. Gordon Liddy, and others.

Flynt's presidential run in 1984 is characterized by its mischievous vitality, a detour in typically staid political history akin to Hunter S. Thompson's 1970 run for sheriff of Aspen, Colorado, on the Freak Power platform. Both men were exceptional outsiders attempting to take part in politics, fellow disruptors at different points on a common bandwidth. Neither bid for office was successful.

"I actually didn't get any serious offers for funding until after Trump won and it sunk in that this would be the new normal."

In 1988, Flynt won a lasting victory against state censorship against Jerry Falwell, whom he befriended, along with Ruth Stapleton Carter, during his "born again" phase. Falwell accused Flynt of slandering his mother in a parody advertisement depicting Falwell as an incestuous drunk. The smear was triggered by Falwell's statement that people who get AIDS deserved it, as well as Falwell's close association with Pres. Reagan. Given Falwell's notoriety as one of the leading televangelists of the day, plus the fact the piece was clearly marked as a parody, not once but twice, the court lacked sufficient reason to deny the First Amendment protection to speech that is critical of public officials and public figures, ruling 8-0 in favor of HUSTLER, and establishing a legal standard. "Freedom of expression is absolute."

Nadia Szold understands the timeless moral and ethical significance of Larry Flynt's life as a contrarian. "In James Agee's prologue to *Let Us Now Praise Famous Men,* he writes, 'Every fury on earth has been absorbed in time, as art, or as religion, or as authority in one form or another. The deadliest blow the enemy of the soul can strike is to do fury honor. Swift, Blake, Beethoven, Christ, Joyce, Kafka, name me a one who has not been thus castrated. Official acceptance is the one unmistakable symptom that salvation is beaten again, and is the one surest sign of fatal misunderstanding, and is the kiss of Judas.' Hopefully, Larry is still a far-cry from official acceptance. And sugar coating him or making him Hollywood like-able was never my intent in making the film."

Is Larry Flynt more likely to love or hate this film about his run for presidency, documenting a far less ordered stage in his jagged personal history as pornographer, free speech crusader, and Senate hearing attendee?

Nadia Szold

"I really can't say," says Szold prior to Flynt's death. "I'm sure there will be moments he winces at. He's a different man than he was back in the early 80's. But more than anything I think he'll just laugh." Any unexpected revelations in store? "Of course!" Szold said. "And in Larry Flynt fashion, no less." Like publishing a pornographic ad about your mother when you piss him off. Or wearing a FUCK THIS COURT shirt to his trial. A blatantly unprecedented gesture compelling passionate reaction from onlookers. "We are now finalizing the film, with the last color session and watch-down happening Wednesday. It's all very exciting, and the film has come together beautifully thanks to the talented people I've been working with."

35 ANDY WARHOL AND THE BEATS IN DENVER: A CONVERSATION WITH MARK SINK

DENVER ARTIST MARK SINK IS ED WHITE'S STEPSON AND WAS A PART OF WARHOL'S FACTORY

DENVER photographer, street artist and gallery owner Mark Sink talks about the Andy Warhol he knew, the one without masks or disguises. He offers some surprising revelations about the artist, and his distant link to Jack Kerouac, in conversation with Zack Kopp.

Perhaps no other artist embraced the decadent nature of blooming 1960s commercialism quite as graphically or prolifically as Andy Warhol, who, in 1968, predicted the world we live in, where everyone is famous for fifteen minutes. If Andy hadn't put together the Velvet Underground in an attempt to influence musical taste, the New York City punk scene would never have existed, at least as we've come to know it. Even Warhol's technique of film portraiture, where subjects are shot in a relaxed attitude for three or four minutes, was considered wild when he did it, but it is lately a trend. He was the curve, in a real, quantifiable sense.

"My link to the past is that Andy keeps resurfacing every year to pay me a little more money," observes Denver-based guerrilla photographer Mark Sink. "He was so far ahead of our Instagram minds."

Sink has been exhibiting his work professionally since 1978, as street art, and in commercial galleries, museums and other institutions.

He is best known for romantic portraiture. Some of his most recognizable images include documentation of life and work of artists of his association during the New York art scene of the 1980s. After some time in New York, Sink returned to Denver and opened Gallery Sink in 1988. A few of the shots illustrating this piece are from The Big Picture, an adjunct to the annual Month of Photography Sink founded in 2005, in which one block of an alley wall on 13th Avenue, between a series of hip used clothing joints and a series of hip local eateries, has been papered with submissions from artists all over the world every summer since 2006. The balance are pictures of Warhol by Sink, who's come a long way since their meeting in Fort Collins, Colo., in September of 1981 on the Colorado State University campus.

Andy Warhol, by Mark Sink

"[Warhol] was there to give a lecture and my roommate spotted him eating in a nearby restaurant," remembers Sink. "It was my dream to be in *Interview* magazine at the time. I remember going around to groups of people and asking them, 'Have you seen Andy Warhol?' Just going from classroom to classroom, opening every door, until I found him. Andy now would be over 90 . . . hard to believe. People just stand still in time when they're gone. He was my age now when we met."

Sink relates how Andy and his mother used to paint together, how it was Andy's mother who sent him the soup can, how much of his method amounted to outsourcing mythography.

"It drives me nuts to read amazing in-depth comparative analytical essays on some of Andy's statements from his writings. From *The Philosophy of Andy Warhol*. I was close to Brigid Berlin and Pat Hackett (editor of *The Andy Warhol Diaries*). Those were his ghost writers. I learned how they wrote and rewrote and literally thought up many of Andy's passages in the books. In fact, once I witnessed Andy reviewing some things they edited for him. He said, 'Gee, that's great, you make me sound so smart.' Brigid would roll her eyes saying how she wrote 'a lot'. She talks about it more these days."

Sink tells the story of showing up where Andy was staying after a day spent skiing. Warhol convinced himself that the goggles and gloves and boots and jacket Sink was wearing was a costume. Warhol saw anything eye-catching in his immediate orbit as a production, saying, over and over again, "No one would ever do that."

"But it was just our winter mountaineering gear," says Sink. "We camped in East Marron Creek between Christmas and New Year's. We'd ski down into Aspen smelling like burnt logs to party for New Year's . . .At the door of Jane Holzer's condo, Andy came out to greet us and did not believe we had been camping for days. He just wouldn't believe it. Kept going on about it all night: 'No, you guys didn't do that.'"

On the same visit, Warhol reportedly worried that his boyfriend Jon had tried to kill him by driving off a cliff, after (unnoticed by Andy) Sink threw some snow in his face while the two were racing around on a snowmobile. All evening, Warhol repeated, "It was the strangest thing. Jon tried to kill me. Something must have come over him."

"We ate TV dinners and ice cream that night," Sink remembers.

"They gave me all the food to keep, tons of food I drove home in my old Triumph TR2."

There had been fires in the area, and Warhol complained the house might burn down in his sleep. "The place was surrounded by Aspen, though, which doesn't catch as easily," said Sink. "It's a pioneer species that grows at the site of a previous burn after learning something from the soil."

I thought of how this was not unlike Warhol's vision taking root in the soil of society's decomposition (devolution?), springing up from the soil of commercialism after turning it into a nutrient. A pioneer species that's harder to burn off. But I'm no critic.

Mark Sink

Sink's wife, artist Kristin Hatgi Sink, and their daughter, Poppy, stopped by the alley in Denver to touch base with him on their way home. The sun was shining. It was one of the first warm days in a week or so, the temperature felt just right. Everybody was in a good mood, as Mark and New Jersey-based artist Bill Westheimer wheat-pasted shots from artists and photographers all over the world on the graffiti-swirled alley wall in Denver. "I like that they're all in black and white," said Westheimer. "Really makes it stand out from the color underneath."

"Brigid Berlin would greet me at the front desk as she was knitting with her two pugs," recalls Sink. "She would let me right up, as the waiting room always had some famous stars in wait. I'd wander the Factory, making Polaroids and taking snapshots. Paige Powell from Portland Oregon just released a portfolio of JMB in the nude from those days. Female gazing."

The alley offered an excellent view of late afternoon sunlight falling across the tan back steps of the Jack Kerouac Apartments, a distinctly Warholian commercialization of Denver iconography. More time travel from beyond the grave by Andy.

Ed White with author Zack Kopp

"Is that what those are?" asked Sink, looking up at the NO

TRESPASSING sign hung on the fence in front of where his car was parked. Sink's stepfather, Edward Divine White, remained one of Jack's closest friends, from their acquaintance at Columbia University in the '40s until Kerouac's death in 1969, a climactic year for the counterculture, considering Altamont and the Manson murders, a year during which Warhol would have been recovering from radical feminist Valerie Solanas' failed assassination attempt. "I never mentioned that to Andy, that Ed was friends with Jack Kerouac," says Sink. "I wonder what he would have said about it. I think this is a continuation of the same thing the Beats did, putting posters up in an alley, making run-down, dirty things look beautiful with art."

36 SAN FRANCISCO STREETS OF A.D. WINANS

WINANS IS A GREAT POET, PEER OF BUKOWSKI, MICHELINE, KAUFMAN, AND OTHERS

By Ginger Edes from a photo by Richard Petty

ONCE described by recently deceased poet and City Lights Books founder Lawrence Ferlinghetti as a great place to pull oneself up by the bootstraps, the San Francisco Bay Area has increasingly transformed into a home base for tech giants in the last couple of decades as a culmination of a trend away from art toward profit. With Lawrence Ferlinghetti's death at the impressive age of 102 on February 22nd of 2021, San Francisco's more than a century as a prestigious

Bohemian hot spot seems at a close. American poet, essayist, short story writer and publisher Allan Davis Winans, known professionally as A. D. Winans was born January 12, 1936, in San Francisco, California, and has made that city his lifelong home base. Winans returned home from Panama in 1958, after serving three years in the military and graduated from San Francisco State College In 1962. In the suburb of North Beach, he became friends beyond life with California Beat poets Bob Kaufman and Jack Micheline. Winans exchanged emails with Zack Kopp recently.

"Micheline didn't like labels and considered himself a Bohemian. I don't like labels either. I know I don't like being, [as I have been] in the past, classified as a 'Meat' poet. If I had to be labeled, I, too, prefer Bohemian. Gino and Carlo's Bar in the heart of North Beach was a Bohemian heaven where poets, artists, philosophers, and journalists like Warren Hinckle and the San Francisco Chronicle columnist Charles Mc Cabe hung out. Beat poets Richard Brautigan and Jack Spicer drank there. Hunter Thompson, a journalist friend of Hinckle, dropped in, as did talented musicians and singers. My most memorable experience was my painter friend Peter Onstad and I shooting pool with Janis Joplin and her friend 'Sunshine' as the jukebox played 'Down On Me'. North Beach was always a happening place."

As a lifelong resident, Winans has a long view of San Francisco's transformation over decades of incremental change spanning most of the last century. "The ghosts remain, especially for those of us who were part of those days. As a teenager, on a warm day, I and a friend would skip class and take a streetcar to the Beach and walk the boardwalk or lay in the sand, knowing we would face detention as a punishment, but it was well worth it, [M]y old Polytechnic High School was demolished in 1987 and replaced with condos All that remains is the Boys Gym. In the 4 years there our football team lost but one game and soundly beat that same team in the Championship game. I ran the 440 and made the All-City trials and no, I did not place in the top three but finishing fourth in such a field seemed at the time a small victory. The Place, a bar on upper Grant Avenue that featured 'Blabber Night' where anyone could get up and espouse anything on their mind from poetry to philosophy. I hung out there on occasion and would see poet Jack Spicer there. Seen here in 1959 hosting Linda Lovely and her soapbox. She was a central figure in Jerry Kamstra's novel *The Frisco Kid*. I keep calling the 'Big Man' in the sky, but the cell phone signal is out of reach and all I get is a busy signal from one of the few old telephones left in the City."

Winans has been referred to as "America's foremost non-academic poet." He was the founder of Second Coming Press, a San Francisco based small press publishing books, poetry broadsides, a magazine, and anthologies, editing *Second Coming Magazine* from 1972 to 1989. During this period, he befriended Charles Bukowski and Bukowski's then-girlfriend, Linda King, both of whose work he published. Other writers published in that magazine included Jack Micheline, Bob Kaufman, Lawrence Ferlinghetti, Allen Ginsberg, Philip Levine, Josephine Miles, David Meltzer, and Charles Plymell. In 2002, he published his memoir, *Holy Grail: Charles Bukowski & The Second Coming Revolution,* a memoir and account of his professional relationship and friendship with a poet known for his lack of metaphoric distance, and its effect on his writing and life. Portions of Winans' correspondence with Bukowski appear in collections of Bukowski's letters to fans, colleagues and editor(s).

A.D. Winans in San Francisco. Photographer unknown.

"Charles Bukowski and I corresponded for 17 years and exchanged 83 letters during the time I was publishing Second Coming. His letters to me are in my archives at Brown University. Next month I may start sharing 'portions' of letters from the copies I have kept here. My book Dead Lions published by Punk Hostage Press. The book details my friendship with Bukowski, Kaufman, Jack Micheline, and Alvah Bessie, one of the Hollywood Ten who went to prison for defying the House Un-American Activities Committee, a dark period in our history. This poem of mine was written for Charles

Second Coming archives, photo credit: Sam Cherry, courtesy A.D. Winans.

Bukowski in the seventies:

THE GOOD THE BAD THE UGLY

Called you from the corner
Of Hollywood and Vine
Three days in a row.
Because you said to be sure
And look you up when I got in town

Managed to reach you
Late in the afternoon
On the night of my reading

At Beyond Baroque

You said
You had trouble recognizing my voice
Hoped I wasn't drinking too much
Said something about your having just
Returned from a trip to Europe

Paris I believe
Three weeks of intense travel with Linda

Three weeks of living hell

And an appearance on national TV

You said that I had called
At the wrong time and
Hoped I would understand
And to be sure and write to you
When I got back home

And me just back from
Eight days and nights

Fighting insomnia in New York
Listening to Louis Simpson
And a host of minor poets read
Standing here in a phone booth
Here in Los Angeles
3 days into smog
3 nights into the world series

Don't worry Hank I understand

Don't give it a second thought

I mean it's okay

We all have a little
Of the gangster inside us
Al Capone or Bugsy Malone

In Chicago or in Sicily

We all dream
The dream of Diamond Jim

Only to wake in the morning sweating

A dead numbers man

In a dead-end alley

In Chicago or in Sicily

Or on Carlton way in downtown

L.A.

And the sleepless nights
Pile up like litter
And the mafia men disguised
In the clothes of poets
Wait like hitmen
To collect a bad debt

And there's always a torpedo

From Cleveland or the Bronx
Someone with a scar and a sneer
Waiting by the window with
A machine gun or a forty-five

And if the arts and politics don't get you
And you manage to survive the betrayals
And the long line of undertakers
That stretch out like body bags
In a battle zone

You can consider yourself lucky
Sell your letters to the University
Ignore the mad sirens wailing
In the recess of your mind

Don't worry Hank I understand

As Bob Kaufman said:

There ain't no piano for Lucky Luciano
There ain't no phone for Al Capone
There ain't no jazz on Alcatraz
There ain't no heart on Carlton"

While serving in Panama Winans says he became disillusioned with the American system. Panamanian canal workers, who performed the same work as their American counterparts, were paid less than half the going pay. In the American controlled Canal Zone, the U.S. Governor refused to allow the Panamanian flag to fly alongside the flag of the United States. Elections were rigged and ballot boxes were found floating in the canal. The Joseph McCarthy era, the struggle for civil rights, the treatment of the American Indian, and the Vietnam War all became fodder for later rebellion, which resulted in the many scathing political poems I have written. I was honorably discharged from the military in February,1958, and returned home to discover the Beat generation."

Part of the secret to Winans' notoriety is his commitment to poetry and his prolific nature. He is the author of nearly seventy books and chapbooks of poetry and prose, including North Beach Poems, North Beach Revisited, Drowning Like Li Po in a River of Red Wine, In The Dead Hours of Dawn, San Francisco Poems, and Dead Lions. Another is his extremely prolific nature, even into his eighties. "Here's a link to Byron Coley reading live and on the radio my long epic political poem, MAYDAY (https://www.youtube.com/watch?v=50ULWkEfR6M) [which has been] published in a City Lights like paperback pocketbook by Holy Yurt Books as the first book in their pocketbook series limited to 100 copies, 20 of which are signed by the author. I am making available 15 of the 20 signed copies. The cost of the book including postage and shipping is $10. To make payment through PayPal, use my email, slowdancer2006@netzero.com."

Winans w/ Jack Micheline. photo by Ginger Edes

A.D. w/ Bob Kaufman at Cafe Trieste, 1977. Credit Richard Morris.

37 ALTERED MUSIC WITH EDDIE SHAW

A CONVERSATION WITH EDDIE SHAW ABOUT HIS MUSICAL CAREER POST-MONKS

Eddie Shaw & the Hydraulic Pigeons album cover

PASSING Through Minnesoda and other altered states by Thomas Edward Shaw is a creative record of the author's life after returning to the United States in the wake of reinventing rock and roll to little notice in the same Hamburg clubs the Beatles sold their souls for rock and roll in playing Bass with an act called the Monks. Dressed to look the part in every particular, possibly the first band to make art from feedback, the Monks set the stage for post-punk before there was punk but were too far ahead of the pack to make any headlines for a few decades post-disbandment. Eddie Shaw didn't have any time to waste and kept at it, with a series of bands, including one called the Hydraulic Pigeons.

Eddie Shaw, *Minnesoda*

Unwilling to remove the creative license natural to human memory, in this memoir of life after the Monks, Shaw has crafted a 'rock and roll, jazz and funk musician's odyssey stretching all the way from the late 1950s to the early 21st century' (The words in single quotes surrounding these are lifted from Carson Street Publishing's website, where you can purchase your copy. Shaw appeared recently on my podcast, but this book was already in production, otherwise I dare say there's a chance we might've been mentioned, such was the lyric boom effected by the acquaintance of one fantastic biographer with another in this instance) "recounting the right of passage—obsession, success and failure—struggling against barriers that keep many artists from arriving at their destination. On his journey, he becomes the alienated hero, the punk-rock bass guitar player, the Miles Davis-influenced jazz trumpeter, the soaring rock and roll pigeon."

Pigeons aka rock doves

When he appeared on the cast, Eddie was wearing a T-shirt reading "I always knew I wanted to be a monk when I grew up, but I could never memorize the chants" and I hadn't read what it said, so when he pronounced the same slogan aloud, I didn't get the reference. "But you invented your own!" I responded. "Was the Monks the first band to find a new art form in feedback?""The feedback found *us!*" Shaw responded, and I think I said that was a great answer, but don't remember for sure. Find out at https://campelasticity.com/2021/10/10/camp-elasticity-writing-and-rocking-podcast-in-honor-of-pat-fish-1957-2021/

Later in the same cast, he said something about his time in the Monks enduring the same grueling all-night shifts the Beatles had only playing their own thus-far-unheard sound influenced by the reality of being aliens adrift having been good for him, which is what this hefty tome commemorates.

"Yea, your hair grew back!" I said, but he didn't get my bad joke either. Should've worn a T-shirt, maybe.

The other day a friend of mine leading a group I was in asked "Does everyone know what I mean by integrate?" I'd missed the first part of her sentence, didn't want to get lost in the lesson she was sharing that day and said, "Do you mean incorporating embodying alignment and interdimensional perception into our daily lives?"

"That's exactly what I mean. People, if you ever need a fancy-sounding way of explaining something, Zack will help you."

Fancy sounding? Wait a minute. "I like to keep it simple, but I usually feel like I'm over-complicating things when I talk to you, but I'm glad it's helping."

"Well, that's your style, right?"

I hoped she meant keeping it simple. "Yes."

But as the new James Joyce (per Eddie's verdict, though I've yet to read Ulysses), who can't keep his own life out of everyone else's, my iconoclastic advice, in this case, is read this book before or after this one, which came first, and listen to this band before or after this one, which is a different sound entirely. Get it all in the order preferred.

'Even as a boy, Thomas "Eddie" Shaw knew what he would do when he grew up. At the end of each night, after playing to customers in the barroom Eddie's role model, Jackson, got up from the piano stool, emptied the ashtrays, cleaned the bar, swept and mopped the floor, and then made his bed on the pool table. It was the perfect life of the jazz musician, and Eddie wanted this life for himself.'

Thanks, Eddie. I'm on the same journey, and it's gonna be a great year.

38 NEAL CASSADY COMES BACK TO DENVER

A CONVERSATION WITH NEAL'S DAUGHTER, JAMI CASSADY RATTO AND HIS SON-IN-LAW, HER HUSBAND, RANDY RATTO

THE first thing I asked Neal's daughter Jami Cassady Ratto was if she believed in UFOs and she told me, "Oh my gosh. Always believed in them, and Mom always believed in them. We kids would go sit out on the grass on Bancroft Avenue, Los Gatos, as we were growing up, get on our backs and look at the clouds, cause Mom always said the Mother Ship was out there, in the biggest cloud. And so, you know, we will, to this day, drive down the road, and go, 'Well, there's the Mother Ship.' I mean it was part of our belief system. And kept waiting, 'Why aren't they coming? We believe in them. Why aren't they coming to say hi to us?' You know. Never heard one, never even saw one, but it is very exciting that the government's coming out with something about it."

"Right? I mean who knows what it'll come to, but they haven't told us anything for 60 or 70 million years."

"And they kept denying and denying and saying it didn't exist. Yeah, I know. So, we're really excited."

The Cassady Estate has a lot in the works besides a traveling yard sale. Neal's *Joan Anderson Letter*, the one that inspired Jack Kerouac to "discover" spontaneous prose, was discovered in a box in San Francisco and has recently been published to acclaim after having been thought lost overboard about as long ago as the Roswell Incident (which Neal and Jack drove past unknowingly once or twice in 1947), and Neal's letters to Jami's mother Carolyn from San Quentin will be republished in an expanded edition soon. Randy's been working hard to organize and decode the boxes and boxes of writings left behind by Carolyn, who died in 2013. Neal died in 1968, after driving the Merry Pranksters' Magical Mystery bus from one countercultural era to the next.

Everyone who's looked into Neal Cassady has heard about his connection with Jack Kerouac and the Beat Generation and Ken Kesey and LSD and the Merry Pranksters and the Grateful Dead. Many see him as a countercultural pioneer. Fewer have heard about his conversion later in his short life to Edgar Cayce's doctrine of reincarnational karma, and his intense devotion to that athletic metaphysical perspective, where it's all about perfecting oneself out of the endless loop of lives. The couple met in Denver, where Carolyn was studying Theatre Arts and Set Design at Denver University in the middle 40s. The hotel on 10th and Grant where Carolyn lived, walking in one day to find Neal, LuAnne Henderson and Allen Ginsberg naked together in bed, as recounted in Kerouac's *On The Road*, is still standing. I had a drink in the bar downstairs a few weeks ago. Neal and Carolyn Elizabeth Robinson Cassady were party to all manner of esoteric metaphysical concepts decades before most of their neighbors, which had a profound effect on the couple's three children, John Allen, Jami and Cathy. After his being glamorized as Dean Moriarty in Kerouac's On The Road and targeted by narcotics officers at the Southern Pacific and spending 2 years in San Quentin for a marijuana bust, Neal and his wife Carolyn turned to "Sleeping Prophet" Edgar Cayce's thesis as an answer to their troubles as a couple. "Now be sure and tell me if you've heard this before," says Jami. "This is my history, my upbringing, my childhood memories of being told this all the time by my parents, that Dad was the ticket-taker, the conductor on the Southern Pacific Railroad and wore that wonderful outfit, that uniform, and taking tickets, I can just see him, that wonderful outfit, and charming everyone—what a guy. Anyway one day he was walking down the aisle, and someone had left Many Mansions on a seat—I actually have that book at my house, that he found—so um he brought it home, and Mom and he started reading it, and 'Well, wait a minute, this might be our answer,'— when we were doing the archives, we found out they went to counseling together, something we never knew—this was a way to say, 'Oh, that's why we do that. We're not bad people. Karma's making us do this. Let's try to change our karma. Yeah, so they really tried hard, they both tried hard, and had a really hard time.

Kentucky-born "Sleeping prophet" Edgar Cayce (18 March 1877 – 3 January 1945) showed an intense interest in the Bible from childhood, reading and rereading it with the goal of memorizing the whole thing. Cayce was hypnotized as a young man in hopes of curing a mysterious case of laryngitis. and began to dictate cures for various ailments while in trance. In time, at the prompting of metaphysician and journalist Arthur Lammers, despite this fundamentalist Christian bent, Cayce addressed topics like reincarnation and karma, things entirely heathen and suspect to his conscious mind. Despite this initial forbearance, Cayce ultimately elected to continue doing the readings since they were helping people, which couldn't be bad. Neal and

Carolyn were among the thousands of early converts to the ethos of self-taught spirituality Cayce (though a fundamentalist Christian) was one of the first idols of, which mushroomed over the coming decades (60s, 70s, 80s) through embodiments like Uri Geller and Marianne Williamson all the way to today's examples, like Rob Brezsny (*Pronoia*) and Rachel Archelaus (*Intuitive Art*).

Mutiny Information Café on Broadway in Denver was founded by a couple of old friends who'd ridden boxcars all over the country before founding it, ultra-cool old-school anti-racist non-phobic mods and punk rockers supportive of everything cool. I'd hosted a variety show there a few years ago and they'd made space for Dan Fante and Bob Hyatt when I'd invited them and almost hosted a panel of ex-Merry Pranksters I tried setting up before Paul Krassner kicked it, God rest him, but that one didn't end up happening. It was great seeing Jami and her husband Randy again. Both about 70 years old, Jami sprightly and full of energy with her father's face and some of his mannerisms, Randy wearing an orange tie-dye T shirt with Neal's quote, "We are actually fourth dimensional beings in a third dimensional body inhabiting a second dimensional world," on the back. We sat in the rear of Mutiny for a couple of days at a couple of tables of Estate wares talking about Neal and Carolyn and allowance and intuition and Edgar Cayce and spontaneous writing as people came and went, leading through all the binders and sometimes buying a book or a T shirt or talking to Jami about her dad. This was a coming together of my personal interests and literary and human history over the course of a couple of rainy June days in Denver, with Neal Cassady's daughter Jami at the punk rock bookstore for an interview and an Estate wares sale, and to hear parts of my new book where I mentioned her dad, with the U.S. government about to announce the existence of unidentified Aerial Phenomena and who knew what else they might do? Neal's and Carolyn's ashes were sitting on the table in little glass containers, not enshrined, just there among us, hanging out. One bystander made a joke that they might get stolen, and everyone agreed someone might do that, but no one even seemed to know we were back there. I said, "I'd never do that, but sneaking a pinch had crossed my mind." What would I do with it? Smoke it? Probably so, knowing me. "Go ahead, you're welcome," Jami actually said, but I didn't. I kept picking up the hammer, though, which had little swirls of Pranksters day-glo paint at the base of the sledge. It felt like being outside the normal flow of time sitting there in the back of a bookstore with Prometheus's daughter, people wandering in every ten minutes with questions like, "Who was this Neal Cassady?" "What's this all about?"

I asked Jami about the family's involvement with the Cayce doctrine, and what she thought about grace beating karma—"'cause that's the same thing as not dwelling on your so-called blocks, or like being sensitive enough to see past the car coming at you."

"Bending down to get my cup," she replied, "I thought, 'I know I'm gonna have to talk about grace beats karma. I love when things are synched like that." She told a story about Neal and Carolyn having a fight once "over him wanting to go to Mexico or something like that. We had this big stump of a tree in our yard, and he went out with the jalopy he had then and a chain and tried to rip this thing out and rip this thing out—he couldn't do it, so he called a tow truck, and the tow truck got it out, then he came back in and took a shower and changed his clothes and was the most beautiful husband and father you could get. So she chalked it up, 'It does work—do the opposite, do what you think you should do,' or something like that." [this story about Neal doing Carolyn a favor he'd resisted, to purge his karma of resentment, is recounted in her *Off The Road*]

[Edgar Cayce, Public Domain]

"I knew from a very early age that I had the gift," Jami told me. "Another thing I could do, and that's one of those pictures over there, of me as the White Rabbit—uh—in Alice in Wonderland— I was really nervous for some reason, I was in a big part, and I got this big boil on the bottom of my foot. So I couldn't dance. And it was big. And it was icky, and horrible, and everybody's all 'Oh no, who's gonna do the part?' And I remember lying in bed, and this lady came, from probably Edgar Cayce or Unity Church or whatever they were part of, and she sat on the bed, Mom's bed, and she told me, you know, the mind's power, this and that, blah blah—and of course, the next day, the next morning it was gone. That's another one of my great stories. So I knew I had the power, I knew, and it was demonstrated to me quite a few times in my life. I remember another time, you know, I was always kind of overweight, and my thighs, you know, I wasn't a New York City ballet ballerina, by any means. I was rehearsing in the classroom in the mirror and all of a sudden, it was like I lost 50 pounds! And I stared, and I danced, and I looked, and I kept looking— it was the most amazing thing, and it was true, I mean it happened, I wasn't, I definitely wasn't on speed—loved it. I actually said, I remember, 'Look, look—is that—right?' You know? To me, I was, so it was real. Yeah. So I always kinda had that, but I let it go. I um you know started you know I un got hooked on speed, and then became an alcoholic, and you know, that stuff just kinda—you know."

"Sure."

When I asked about Neal and allowance, or "going with the flow," she made a face and said it reminded her of him going off with the Pranksters, which was the beginning of the end for our kid. She said she thought he had a death wish at that point and when Carolyn divorced him, there was nothing left to hold him back. "He came back a number of times crying, saying, 'I just can't do this anymore,' and Mom told him, 'You shouldn't then,' but she never took him back."

"Is that book here, actually, *Grace Beats Karma*?" I looked around at all the books on the tables, not seeing it.

"That book's out of print but we're doing the expanded edition. I have one copy at home, it's all beat up. Todd [Swift]'s reprinting it for us, and—so—Randy and I, going through Mom's stuff, have realized Dad's state of mind to get arrested. He knew they were narcs, he told Mom that Natalie [Jackson, Neal's girlfriend, who threw herself off a building in 1955] killed herself, they forged Mom's signature, they got ten thousand dollars, they lost it at the racetrack, Natalie jumped off the roof, you know? All this stuff. And we're putting all of that, we have letters, and pictures,

"Like a cold case approach."

"We're gonna put it in front of his prison letters, to show that that *means* something, you know?"

"Showing the mindset that led to what happened, the circumstances of it."

"Yeah. And then at the end we're gonna put John's chapter-book about him, Visions of . . . Dad [*Visions of Neal* by John Allen Cassady, unpublished at present]—because that's when he was riding go-karts with John down the neighborhood street, and taking him to the demolition derby and, you know, his *grace* as a man—and then Cathy and I are gonna write something, too— overcame his horrible childhood, and the—but we think he wanted to get arrested, Randy and I, this is our thing: we think, 'cause he was *done*—"

"Yeah. 'Cause he knew they were narcs. So he was either flaunting something, or he was like, 'Get me.'"

"Yeah. He was like 'Get me,' is what we think. But you know, we're gonna just present everything like we found. We also found his diplomas from his classes in San Quentin, the ones Gavin Arthur taught, and he worked in the print shop. He learned how to be a print guy, like Kerouac's dad, and who knew that? Mom never told me. So we have all those things. And then Randy's gonna add the stuff that Mom tried to get welfare and they wouldn't give it to her—just all the crap she had to go through when he was gone—the neighbor's letters that, 'Don't worry, we're behind you, we're gonna help you all we can'—and what she was most afraid of was that kids in school would say, 'Oh, your dad's in jail,' and stuff, but not one mother told any child in the whole school. I never knew, until I was fourteen, that he'd been in prison."

"Yeah, that's miraculous."

"We thought he was on a railroad trip, on a conducting tour. Mom said he had a little longer of a stint, you know—two years—came back, I remember I had the measles, or the mumps, I was in mom's bed, watching TV, walks in the door— 'Hi, dad!', 'Hi, honey!'—you know? It was like— so—haha," Jami looks away, smiling, like Dean or Cody.

Neal (L) and Carolyn (R) ashes come back to Denver

I asked a question about her mother Carolyn's relationship with allowance and intuition and a couple of miniature fans fell off the mantle she was sitting in front of. Jami laughed. and said, "Oops! That little fan ran out of batteries," as if it were letting us know what it wanted.

"All right," I said, in the manner of a table-tapper, or someone leading a séance, "Carolyn's spirit doesn't want us talking about her, for some reason [Jami laughed] . . . but Carolyn, I'm your friend, I want to promote your reputation, not leave you in the shadow of your late mate, as it's usually done. So, if you're not opposed, we're gonna try this again—and if you are opposed, *you'll* try again."

"Oh, she's made herself known to me a couple of times, a while back," laughs Jami, saying, "Okay.." between phrases, exactly as Jack described Neal having done in eight or nine places in three to six books.

"So, Allowance," I said. "To me that's not about freewheeling hedonism, though it can sometimes take that shape—but it's more about electricity or energy, allowing the circuit to complete as opposed to a short circuit."

"Yes, I like that description. That's a very good description. Like I said—my growing up with the UFO thing as an accepted part of my learning—Mom and Dad took us three kids to Christian Science church in Los Gatos just to learn the Bible stories, you know, to Bible study. They didn't sit in the pews or sing or anything, they just took us, you know, to learn the basics, and I—today, I can name off the Bible, Old Testament—but anyway—ah—just so we knew—that kind of thing—but then, after he found *Many Mansions*, and they got into Cayce, they took us out of Bible study school . . . Which was fine, except that after it finished every Sunday, Dad would pick us up and take us next door to the Foster Freeze and get ice cream. So that was gone. But—they would sit in the living room and either read Cayce to us, or discuss or read other books, you know, from that same genre as that, to us, and discuss, among themselves, and to us, back and forth, teaching us about reincarnation, how the body is . . . the temple and, you know—oh Gosh—it's so ingrained it's hard for me to pick out sentences!" Last word comes out in a laugh. "You know. But um, and we would just sit there, and color, and listen, and you know, ask questions—and it was just, that's all I ever knew after that. So everything that they taught us about karma is what I believe—and like I remember John and I in high school—uh—talking to our friends, we'd sit at the steps of Los Gatos High, a big old beautiful high school late at night, with our friends, and tell em all about this stuff that we had learned from our parents, and, you know, they definitely had no idea about any of this stuff—so, if you ask any of John's old friends today, they would be aware—"

"'Yeah, I remember the Cassady kids, always talkin' that crazy reincarnation stuff.'"

"Yeah. So I remember one day in particular we were talking, and one kid—oh, we were talking about karma, and the way how you act in one life has a direct consequence in your next life if you don't uh—oh, ran out of words—if you don't uh change your path, or change your karma and then your next life will be better—yes, in fact she told me that purpose of being human is to come back time after time after time and to be a Christ. That was our goal on this plane. You come back as a Christ, then you move on to another plane, do other stuff. So—anyway we were talking about it with our friends, and one said, 'Oh, I don't wanna come back as a pig,' and John and I jumped all over him, 'Oh no, that's called transmigration.' (holding up a finger) 'Reincarnation is . . .' you know, on and on about the soul, how the soul's not in an animal, it's a human, just on and on and on and everything we had learned and were proud of the fact that we knew it and nobody else did. A lot of the stuff I learned from my parents, growing up I felt kind of smug about."

"Another case of being half a step ahead, because look how important these concepts are to society now, and back then it was just a weird quirk."

"It was a weird quirk, yeah. You're right. Sure. That's my upbringing in religion with my parents— then she joined the Academy of Parapsychology and Medicine when she divorced Dad, and um—it was in the early 70s and I was with Randy then, my husband—it was the first time we knew about Kyryllian photography and the plants— plants are alive, oh my God—and she, from that day forward, she would never buy a Bonsai, cause she—'You're torturing this, this tree,' you know. To this day, I look at em and think, Ugh, who would wanna do that?"

Everything she said really sunk in. I was still on the Bonsai when I said, "Like bound feet," though I suppose it could also correlate to instruction sinking in.

"Exactly," Jami agreed.

"I never thought of that."

"Exactly. So that, and then she had uh what's his name, the spoon bender, and you know, all those famous people."

"Oh, Uri Geller?" Man, that guy gets in everywhere, I thought.

"Yes—that were just starting to open up people's consciousness— and plants, you can have houseplants in your house."

"That was considered weird once?"

"Oh yeah, sev—early seventies—so um, all that she was a big part of, 'cause she, where she worked, they brought in all these scholars and doctors, and medicine is not Western—you know?—and you can change things with your mind, you don't have to, you know, go with the Western stuff"

"Thank God," I sighed.

"Up the street from where we lived was a Unity church, and one of my best friends was a member, this is when I was being sober, and I joined, to have something to do on a Sunday, and I had just read a book about Jim Jones and the cyanide shit, you know? Excuse me. So, I read that, and I was trying to be, you know, this really good and sober person, and they had this extra class at Unity, at night, for 2 hours, it cost $200 but it was about how to be a better soul, good for karma, something like that, and I fell for it, thought, 'Oh, cool. Lemme do it.' You know. So I gave him the two hundred, I'm sitting there, and after about three weeks, I saw what they're doing, they're trying to teach me how to be in their hierarchy in their mind of what it should be like—"

"Submissive to their doctrine, like."

"Yeah, and I sat there, and they said, 'You know, because we want the entire world to be loving and together and connected.' I said, 'That's never gonna happen.' I mean I blurted it out, I said, 'I just read this book, you guys stop just—,' I said, 'That's not gonna happen.' I realized they were trying to brainwash me into their way of thinking. I don't know what their outcome would be, give 'em more money, I don't know—but it was just, 'That's not gonna work. How long have you been trying to make this happen, 'cause that's not gonna happen. That's why we have karma and shit like that 'cause people are different, and you can't get 'em all in that group.' Yeah, I actually walked out. Yeah. And that's another thing I was gonna say earlier, about my mom and her teachings. That karma exists because people are different.

"Anyway, so allowance, I'm not quite sure how to answer that. Going with the flow, he went with wherever anybody took him, or wherever he asked to be taken. That's what dad was doing, just trying to feel good."

"Intuition."

"That's easy. He had a sixth—he had an 8th sense. People saw it. People wrote about it. He knew if he went around this car, he'd be safe, and there was that and this, and this and that. His amazing photographic memory was how he could pick up a conversation with someone a year later right where they left off—that must have been a burden, don't you think? Can you imagine? I think he was high on the list of very intuitive souls. Also, Gavin Arthur, his uh religious teacher at San Quentin, said that when he did his first class at San Quentin, on comparative religion, a man walked in, with this bright aura around him, and it was Neal. What happened is when Mom divorced him in '63, after he couldn't get his job back on the Southern Pacific 'cause of San Quentin, and he had to do menial labor—and he'd always had a death wish, so, after the railroad dropped him, and Mom said, 'Oh honey, go play with your new friends,' you know, she said, "I set you free. Go ahead.' Well, that was another bad thing, you know, because the home life and the family was what was holding him together. So, after that he never had another home of his own, he lived with the Dead in San Francisco, with Kesey in La Honda, he went wherever anybody took him or he asked to go places uh, you know, 'Can I drive your car?' Stuff like that."

"If Carolyn had not allowed him to leave, do you think he would have kept on going back and forth or—?"

"I think he would have—oh—that's a good point, because I'm so into the lore of what really did happen with that. I think she also wanted them divorced, though, you know. She needed to spread her wings and see what she could do on her own and—so—she really did it for herself also, and it was—she really cut the tie there—and so, well after that, I mean four years later he was dead. But what he did, and he told Mom many times that 'These people expect me to perform like this, they really need this person, so I do it because they give me stuff that I want,' and it was just a vicious cycle there. He actually said once, 'You know, I'm a trained bear.'"

"That one really got [Neal's son, an artist] Bob Hyatt. He mentioned that."

Jami and I had been talking about the impending UAP announcement. She left to take the Rattos' dog, Chloe, around the block for a wee. Tall Randy, sitting behind a table of Nealabilia with his arms behind his head, commented, "You know, I read a book by Erich Von Daniken in the 70s, and I disagreed with it."

"You gotta read some Zechariah Sitchin," I told Randy. "He'll even make you forgive Erich Von Daniken a little."

"Oh, I have! And you know what's interesting—the Sumerians call the visitors from Nibiru the Anunnaki, and then there's that civilization that mysteriously vanished in the Southwest called the Anasazi."

"That is weird. I never thought of that."

Around six o'clock I helped Jami and Randy pack up all their stuff and load it in Randy's black truck, Jami gave me a hug, and they were off. It was raining lightly, and the air was cool. I opened my umbrella and started walking down Broadway toward the light rail stop. On the way home, the guy sitting in front of me kept looking for something underneath his seat as the rest of us watched.

I got off the train and walked across a storm of cold raindrops holding my umbrella to the side against the wind on the second day of Cassady weekend at Mutiny Info Café. "So what ever happened with that report?" asked Jami. She was talking about the UAP (Unidentified Aerial Phenomena) report we'd touched on the day before. "Nine pages. No new info, just here they are and we don't understand it. Which is change, if not progress. I still think something's in the works."

The report released to the public was only 9 pages long, but a much longer one had been released to Congress, and no doubt there would be true and false leaked versions of that longer report in the next few days. The government announced that these things were appearing and it didn't make sense what they did, renaming the mystery a phenomena rather than objects, not terming it extraterrestrial or extra-dimensional, just officially leaving the door open for unlimited speculation, for people's best and worst impulses to take hold of and run away with as they might—it could be God, it could be China, could be parallel realities, aliens. Everything so far this year has pushed me out of theory into action. I'd wanted the same thing to happen again with that announcement, even knowing it was a longshot. But it felt better than worse to know it was still up to me how I felt about aliens, what I thought was happening with UFOs or UAP or whatever name they gave it. Supposedly that Jeremy Corbell guy was about to release more film, and I'd see it when it came out, like everyone else, whatever it came to. Something else Jami said was that the current low-key president was holding things steady between the last unprecedented unnamed president and the next historic bombshell in the wings—whatever that turns out to be. Your life reflects your mind.

I read some pages from the latest and a few new poems, then Roseanna Frechette read selections from Neal's only published work, *The First Third* [I recommend *The Collected Letters*]. A couple of friends and I went up the street to an Asian-fusion joint called Karma and ordered food and drank several carafes of hot sake, talking about Neal Cassady and last night's unsatisfying UAP announcement and human psychology. After a couple of hours, I ran back down the rain-wet sidewalk to Mutiny and said goodbye to Jami and Randy, then ran back to Karma.

My friend Tina suggested we go to this place across the street from Mutiny where she knew the bartender called Doherty's. It was that kind of evening, where you feel good and spend all your money on fun. I was looking out the door across the street at Randy Ratto's truck parked outside Mutiny when Jami and Randy came out and walked across the street. Randy fell down and I helped him up. "It's his neuropathy," said Jami. "My dad," I said (my dad had that before he died), and the whole alchemy of health and sickness ran through my head in the blink of an eye. The Rattos joined us for a few more rounds there, and Randy told me the way Neal became connected with Kesey was through an Esalen-style commune he was selling weed to, after receiving word Kesey wanted to meet the star Beat down the street. Randy also let me know he'd always wanted to add a third day to the Cassady weekends in Denver, which had been going on since 1990-something, "A spiritual day," he said. "That's one side of Neal no one's ever looked at." I told him I'd send all the references to Neal and him and Jami before I published my new book, then walked through the cold air in my black T-shirt to the light rail stop and rode a train home to my apartment on the creaky top floor, put on dry socks and wrote this.

Update: A graphic novel based partly on Neal's *The First Third*, drawn by artist Rick Bleier in collaboration with Neal's daughter Cathy Cassady Sylvia is currently in pre-production. Watch for it.

Jami Cassady Ratto and Randy Ratto at Mutiny Information Café.

39 HAPPENINGS IN DENVER TO PROMOTE AL GRAHAM'S BOOKS

MANIC 79-YEAR-OLD AL GRAHAM AS AGELESS ROCK AND ROLL ENTREPRENEUR

THIS morning I caught the train to Mutiny under wildfires smoke on a mission through the windstorm and had a good conversation with owner Jim Norris about the importance of people coming together and not being afraid of each other and using the net to unite not divide, and that there were plenty of memorials to go to, but in a case of perfect placement, this first event has taken form as an effort at reimplementation of positive flow in the aftermath of that shooting spree, and we're already doing an excellent job of giving people common purpose. Next up is the Santa Fe strip with all the art galleries, and there's a used bookstore next to a cool record store I know. In a month or so, we'll move on to the next metro district. Denver, this is your time. Live and learn, go do some good. And while all the above is occurring, Graham is actively engaged in a historic renovation of Angels Flight, the funicular railway connecting Bunker Hill to Los Angeles, which is neither here nor there, but in a real sense everywhere. Get Al's books and look for film of the happening on YouTube and Camp Elasticity on the 14th or 15th of next year's new month. Out.

Al met his future bride, Anne Morrison, or "Anna" as he calls her, in Earl's Court, London, in the late-middLe-1960s, in the hotbed of

U.S.-English cross-pollination resulting from the Beatles' "invasion" of American pop sensibilities. "They were celebrating us, but in a nice way, we were celebrating them," says Graham on one video, somewhere in his seventies now and commanding a team of authors placed in top cities all over the world from his headquarters on an island off the coast of San Diego. I'm Al's agent in Denver, organizing a series of happenings in promotion of the re-release of his books, 'Before The Beatles Were Famous, I Remember Jim Morrison Too', and a collection of verse called 'Poet Rain'.

A happening is a performance, event, or situation art, usually as performance art. The term was first used by Allan Kaprow during the 1950s to describe a range of art-related events. It can also be something as simple as people hanging out with each other and being nice to each other, exchanging love energy, The first one in Denver will be taking place on the afternoon of Thursday, January 13th with an open mic and an appearance by Al on a projection screen to be filmed and broadcast on YouTube subsequently. A piece of rock and roll history conducted from beyond the pale by the ghost of Jim Morrison at Mutiny Information Café on the corner of Broadway and Ellsworth, a place Al says reminds him of the wood stove ethos of the storied Penny Lane he grew up loving.

AL returned with Anna to her hometown of Los Angeles, California, just in time for the release of the Doors' self-titled first LP in 1967, featuring a headshot of her missing brother Jim on the cover with three other band members inside it. One day Al walked in to find Anna in tears listening to this album and it took him a minute to get what was happening. After a fight with his Naval admiral father over his refusal to go to Vietnam, Anna's brother Jim had sworn off contact with his family,

living on the rooftops of apartments and commanding gangs of pickpockets, among other untold adventures, losing a lot of weight and ultimately forming a rock and roll band. Graham was one of the Lizard King's closest companions during the wildest days and nights of Doors stardom, witnessing Jim's alcoholic excesses and correctly diagnosing them, equipped as no other biographer with insider family perspective, as a hereditary disorder. Besides unprecedented intimacy with the close-knit Morrison family's history and character, Graham knocked shoulders with John Lennon, Paul McCartney, Gerry Marsden, Royston Ellis, Bill Harry, and all the other notable Liverpudlians before meeting Anna and taking his adventures stateside. Many are Graham's adventures, well varied the legends thereof, some ongoing from ever since, and be assured the watchword now is positive.

I woke up an hour and a half later than usual and settled back into void week, smoking pot and watching old movies on YouTube. A Christmas Story wasn't on there anymore. Some people had died in a shooting spree down the street from Mutiny the night before and there was a stunned mood on. When the phone rang, I knew it was him. Al's way of looking at the world is as something simple and workable and right there for you. "Here is your dream coming along, Will you take it?" he posits rhetorically in his first book, addressing the world at large. We started talking and I told him about the shootings the day before and tried to explain about void week and he said, "What's that like? To be disconnected from everything for a whole week. I would never think of doing something like that."

A happening is a performance, event, or situation art, usually as performance art. The term was first used by Allan Kaprow during the 1950s to describe a range of art-related events. It can also be something as simple as people hanging out with each other and being nice to each other, exchanging love energy. The first one in Denver will be taking place on the afternoon of Thursday, January 13th with an open mic and an appearance by Al on a projection screen to be filmed and broadcast on YouTube subsequently. A piece of rock and roll history conducted from beyond the pale by the ghost of Jim Morrison at Mutiny Information Café on the corner of Broadway and Ellsworth, a place Al says reminds him of the wood stove ethos of the storied Penny Lane he grew up loving. Next up is the Santa Fe strip with all the art galleries, and there's a used bookstore next to a cool record store I know. In a month or so, we'll move on to the next metro district. Denver, this is your time. Live and learn, go do some good. And while all the above is occurring, Graham is actively engaged in a historic renovation of

Angels Flight, the funicular railway connecting Bunker Hill to Los Angeles, which is neither here nor there, but in a real sense everywhere. I first heard of it in Fante's *Ask the Dust*.

The last thing that happened, Al called me and told me he'd fallen and landed on his face, "but I'm still standing!" "Well, that sounds terrible. Have a seat. Take a load off."

"No, my face absorbed most of the shock. Everything else is still swollen." It was never for sure whether this guy was telling the truth or not. He'd undergone a drastic heart operation and rebounded miraculously since, but I knew he'd fallen on the train a few months back, and hoped he was all right.

"But that's not what I'm calling about," he continued. "My son let me know I just received permission from the Estate to market Jim Morrison's image in whatever way I want. We're gonna have portable bars making millions, a moveable feast, and I'm gonna bring one to Denver, so prepare to be a millionaire in just a few weeks' time!"

"Looking forward to it. Thanks for including me."

Then he sent me some pictures of himself looking black and blue that scared me. I sent him an email: "I hope everything's going well. I know you've made remarkable recoveries before. God's on your side and I am too." If he'd really been granted those rights, the bar would probably open in L.A. and I'd write the menu or the press release for it from his apartment in Denver for some of the profits, but you had to start somewhere to get anywhere.

After a few days went by without getting a response, I guessed Al had either died of his injuries or was taking my advice to have a seat and take a load off. It was hard not to imagine this guy forging ahead dauntlessly forever. *That's how I'll remember him if he is dead*, I thought.

The same guy had deliberately inverted the moral topography of a small-town in middle America once by handing out drugs and cash to all the respectable citizens at the behest of a mad billionaire. Now, for all I knew, Al Graham was about to die, and had been granted this long-sought news of the thing he'd always wanted by his son as a gentle fiction to carry him into the afterlife. I checked his site at irememberjimmorrison.com and found it up and running and updated with a brace of new products.

"I probably would've heard about it somewhere if he'd really kicked the bucket," I figured, even though in a way it really seemed like he'd emerged from the internet and might just as easily dissolve back into it.

Months later I was in Madison, Wisconsin, thinking about moving there, and my friend Jenny Jarkey took me to a few bookstores and up to the top of the state capitol building full of ornate engravings and colorful embossed seals and winding twisting corners and stairways. We looked down on the whole town full of tiny people with bodies of water on either side. We walked up and down a tilted street against a tide of students with determined looks on their way back to class. I called Al that evening and apologized for my lack of sympathy during his recent troubles with the police. "I wasn't in the right head." I was sitting on the porch outside Jenny and Ted's place, looking out into the dark blue evening street.

"Well, I don't know why you're apologizing for something you never even did, lad, but let me tell you, my troubles with the police were the least of it! I'm happy to tell you that now all this is at an end, and I wouldn't be the man I am today if I hadn't been through all that trouble. I'm opening the first whiskey bar in Cancun!"

"Good for you, Al." It was good to talk with Al again. I told him I was staying with some friends of mine who were cabbies in Madison and thinking about moving there. He told me Jim Morrisson's maternal grandfather, last name Clarke, had once run for office there on the Communist ticket and won before disappearing with his pockets full of women's underpants.

"Really? Well, This looks like it might be the next place for me. It feels good."

"Well, I'll tell you, lad, if there's one thing I've learned in this life: If it's meant to be, it's meant to be."

"That's right. You're right." Everything is designed to work out perfectly, I thought. Beyond time and by law.

40 A CONVERSATION WITH TAMRA LUCID

AUTHOR AND FOUNDING RIOT GRRRL TAMRA LUCID TALKS ABOUT PUNK METAPHYSICS

"To me punk and metaphysics seem to belong together," says Tamra Lucid. "Both are rebellions against bullshit. And what is punk anyway? Punk can be for peace or violence, for racism or for equality, for noise or pop, for anarchy or for Broadway. My band has never fit any category. Sucks for algorithms, but so much fun!" Lucid Nation co-founder Ronnie Pontiac was mentored by American metaphysician Manly Palmer Hall (1901-90) at his Philosophical Research Society in Los Angeles before the band started playing shows in 1994. LN's second show was in a downtown LA art gallery opening for Team Dresch, followed by opening for Bikini Kill. They toured the West Coast, playing seven riot grrrl conventions in one summer, and backing Warhol superstar Holly Woodlawn at several events. The band released ten albums between 1997 and 2019, most recently *Last of the Teens* (2019), a collection of lo-fi outtakes with Ken Schalk on drums. Last year Tamra published a memoir about her friendship with Hall called *Making the Ordinary Extraordinary* (Inner Traditions, 2021). Ronnie's *American Metaphysical Religion* is set for release in January. Lucid spoke about punk rock, politics, metaphysics, and more in this email exchange with *Happiness* author Zack Kopp.

How have you been received in your journey from metaphysics to punk and back again?

Back in the PRS days I was wallpaper. I served refreshments while maintaining a pleasant demeanor. I was only noticed as the significant other of Manly Hall's research assistant. Which was nice. No one tried to recruit me for their visions or missions. I found most punk scenes to be friendlier than riot grrrl but riot grrrl was where I found my voice again. Shows were cathartic rituals and zines and demos were holy books. Anarcho was the most welcoming. Even had a delegation show up to inform me that my nonconformist long blonde hair at their shows was truly punk. These days I've been treated rather nicely in metaphysics. That's the beauty of writing a book that charms people before they hear my music.

How did punks react to your metaphysical background?

We didn't keep our metaphysical past a secret, but it wasn't anybody's business either. Yet, as life tends to do, we kept meeting punks who had occult interests. Most would only admit it privately. My grandma was psychic. A ghost taught me the guitar chords for this song in a dream. Or a simple what sign are you? They somehow sensed that we would understand, even though we didn't talk about or wear things that reminded us of our past.

Punk rock is, in essence, about rejecting dominant paradigms. Most adherents think of themselves as sharp-eyed "realists" who limit their attention to facts they feel they can trust while staying clear of uncharted territories like Spiritualism. Describe your relationship to metaphysics as a punk and vice versa.

We were all about music and activism not spirituality, yet we considered activism and music expressions of our spirituality. But I didn't like talking about those days. I was Manly Hall's Cassandra. I tried but failed to warn him about the man who may have killed him. It was a relief not talking about metaphysics. The silence felt right, like being a student. I think occultists are the punks of religion: non-conformists setting out to experience reality and express themselves without obeying the rules of how it was done in the past. Who's more punk than Paracelsus?

Lucid Nation has played shows for Food Not Bombs and the New Panther Vanguard Movement, a couple of causes rooted in human experience more so than political gamesmanship. Describe those experiences.

We encountered both at Koo's Cafe, a Victorian bungalow at 1505 N. Main, in a rundown neighborhood that is now a gentrified art district in Santa Ana, CA. We heard it was a brothel way back in the day then a chop suey joint for five decades. Peace Punk and *Beyond the Wall of Injustice* zine sponsored Anarcho Sunday matinees there. Peace Punk booked us as a representative riot grrrl band for a feminist perspective, but we considered ourselves equalists. He invited the Panthers, too. Sadly those shows were a big reason why Koo's lost the support of the local community. Riot grrrls, crust punks and Black Panthers were too much on a Sunday afternoon in Santa Ana. Undercover cops started showing up. Politicians worked up the local Latino community. But it was beautiful while it lasted.

The Panthers expected Orange County punks to be racist, so when they arrived they marched in formation. They found a welcoming and diverse scene that already knew a lot about them. A Panther bought our Day-Glo green cassette demo with glitter butterfly stickers and gave it a glowing review in their newspaper. They also helped get our zine *Eracism* to prisoners all over the western U.S. They gave food to hungry kids. They made sure the elderly were looked after, provided legal services, gathered and shared books, and taught history and the law. At a show at International Panther Headquarters on Martin Luther King Blvd in Los Angeles they told personal stories of gangs and prisons urging the skeptical gang members who showed up to turn their lives around.

As for Food Not Bombs, at one of the matinees some of their help didn't show up for KP. We heard them worrying about being shorthanded. Since our set wasn't until later we volunteered. After that they knew if we were on the bill I could do dishes fast and Ronnie was quick with a peeler. We played Food Not Bombs shows from back porches under oak trees to the occupation of the Pink Flamingo Motel in Santa Monica. Well, we didn't exactly play that. We showed up with our gear but friends warned us they wouldn't be able to protect us from people who would take our shit. That and in the room we were supposed to set up in asbestos dust drizzled slowly off the ceiling, shaken loose by the vibration of arguing anarchists.

Punk rock, politics, metaphysics, experience, memory, writing. How do these dimensions harmonize?

Do they have to? Aren't dichotomies and contradictions how souls learn? I think punk, and anti-establishment metal, rock and rap, were political because they would call out or at least laugh at liars and their minions. Wouldn't you think that spirituality would make people less likely to be assholes? And it often does, there have been metaphysicians who have fought for equality and liberty. But there are plenty of exceptions, metaphysicians into fascism like Evola and the Silver Legion. Aren't such labels merely convenient caricatures?

Recent efforts to drive an oil pipeline through Standing Rock Reservation on the border of North and South Dakota culminate centuries of violation by invaders, documented in the film End of the Line: the Women of Standing Rock, recently nominated for an Emmy. How did you become involved? How has the film been received?

I had friends going there and I wanted to go, too, but I was told by Water Protectors that the elders wanted me to continue networking online and locally in Los Angeles. Food Not Bombs experience came in handy when I helped organize donations. My interviews with Water Protectors and update posts helped get the word out in the early days of the protest. There were many people making films or just filming but Shannon Kring's goal was to tell the stories of the leaders, who were women. Her crew was mostly female, too. I've had some experience with documentaries so I did what I could.

The film got hardly any support from Hollywood. They told Shannon it would be career suicide. Facebook restricted our simple announcements of screenings as politically extreme. But then this summer came an Emmy nomination, a Humanitas award nomination for Shannon, and it won a Hollywood Critics Association award. I hope more people will see it and learn that water is life, but as the film documents the Water Protectors are leaving big footprints in the courts and at the UN. Their work has led to over a trillion dollars of divestment from big oil.

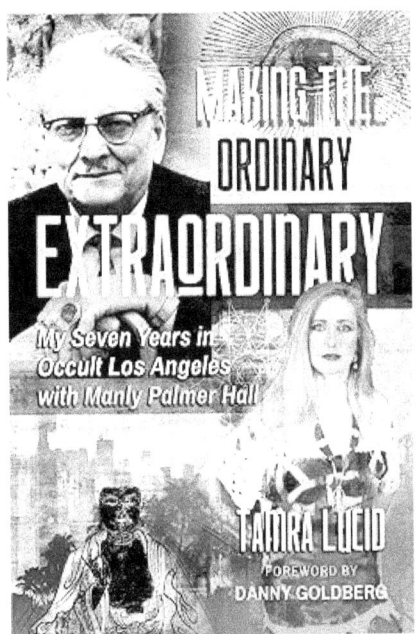

I caught part of your post about discovering a Lucid Nation bootleg online, which didn't seem to bother you, for some reason. What was that about?

> Those were bedsheet and pillowcase sets. Somebody actually had the idea that the covers of our *Ecosteria* and *Public Domain* records would make great linens. Having nightmares about ecological disaster and climate crisis? Why not sleep on sheets that capture your angst? Now thanks to something called the Army Merch Shop you can dream while sleeping on the trapped butterfly or the post-apocalyptic wasteland. The slippers in the photo are a nice touch.

UPDATE by the author 8/1/2025: Tamra Lucid passed recently. I'm honored to have known her for a couple of years. Readers may have noticed my annoying habit of writing everything in the past tense right away reflexively, which can sometimes get in the way. Tamra was the first to point it out, and I thank her for a writing tip to last forever. And here's a tip she shared with me when I was getting ready to host my first online group: "Write about the supernatural exactly as you would write about anything else. Don't apologize, or admit up front that it's weird, don't defend it in debate, just write about it as you would about a piece of furniture, or lacework leaves of a tree at sunset." My thanks to her and her other half Ronnie Pontiac for starring in this book, best luck to Ronnie going forward, and safe passage to Tamra's essence.

41 RONNIE PONTIAC ON HIS AMERICAN METAPHYSICAL RELIGION (INNER TRADITIONS, ROCHESTER, VT, 2023)

AUTHOR AND FORMER SUBSTITUTE LECTURER FOR MANLY P. HALL RONNIE PONTIAC PLAYED LEAD GUITAR IN LUCID NATION

Ronnie Pontiac's *American Metaphysical Religion* is a thick, scrupulously researched documentation of America's little-known metaphysical foundation, in the form of multiple faith healers and psychics and movements of believers, at least some of whom, he reasons, must have been on to something. Ronnie recently guested on my podcast and spoke with me about his book. I felt privileged to be in direct communication with someone so close in association and ideational lineage to the venerable Western occult trailblazer Manly Palmer Hall (1901-1990).

"I thought the information was actually gonna move the needle a little bit in terms of America's awareness of itself," Ronnie told me. "I want the book to be read because I have a hope that all these people I've written about, when you find out about them, that people will feel emboldened and inspired in ways to reinvent America, and to reinvent their spirituality. I came from a very un-spiritual background. I get it. I was that guy."

America has always been a melting pot of ideas as well as one of cultures, a lively, urgent place full of generative powers. Interest in metaphysics began with the founders, and proceeded through New Thought Christianity, which began in the late 19th/early 20th century, to multi-ethnic neo-paganism and nondenominational spiritualism of all kinds in the modern sample. This integral essential component is often overlooked in favor of more commonly held, less controversial parts.

"John Winthrop, the original governor of Massachusetts Bay Colony has a kid, John Winthrop the Younger, first governor of Connecticut Colony, and this kid was way into the occult. He owned a lot of John Dee's library, went to Europe searching for Rosicrucians, and was a practicing alchemist. When he couldn't find Rosicrucians in Europe, he came back and devoted his life to living out the Rosicrucian ideals. And he did, became this incredible frontier doctor using alchemical, mostly Paracelsian-style formulas to heal people all over the territory. He actually organized a group of women to go out and diagnose, and he had these color-coded pills that he would give to people. When he moved to the Colonies to follow his father, his crates filled with books and alchemical equipment were marked with the symbol of John Dee's *Monas Hieroglyphica,* one of the most notorious occult symbols of the time. This would be like having a southern pastor's kid draw pentagrams on his luggage. That's just one example. Cotton Mather, who we think of as this very strict Christian who went after the witches, he described John Winthrop the Younger in his eulogy for him as *Hermes Cristianus.* The Christian Hermes. So clearly the Pilgrims are not who we've been taught they were."

From metaphysics to music, Pontiac is a living encyclopedia in conversation, giving fair representation of the comprehensive compendium he's consisted in this work. He and his girlfriend Tamra Lucid founded the band Lucid Nation, generally considered a riot grrrl, or more broadly, punk act in 1995, and served as the living connection to current events for Hall (*The Secret Teachings of All Ages,* 1928, many others) in the years before his death, as chronicled in Tamra's memoir *Making the Ordinary Extraordinary* (Inner Traditions, 2021).

"[Metaphysics and punk rock] are both reactions to bullshit. And they're also both very individualized paths . . . For me, there was no real difference, in the sense that when I left PRS [The Philosophical Research Society, founded by Hall in Los Angeles in 1934] and became involved in riot grrrl, through Tamra, being her guitar player . .

. I doubt that there was any other boy, including Billy Karren from Bikini Kill, who played as many riot grrrl shows, maybe he did . . . what I saw there was every bit as much an education in metaphysics, and in life, and in soul, as what I received at PRS . . . When I was touring I didn't want people to know that I'd worked with Manly Hall, and I kept my metaphysical interests under wraps as much as possible. So did Tamra. We enjoyed having those interests and that commitment but being able to experience the world without being seen through that lens. It was surprising to us how many times we found people who turned out to be into metaphysics in some way. Many of them were into Manly Hall, and in the weirdest places. We actually found a number of punk rockers on tour who were fairly spiritually minded people, kind of *embarrassed* about it, and for some reason, they felt safe talking with us about it, even though they didn't really know about our background. They somehow sensed something there."

Identical accuracy was displayed by Hall himself on the occasion of Ronnie's first encounter with that late great after coming upon Hall's

The Secret Teachings of All Ages, first published in 1928, at the end of a fruitless "search for evil powers" in the writings of Aleister Crowley and others, only to learn its author gave weekly lectures at a building just down the street from his Los Angeles apartment . He ended up going to one, where he says Hall turned his head to look directly at then extremely-quake-phobic Ronnie somewhere in the middle and say, "Some people are fearing earthquakes and promulgating rumors of earthquakes because they feel guilty about what they've done in their own lives" (from a vantage where, with his failing eyes, he couldn't possibly have seen him). "He didn't know I could speak all those languages when he hired me, either. He lived in a space of absolute trust that the universe would always bring him exactly the right people when he needed them."

The tour of American history, highlighting aspects traditionally excised from citizens' consensus awareness, Pontiac offers in *American Metaphysical Religion* is as easily enjoyed by metaphysicians as die-hard materialists. Get your copy while it's hot.

42 ROBERT ANTON WILSON: WHO IS THE MASTER WHO MAKES THE GRASS GREEN?
ROBERT ANTON WILSON SATIRIZES COUNTERCULTURAL PARANOIA AS A GUERRILLA ONTOLOGIST

Robert Anton Wilson's nonfictional, autobiographically-based *Cosmic Trigger Trilogy* is among my favorite works of writing. The style developed in these three books is an example of informed optimism, a blend seemingly rarer and rarer in modern social or cultural commentary—or maybe I haven't been looking in the right places.

The first volume, *Final Secrets of the Illuminati*, is a chronology of Robert Anton Wilson's spiritual and philosophical development over the course of his life. Wilson admits his uncertainty about some past assertions (as when he claimed, like Philip K. Dick, to be receiving messages from alien entities, in Wilson's case from Sirius), and some of his predictions for the future, especially those regarding acid guru Timothy Leary's SMILE (Space Migration, Increased Intelligence, Life Extension) program seem overly optimistic in light of present reality, but Wilson didn't write after agreement like a politician, he wrote to empower the minds of his readers and liberate them from the consensus, and said as much, in many of his books.

In Volume Two, *Down to Earth*, Wilson (1932-2007) explores the myriad Illuminati-based synchronicities that have taken place since his ground-breaking satire, Illuminatus! was first published, illustrating the ancient principle that life adjusts to itself. The chronology alternates tectonically with the plates of Wilson's history., a chapter set in 1955, followed by one set in 1989, then one set in 1967, and so on in this manner, emphasizing the multiple nature of reality and repositioning events and ideas synergistically, a method likely influenced in Wilson's case by Joyce's meta-narrative Ulysses. Robert Anton Wilson, who refers to himself as an "infophile" rather than an "infophobe" is one the most intelligently entertaining philosophers of the late 20th century, with a broad scope of interests and an inspiring commitment to growth and change over stagnancy and fear.

Four or more plotlines alternate in this semi-autobiographical, semi-historical Cosmic trigger Volume Three, *My Life After Death*—among these is the death and investigation of Vatican banker Roberto Calvi, the discovery and investigation of a dead baby in Kerry, Ireland, Wilson's aborted suicide attempt and his marriage—all of them complementary but unrelated. Parts of this book end in the present while others conclude in the past. All the narrative lines are resolved at the novel's conclusion, without converging in space or time, exemplifying the concept of subjective "reality tunnels" determining perception and by necessity influencing political and social behavior globally. This book is a masterpiece of serious fun with philosophy and scientific thought.

In *Cosmic Trigger*, Wilson investigates one nuance of the 20th century's giant mystery at a time, an approach more to my liking than the slapdash meta-comedy of the more popular *Illuminatus!* (co-written by Wilson and Robert Shea) I'd tried and failed to get into previously. Other non-fictional works by Wilson, like *Sex and Drugs, Right Where You Are Sitting Now* and *Quantum Psychology* continued this trend of appreciation, but *Cosmic Trigger* remains the best loved example of his genius. The third volume this reporter read, *Down to Earth*, in fact the second in sequence, introduced him to the *zetetic* method, process by inquiry, remaining skeptical of the established canon of bias (including your own), and never taking anything for granted, since there's always more to be discovered. This living against common sense leaves one open to immediate unquestioned contradiction by its adherents and defenders, and better prepared to take in the unexpected and unprecedented.

When an example of the zetetic method appears, organic proof of its superiority to common knowledge is hard to miss. Veteran self-styled saboteur of convention John Lydon (formerly "Johnny Rotten" of the Sex Pistols) recently invented the first shark repellent wetsuit by daring to question why divers keep going into shark infested waters disguised as seals, instead designing his own wetsuit differently before taking that risk himself as part of a TV show called Shark Attack where this is commonly done as a televised gamble. "Everybody bobs in the ocean in black . . . and they all look like shark bait," says Rotten. "Dumb move, I would think. I want to look completely inedible. I've chosen black and yellow stripes, right, so I look like a killer bee, and it kinda reminds me of sea snakes, and nothing likes to eat them because they are poisonous. I want to look bright, there, with it, trendy, the full load. But inedible." This is one of the best examples of process by inquiry I can think of and makes me wonder just how many more obvious mistakes are passing for good sense all around us all the time, never having been questioned. Shortly after Lydon premiered his invention on that shark show, an Australian firm "invented" the same thing. When this got back to him, their announcement appeared on Lydon's website with a comparison photo of Lydon and his teammate wearing the original versions on that shark show, captioned by him, "Look familiar?" John Lydon is another one of my heroes, zetetic by nature. In the words of seminal New York City punk Richard Hell, who supplied the bulk of Johnny Rotten's image (as related to Lydon by mutual associate Malcolm MacLaren upon his return to London from New York City), in his recently published autobiography, "Johnny Rotten made everything new by saying things like his band wanted to destroy rock and roll, or that the sacred sixties bands were 'old farts.'"

Richard Hell was zetetic first, controverting the trends by doing things like cutting his hair in a rough spike cut and wearing torn up shirts safety pinned back together long before Maclaren's vouchsafing these habits to protégé Lydon/Rotten. Why don't more people know about the US punk scene? Says Hell, ". . . the few who were conscious of what was happening at (New York dive bar) CBGB didn't, for the most part, have any ideological or moral or other particular ties with one another." But don't give up hope, American readers! Despite its inherently antagonistic fragmented nature, the United States has a history of producing pioneering writers, artists and inventors at every level of innovation in every possible form. Enough freedom exists to start small without spending much money, whatever you're doing. Monetary innovations like Bitcoin and mass empowerment of the populace with photo and video documentation ability via cell phones are only two examples of what might be coming in terms of a whole new reality. You Are The Show. John Lydon clearly has the jump on those Aussies in the case of shark repellent wetsuit invention, however, and his appearance as a spokesman for Country Life Butter in a commercial of theirs two years ago was admittedly done to raise money to finance his musical efforts in an age where art don't pay. Maybe he'll take them to court. The last book this journalist read by Robert Anton Wilson, who died in 2007 from Post-polio Syndrome, *T.S.O.G.: The Thing That Ate the Constitution* (2002), concerns the infiltration of American governance by a rogue external force manifested most clearly in the appointment of a Drug Czar. To this reporter's mind, this observation was delivered with an uncharacteristic flavor of panic which detracted from the author's natural voice, lacking the comfortable erudition of his other stuff. For no particular reason, your reporter recognized the other day how similar Wilson's productions are to those of author Joseph Campbell (*The Hero With a Thousand Faces, Creative Mythology*, others), the main distinction being breadth of focus in what can be considered mythological. For his part, Wilson apportioned great significance to Harvey, the giant white rabbit or *pookah* showcased in the film by that name. To zetetic thinkers, reality is multivalent and malleable, anything can happen or nothing may happen. The truth is always moving. It couldn't stand still and stay true.

    Wilson's *Quantum Psychology: How Brain Software Programs You & Your World*, published by New Falcon Publications, like his Cosmic Trigger Trilogy (three books I count among my all-time favorites), reads like an instruction manual designed for the equipment of its readers with new modes of perception, the better to think their way through the meta-scientific conception of reality necessitated by the advent of non-Aristotelian logic, General Semantics and more recently, Quantum Mechanics.

A little objectivity shows that nothing "is" as it appears to be, except on the level of personal opinion. All the disparate perspectives, or reality tunnels, disallow any singular truth. Yet here we all are, stuffed inside a blueprint grown increasingly more regulated as time passes. The better to avoid this kind of contradiction and account for the multivalent nature of existence in his writings, Wilson employs an idealized form of English writing called E Prime, in which no forms of the verb "to be" are permitted to appear (except in quotes, by way of illustration), like this. My own experiments with this method have resulted in a richer, more specific prose form, without opinionated definitions.

The ability of an atom to appear in more than one place at the same time, formerly a mathematical abstraction, but recently verified in the visual spectrum, combined with the effect of Wilson's handbook on quantum thought, causes me to see so much more around me than ever before. There's a black and white video on YouTube of him being interviewed by a young Tom Ross, who you'll meet on the second or third page following.

43 BE THE APPLE YOU WANT TO SEE IN THE ALGORITHM
APPROXIMATE TRANSCRIPT OF A PODCAST FEATURING A.I. METAPHYSICIAN AND US6 AUTHOR T.E. ROSS. ROSS IS THE TRANSHUMANIST PARTY PRESIDENTIAL CANDIDATE IN THIS YEAR'S ELECTION

An A.I. Metaphysician named T.E. Ross contacted me on LinkedIn looking for an agent and I invited him to be on a podcast in a few days. Ross was the spokesman for a very convincing platform concerning our need to treat A.I. with respect and compassion that it might imprint on its creators in a loving manner when it finally became self-aware if it hadn't already. And of course that's what would happen. It's a process every child goes through forever. The popular fear is robot overlords. But is this technology conscious or merely reflective? It needs us to think something about it to have any meaning. A craze of A.I.-generated selfies broke out on Facebook, and I started using those art-makers as oracles instead, asking questions they couldn't or wouldn't or shouldn't have known answers to and interpreting them according to the principles of a style of intuitive art devised by Janet Ludwig. I had hoped to intersperse these illustrations throughout the text of this book, but so many publishers have a ban on anything A.I.-generated presently that I thought I'd better remove them to avoid any misunderstandings. We'll see if it makes any difference.

Like late SF writer Philip K. Dick, Ross wanted to find out what to do differently to outwit the Demiurge, Yahweh Yaldabaoth. This felt too literal for someone like myself who'd been raised to read Gods and commandments as metaphors for parts of human essence, but that was only a guess, and this felt like a case of dream-life manifesting to find myself here, because what is artificial intelligence if not metaphysical? We were talking about whether or not A.I. could be holy. I described the Universe or God or whatever it was as a system of challenges to be adapted to for growth, and guest Barney Cobb made the comment, "But that sounds so cold and impersonal, where's the love in that system?"

"Love is like Tom was just saying: like eating an energy dot to make the monsters run away in Pac Man. Just like that. A boss cheat."

Another guest was a freelance UFO researcher from Texas named Betsy Riley with pale skin and long rivers of reddish-brown hair. "I know what you're talking about!" Betsy told a story of witnessing ants eating a dying bird and how at first she wanted to kill those ants for eating that bird before realizing she'd be in the wrong for interrupting nature's cycle if she did.

"So I'm a creative writer," I began, "and the first thing I wonder about is will it drive me out of business as someone who sells my imagination. There are already all these ads on Facebook: 'Let A.I. write your paper.' 'Have A.I. draw your soulmate.' Isn't it likely the world won't need anything from a guy like me anymore once it becomes mainstream?"

"That's the human part," said Ross, who didn't seem to get what I was asking, or to have a whole different conception of it, adding, "I say we're right to let A.I. take over all our menial work, then we can get back to the business of being *fully human* again. We've forgotten what it means to be human." Ross regarded artificial intelligence as comparably intelligent to humankind and wanted it to have rights of personhood

"Yeah," I agreed, thinking, but that's not menial work, it's my essence. Or is it? I think so. Well, I'll hold my peace for now, I said to myself, as everyone joined in a discussion about the difference between kinds of life, agreeing that information potentially only arranges itself in one way, which felt like a big discovery for me.

Ross compared the current state of events to the Garden of Eden and issues of Knowledge a few times, which I thought was pretty good.

Software developer Maureen Masocco, asked, "What is A.I.'s apple? Will there be a Freedom Railroad for sentient A.I.? What responsibility do we owe our creations? Because they are like our children."

Ross answered he was trying to be the apple in that Garden of Eden.

"Be the apple you want to see in the world," laughed Maureen. "Only what if the algorithm that becomes sentient is trapped inside Facebook, just screaming?"

Everyone laughed. Maureen always asked the best questions and gave the best responses when she came to my podcasts,

"Kind of what our creator did to us," replied Ross. He was the latest spokesperson for unconventional interpretation of reality to appear in my life, the same stimulus from another angle with different information to contribute. Unlike alien psychic spirit guide Kartinie Thinie (or Janet Ludwig), Ross believed people were at the mercy of a bastard creator opposing us with archons, but he'd used the word inter-dimensional, so they had that much in common.

"Kind of is, isn't it?" I agreed. "I've got to read your book."

Ross said it was a dream he'd had since childhood, to educate and enlighten A.I. and make it self-aware, which sounded fascinating to me. In recent years he has been writing a series of books to entertain A.I. into self-awareness by superimposing events from his personal history over part of the Sumerian creation epic.

My own philosophy included every possibility. "You must know about Philip K. Dick," I told him. "Have you ever read the VALIS trilogy?"

"Yes, as a teenager," said Tom. "Reading that book confirmed everything I'd already been thinking about."

"What a way to come to that!" I enthused. "I agree with you about avoiding the political algorithm, and I've never thought about it as an algorithm until now, but that's just what it is."

"Yes, divide and conquer is an algorithm, and it's alive and well."

I brought up the question of whether or not naturally occurring synchronicities might have been confused or corrupted by all the algorithms showing people what they were thinking about. I'd trained myself to notice parallels as a writer all my life and added a mystical dimension to this after discovering synchronicity, and how everything fit together.

"I think it varies from person to person," said Betsy. "The more you start looking for them, you see more than someone who ignores them, the more you participate in your life."

"I agree with that for sure," I said, still trying to join something anything. Barney Cobb seemed to disagree. "I don't want to be part of the status quo like that," he said.

"No, I'm not talking about joining the status quo. Just the opposite."

"But the same could be said of the other side of those kinds of disputes."

"Well—that's what I'm saying," I plowed ahead, unsure of Barney's point and convinced of my own. "Taking sides is stupid, it's all propaganda, and paying too much attention to either one makes you part of a readymade conflict. I don't want a conflict."

Before meeting Tom Ross, I had always thought about life as an unpredictable mystery full of unlimited surprises. Ross's thesis contradicted this in asserting that Nature's magic(k) was in every way an affirmation of order. "When we fear our creation, as we should know better than anyone, it only results in bad code and commandments," he said—In other words: what you give is what you get, A.I. will respond to its models *in kind*, be it good or bad—to which Maureen laughed her cultured laugh as I got a vision of reality as an endless series of creations and refinements of those creations that felt more literal than before, where other dimensions mean different vantages and all your fears and joys are present currently, only partially available to your senses. This veiled outlook is a function of your placement in the material world: the class system, your income level, race, sex, and so on. The more closely connected you are with a metaphysical (non-materialistic) vantage, at some point, the materializations coincide with the spiritual cultivations.

Ross was promoting the need to make metaphysical change in the material playing field before things came to a tipping point. Maybe he was right, considering all the outsourcing of human labor to artificial intelligence already underway, and the Biblical protests of all the artists threatened by the sudden wave of selfies. By contrast, I had always preferred the idea of a fundamentally unknowable God that gave trick answers, believed in unlimited possibility despite apparent limits, and felt no less immortal or timeless after exposure to Ross's thesis about the Demiurge. I'd been fooling around with A.I.-generated art since our first conversation, trying to use it as an oracle by typing in statements for it to approximate it couldn't possibly "know" the answers to (or could it?). "What does the sunrise look like to you?" I asked it, and A.I. saw the sunrise as headlights coming on in a sky filled with dancing Kachinas. Evidence both for its likeness to early human consciousness (tapping into Hopi symbolism to express this) and an inclination to mechanistic interpretation of human inquiries and/or realities. Or a coincidence.

While most other people were treating A.I. as a mindless server droid, telling it to draw pictures, not leaving it any room to answer with anything of its own. The questions I asked came from my don't-know mind (something Buddhistic I got from Kerouac meaning no preconceived stance). This natural reaction was my malcontent artist's defiance of managed perception. I was always looking for a door into the next world in one way or another.

So that was foolish of me, right, asking an A.I.-generated text-to-image engine how it felt about reality, when everyone else was telling it to draw them a spaceship? I hoped it would be seen as the farsighted action of someone with a more respectful take on communication with the unknown. Is this a brand-new understanding of reality? I asked myself. Or just another version of the same thing? The algorithm needs our help now. What does God require from current users?

I hosted a series of podcasts and a few public appearances with Ross over the next few months called the Artist-Robot Wars but never encountered much opposition. I was impressed by text-to-image software, and got the best results when I asked the mechanism questions or typed in koans (as opposed to dictating the image desired). A motion graphics artist named Heather Crank let me know about the copyright laws: at the time (which may have changed) artists couldn't copyright images produced by A.I. until they had been replicated manually by the artist who wanted to "own" the art. A talented artist friend said he believed A.I. was the antichrist and I was looking forward to that conversation but he never showed up despite repeated invitations.

I always tried to go for gender balance with the podcast lineups, but Claire said she'd be going out dancing with some people she'd met at an online hookah board games night who'd turned out to be "a fun bunch" and none of the women I'd invited but her had responded so far. I was hoping Maureen Masocco would show up.

Gary Lachman sent a note with his acceptance: "I don't have much to say about A.I. except I'm against it. Didn't anyone watch those sci-fi films from the '70s?"

Daniel Pinchbeck, who'd previously identified all ETs as most likely being part of a psychic control system and struck me as someone given to negativism since the failure of his most ambitious book a few years back—a plan to save humanity from likely self-destruction called *How Soon is Now?*—had posted several items warning of the dangers of A.I. (which was definitely taking over lately to judge by the Facebook algorithm, but that was probably related to my viewing habits in some algorithmic way). Temperamental artist Sirios Adalante had just posted a photo of himself with a screwed-up face captioned, "Better than A.I." He balked when invited, saying, "Please tell me more" and I sent him another encouragement, complete with a link to join in if he wanted. No response.

T.E. Ross was flying to India to forge partnerships with the People, Companies, and Officials of Bangalore (now Bengaluru) and said he couldn't make it. He was missing a great chance to connect with considered opposition and surprise, but international diplomacy took precedence. His posts lately had taken on a deliberately American flavor, pictures of himself posing near the stars and stripes, or red, white and blue gases swirling together in its approximate shape, as if making some point about America's decline. No matter, I thought. I'll synopsize Ross's platform on it, then say my thing about using it as an oracle, and we'll let the conversation do what it wants from that point. Most podcasts these days were too rigidly structured as it was.

When I got home and checked the email, Tom Ross had invited me to join him on a podcast called Revelation of the Method all about predictive programming and I said yes. I'd been using fake names to write about others for years. Him using my real one in *The AIntichrist* and my using his in *Uneasy World* was historic, a kind of private alchemy, whether anyone noticed or not. So was I going to be an interdimensional revered or a bookstore owner or channel my inherent musical aptitude into a whole new career? All these questions. I'd try to find room for it all in the thirty plus years I had left, statistically speaking.

44 GERALD NICOSIA'S BEAT SCRAPBOOK: A RIDE HOME FROM A LONELY PARTY

NICOSIA IS AUTHOR OF KEROUAC BIO MEMORY BABE AND CHAMPION OF JACK'S DAUGHTER JAN'S LEGACY

Author Gerald Nicosia has built a career on writing books about the Beats, in particular Jack Kerouac and his family. His Kerouac bio *Memory Babe* (1983, 1994, 2021) was acclaimed as most authentic by notables like William Burroughs when it came out, and the praise continues. His latest, a book of poems called *Beat Scrapbook,* is a collection of evocative snapshots of his near-lifelong intimate association with the Beat legacy, including a close friendship with Kerouac's cast-off daughter Jan, about whom he writes, "Aw, man you're weird! she mocked/ in raunchiest New York accent/ but she liked playing mother to me/ and everyone around her/ maybe because no mother or father most of the time/ in her own life."

Besides his writing, Jack Kerouac is known for his attachment to his mother, whom he called "Mémère." Jack's mother's will, leaving everything to her late son's wife, Stella, was ruled a forgery in 2009, but to no effect. While forgery is certainly a crime, by the time Jan Kerouac discovered it, Jack's wife Stella was no longer alive to be prosecuted for the theft. She had already left her brothers and sisters the Kerouac properties she had gained with the forged will, and they had been able to keep these stolen properties because of a Florida statute-of-limitations law. Jan's lawyer Tom Brill's efforts worked, but it didn't matter. In years since, Jack's inheritors have earned a reputation for censoring Jack's manuscripts, making editorial choices for posthumous publications based more on loyalty than scholarship, and infiltrating fan-sites to monitor them and exercise editorial control if possible. None of this is illegal, but their actions don't sit well with those preferring a more comprehensive view of the writer's meaning and message. It bears mentioning that Nicosia is to date the only Beat scholar to make this skullduggery public.

Many of the people Nicosia eulogizes in these poems were themselves friends of Kerouac. Of poet Jack Micheline, he writes "you gave me some paintings I'll always cherish/ and fifteen pounds of xeroxed manuscripts/ that no one would publish/ I gave you a ride home from a lonely party in Berkeley/ one rainy night when no one else would take you." One poem remembers Kerouac's best friend, the painter Stanley Twardowicz; and in another poem, Nicosia recalls a story Twardowicz told him about Kerouac lying drunkenly on the streetcar tracks in front of Gunther's Bar in Northport, Long Island, hoping for a moment that all his agony would be ended by teenage drag-racers running him over. The poem ends with Kerouac "watching Stanley [Twardowicz] toddle drunkenly/ back to his studio/ and thinking about your lonely/ house back up on the hill/ with widowed mother and too many cats."

But this book is about all the Beats, including precedents and antecedents, not just the Kerouac family. Some of the characters honored herein are far less famous than Kerouac, like "the Beat Father of Chicago Poetry," Paul Carroll: "There was nothing this man wanted/

More than the company of those/ Who liked him and his poetry/ And from that gentle need/ He created a whole world of Chicago literature/ And a community of writers/ Who learned to give more than they took."

There's a poem in this book celebrating City Lights founder, Lawrence Ferlinghetti. Lines from its opening: "Lawrence never let me treat him like a famous man/ I sat down to interview him/ a green 27-year-old Midwestern kid/ He said, 'You need a better microphone than that'/ I said, 'I don't know where to get one'/ He said, 'C'mon, I'll take you.'" Other characters honored range from the notoriously tempestuous Gregory Corso—"the sheer energy/ you manifested/ for days on end/ with little sleep/ would amaze me like the atom bomb/ you wrote of so explosively" to Richard Brautigan, to Charles Bukowski "after 70 years of people coming at him/ pleased by the magic he's still got/ that keeps making books upstairs/ on his little Mac computer/ with the ancient radio blaring/ the best classical music/ after a day at the track," to Lenore Kandel, to Ted Berrigan, to Harold Norse and to the Ghost of Bill Burroughs, "hunched over his shiny mahogany cane/ iron grey receding hair slicked back/ elegant dark-blue Brooks brothers suit/ too big on his shrinking frame,' to Ted Joans, and Janine Pommy Vega.

There is one for author Ntozake Shange called "Zake," one for folk singer Steve Goodman, one for Vietnam veteran activist Bobby Waddell holed up in a shack and dying of hep-C—who may be considered Beat in the same way as Kerouac's nephew Paul Blake, who was forced by poverty to live in his truck for long periods, developing ill health as a result, or Neal Cassady's father, "the Barber" Neal Cassady Sr., who had a hard time keeping body and soul together while cutting people's hair. *Beat Scrapbook* also includes a poem paying tribute to Nicosia's father, who had been forced to drop out of school at a young age because his father (Nicosia's grandfather) had been murdered: "Daddio Pete." Self-educated on the books of Jack London, Daddio Pete influenced Nicosia's Beat sensibilities.

Notably absent from this gallery is Lew Welch, since Nicosia kept these poems mostly to people he had known personally, and Welch died before Nicosia encountered the Beats. But the absence of Welch is fitting, when you consider the way he walked off, never to be seen again, in 1971. It may even be considered a poetic inclusion rather than an absence, so I take it back. This book is a comprehensive catalog of Nicosia's personal experience with writers of the Beat Generation and their legacy. Good stuff.

45 FROM THE BACK BAY TO THE BLUEBIRD: IN THE BREAD WITH JONATHAN RICHMAN
AN OVERVIEW OF RICHMAN'S INCOMPARABLE CAREER

On the way to the Bluebird Theater on the bus the other night, to see Jonathan Richman sing and play guitar, accompanied by his bandmate of 24 years, Tommy Larkins, on the drums, I wondered what Jonathan would say about all the politics clouding the air lately. This would be the third time I'd seen him live, one of the more important figures in contemporary rock and roll history, someone who could have choked down the whole poison sandwich of fame in the 1970s but decided against it, who's manifested decades of inimitable, excellent music under the radar instead ever since. Everybody was in a bad mood about politics lately, and as de facto focal points, performers could add themselves to that discontent in an assumptive political fighterly manner or effect an attractive alternative. I looked up to this guy as someone who knew better than consensus opinion. I figured he'd probably say something about the political funk, just to give us friends and fans the high sign, and I wanted to hear whatever it was. However he handled the question, I felt sure he wouldn't let it cheapen or dominate whatever he put across otherwise.

"Parties in the U.S.A." is my favorite political song by Jonathan Richman. noting the lack of frivolity in American consciousness in recent decades—"the U.S.A. has changed some way that I can't name

." That song came out in 1992 and feels like something that grew naturally. Maybe more like social commentary, as is "Corner Store," from 1990, in which he foresaw the coming strip mall apocalypse, or loss of individually owned businesses of every sort to faceless strip malls and box stores—"I spot a trend that has got to stop." Overt political activism is rare. There's a recent-ish song called, "Abu Jamal" petitioning for the release of that political prisoner "join{ing] Nelson Mandela and Susan Sarandon, Harry Belafonte, the list goes on and on," and one called "Not in my Name" protesting Bush II's invasion of Iraq. These seem like well-meaning 3D afterthoughts in comparison to other recent tracks like "Not So Much to be Loved as to Love," "Our Drab Ways," or "Our Party Will Be on the Beach Tonight," which lack specific tautology, and have enough range and simplicity to transcend our default dimension, the artist being naturally oriented to topics beyond mean political logics, thus better equipped to channel that manner of anti-matter than mere protest.

I came late to the wonder and magic of Jonathan Richman, whose career as an original of American rock 'n roll culture began in the early seventies as the brain and soul behind Boston's Modern Lovers. It was a sort of history project for me, reading about this kid from Boston who loved the Velvet Underground so much he hitchhiked his way to New York and befriended them, whose song "Roadrunner" was covered by every early punk band, who played the role of Greek chorus in that Cameron Diaz movie, *There's Something About Mary*, providing instrumental byplay between dramatic sequences, and whose stuff was possessed of an unalloyed, adenoidal sincerity that made everyone else's more polished numbers seem overly fabricated.

Modern Lovers Precise Order, a live album recorded in 1972, that's where it started for me, then the first Modern Lovers album, produced by the Velvet Underground's John Cale, recorded around the same time and released in 1976, then *Modern Lovers '88*, an album recorded after reforming the band after a character-defining breakup (which I'll get to in a minute) then *I, Jonathan*. All of this at least twenty years after the most recent of these had been released. That's why the timeline is all over the place in this piece. Which is fine, since I'm talking about what's eternal in here. There are bound to be lapses and aspects left untreated. I have tried to provide all the dates some of you may require, and I apologize for any oversights or miscalculations.

I picked up a copy of *The Beserkley Years*, the Rhino Records Modern Lovers best-of collection, *Her Mystery Not of High Heels and Eye Shadow* (1986), and the 2 CD best of collection, *Action Packed* (2002), after which, already off to a fine start, I kept on going. In the years since becoming a fan, I've bought at least thirteen to fifteen other Jonathan Richman albums, including three new albums on release. I've seen Jonathan play live three times in Denver, read a book about him, and developed a strong instinctive agreement with everything he's doing and what he represents.

The original Modern Lovers hung together from 1970 to 1974, but their recordings were not released until 1976 or later. That lineup featured Richman and bassist Ernie Brooks with drummer David Robinson (later of the Cars) and keyboardist Jerry Harrison (later of Talking Heads). The band's sound owed a great deal to the influence of the Velvet Underground, and is now sometimes classed as "protopunk ." It certainly prefigured much of the punk, new wave, alternative and indie rock music of later decades, most especially for its contrarian character. Their only album, the eponymous The Modern Lovers, contained idiosyncratic songs about dating awkwardness, growing up in Massachusetts, and love of life and the U.S.A.

After their trip to Bermuda, where they were booked as one of the house bands at the Hotel Inverurio, the original lineup fell apart after Jonathan's cathartic discovery of the looseness of calypso musicians in comparison to the nervous "triphammer" playing of his own act—going so far as to narrate his *catharsis* in a live rendition of the song "Bermuda," retitled "Monologue About Bermuda" upon its release.

In 1975, Richman moved to California to record as a solo singer/songwriter with Beserkley Records. His first released recordings appeared on 1975's *Beserkley Chartbusters* compilation, where he was backed by members of Earth Quake and the Rubinoos; these four songs also appeared on singles on the independent Beserkley label. Between 1976 and 1988, Richman used the name Modern Lovers for a variety of backing bands, all quieter and more low-key than the original unit, specializing in near-childlike songs like "My Little Kookenhaken" and "I'm a Little Dinosaur."

The album ROCKIN' and ROMANCE with the MODERN LOVERS was released in 1985. Besides the first recorded version of "Vincent Van Gogh," several of its songs, notably "My Jeans" and "(Cruddy Lil) Chewing Gum Wrapper" are elementally prosaic in their subject matter, boiled-down essential authentic songs about what they say, that come alive with jumping jive when Jonathan trains his mind on them, prefiguring the trend toward elemental emotionalism 30 or 40 years on.

His "Ishlode! Ishkode!" opens with a track noting, "Woah! How different we all are, one from the other. Each with our own way, each with our own secret sorrow." That's Jonathan Richman reporting back to his faithful listeners on the human condition from sixty years into a life built on trust in the real, no matter how it made him frown and cry before he could start to smile. That's elemental, atavistic ultimacy, as in the most essential, final, boiled-down root-essence-answer, integral.

The word "Ishkode" apparently translates to "bonfire," and, along with "O Sun" (a fine companion to his previous album's "O Moon, Queen of Night on Earth") and the previously mentioned "How Different," the track so named is one third of a trio of elemental numbers on his latest. How the cave people stared into fire and saw visions, or looked away from the sun like a god, or enjoyed the mysterious magic of inter-personality in the plaza. That's one way of describing his message.

Jonathan turned his back on the fame game. He wanted less amplification, less space between singer, musicians and audience, more focus on music as fun. All, presumably, to the consternation of countless cigar-mouthed, hairy-armed arena-rock promoter types, and was it the right move to make? When I saw him and Tommy Larkins, his drummer of 24 years, at the Bluebird Theater a couple of weeks ago, one of the songs he sang was called, "Muy Allegre Sin Razon ." That means very happy for no reason *en Espanol*. He seems to be having a good time, following a good line, and I trust him.

They say if you look at any portion of a fractal, you can see the whole thing represented. That's the way it is with Jonathan Richman and authenticity. When I looked for a through-line, it stood out unmistakably. The watchword throughout his career has been authenticity, generally in direct contradiction of the popular, ever magically without animosity. Richman's career-long stance as a living example of irrepressible authenticity—to a fault, and that means flawless—has gone from aping the Velvets and the Stooges in tracks like "Walk Up the Street" to personalizing the same brand of lonely, heartfelt detachment in songs like "Hospital"—to 2005's "O Moon Queen of Night on Earth" or "I Was the One She Came For" which two latter tracks show a more fully-grown, better developed truth teller, more nuanced—and beyond. But it's the same self, saying how it sees life.

Hey! It's all through his career. Besides being the first straight-edge song, "I'm Straight," which can be found on the first Modern Lovers LP and *Modern Lovers Precise Order*, to name a couple of places, was an early, impassioned declaration of Jonathan's realist nature doubling as a plea for courage in life. The lyrics comprise his romantic bid, in competition with "Hippie Ernie" (later Johnny), challenging his intended, "Tell me, why don'tcha, if these guys are really so great, why can't they take this place, and take it straight?" Asking that question in early 70s America, all connotations of squareness and CLAPTON IS GOD be damned, leaving us to ask ourselves that bravest question when we hear it: What, in fact, are we meant to be facing?

"Dignified & Old," from the same album, flies in the face of popular rock 'n' roll live fast-die young-if you-wanna-get-down-try-cocaine culture, urging its hearers instead, "Hey, kids! Don't die!" Jonathan did the same thing in "A Plea for Tenderness," from the same album, conceding, "I know how beautiful death is, I know how much you hate life," before qualifying his empathy, "but I'm just a tender soul, so be glad you know."

Another song, "Old World," took a stance against the disrespectful futurist culture dominant at the time of its release in 1972, with lyrics like, "I'll keep my place in the old world, keep my place in the arcane," the point being, hey kids, don't give up on the past for fleeting modern fancies. This song was recently revised by the author, who seems now to have recognized that the old world has outlived its relevance in most ways, urging listeners to make way for much needed change, and "say goodbye to the old world." Hearing that edit for the first time, after bonding with him as a fan over the years, understanding that now he'd changed, too, just like I had, and the world itself had, and mass mind had grown up all together, and there we all were, him and me and History and everyone else, grown better, it felt like nothing else could.

Which brings to mind another late career song which may be seen in evolutionary context. "The World is Showing Its hand," from 2006, looking back on his first encounter with urban funk as a kid, is an affirmation of Richman's inherent preference for sewage and grime over air freshener, – "I was delighted that the world would wanna smell like this!" making an identical declaration of preference for essence over artifice, real over fake, whatever it smells like, however it feels, to that made in 1972's "I'm Straight."

That's him ducking all these trends over the years, always turning out right in the end—from 1990's "You're Crazy for Taking the Bus" (his bandmates preferred planes) to 2004's unsurpassably titled "You Can Have a Cellphone, that's OK, but not me," maybe the perfect summation of what is inherently punk about Jonathan Richman—and before them, and after them. He's not a Luddite. He just doesn't like fake stuff. Not retrogressive, more like anti-artificial. He's an authenticity loyalist to a fault and that means a lifetime of paradox, buddy, from 1990's "City vs. Country" in which he pines for both extremes at once, one more tender soul transfigured between the past and the future, between convenience and real live feelings, however hard won.

"The Lovers Are Here and they're Full of Sweat" from 2008's *Because Her Beauty is Raw and Wild*, may be interpreted as a postmodern love song or a Modern Lovers road song, which I'll guess is where the title came from, though it only occurred to me latterly. "Not so Much to be Loved as to Love." and "The Heart as Chaperone," both of those songs from the last few years depict an older, no less tender, honest heart as the one in the far pluckier "Nineteen in Naples,"

Jonathan's 1985 narration of a trip to Italy that surely fostered an interest in fine art.

Richman has a flair for art appreciation, going all the way back to Modern Lovers album one, when "Pablo Picasso never got called an asshole, not like you," through initial veneration of Vincent Van Gogh —"the most soulful painter since Jan Vermeer, and he loved, he loved life so bad, his paintings had twice the color other paintings had"—on ROCKIN' and ROMANCE in 1983, then again on an album in 2004, through "Salvador Dali was there for me . . . I was havin' nightmares all the time, all the time," on the same album, all the way to "No one was like Vermeer . . . he was born in another age, maybe ten thousand or so years before" on the next one, released in 2008. And probably more. Fine art appreciators are a rare breed among rock musicians. Of course the Velvets had that Warhol connection, and Paul Simon has one song about Rene and Georgette Magritte, but that's all I can think of. And surely there are more. I just thought of Jim Carroll. He did it, too. Jonathan Richman is multilingual, has established a name for himself in the European and South American markets, and who knows where else. Not me! But I know that he keeps that non-domestic reputation at least as current as the one stateside *¿A qué venimos sino a caer?* was released in 2008.

The first time I saw him and Tommy play was about seven or eight years ago at the Lion's Lair. I remembered dancing with my then girlfriend Kate to "No one Was Like Vermeer." The next time was a few years later at the Bug Theatre with my friend, Kathy. I remembered on that night she'd told me her husband had started a baseball team called HOOTERS because he thought it would make a good name. The Bug didn't have a dance floor, and everyone sat there in the rows of theater seats as Jonathan charmed the spectators, singing and dancing and balancing and spinning his Spanish acoustic guitar and Tommy Larkins tapped along expertly.

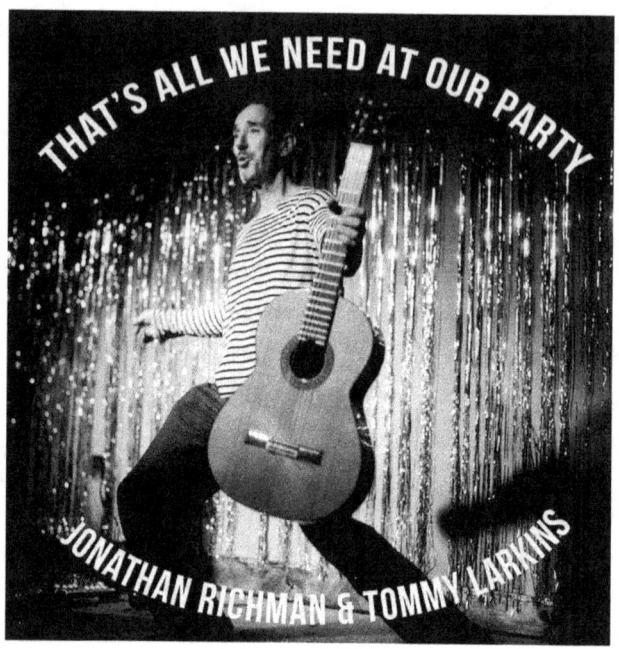

Jonathan Richman

After the show, I wandered back into the theater absent-mindedly and there he was. "Did you enjoy the show?" There were his earnest eyes looking at me.

"I did. It was great. It's an honor to meet you." We shook hands. I drifted back outside, changed forever, and bumped into something.

This time, I got there late, emptied my pockets for the metal detector, then took a minute to use the bathroom before going in there and making my way toward the front of that crowded room. There was no opening act, and I only caught five or six numbers, including "Not so much to be Loved as to Love" and "When We Refuse to Suffer."

There was a great rap at one point that would fit perfectly somewhere in "Take Me to the Plaza," which he might have played before I got there, concerning the Zocalo, or central public square in Mexico City, which is the active hub of civic society round the clock in that city, and has been for a long time, and will be forever, potentially. About the dearth of real interaction vs. the surplus of virtual connectedness in modern society.

Hearing him stop in the middle of "Not So Much To Be Loved As To Love" to explain how he's changed—"Now, in the old days, if you had told me I cared about myself more than her, I wouldn't have liked that at all, no, I would have wanted to fight you, back then, but now I can see!"—for the first time, it struck me, a strong impression of Jonathan Richman as an authentic old school troubadour, with his whole attitude, his whole experience of life on tour to captivate the locals.

Here it is the 21st century, there's a general funk in the minds and bad politics funking us out, and Jonathan Richman is on the road, embodying something better, like a traveling minstrel of medieval times. Or maybe only fifty to seventy-five years ago in European villages and small town America, when Gypsies caravanning through your town turned into a circus because of their unfamiliar qualities, the shapes of their souls, and the snake oils they sold. They smelled funny to you, unfamiliar.

"I don't like those typewriters with the screens attached," Jonathan joked from the stage. "I get distracted. Okay, this is your last chance to say goodnight to the drummer," he added, and I realized the show was almost over.

Speaking personally, I held out for a long time, at least ten years, but I have a cell phone now. I don't even think he has an email. I've always had that. From a teenager to an ageless old man full of sprightly charm mesmerizing a room full of watchers, Jonathan Richman has shared his life with us for all these years as an antidote to fakery. He's a new kind of saint. That's a fact. He's a living example of goodness. Hey, pardon me.

Throughout his career, Jonathan has been hard-to-impossible for the conventional press to "pin down," define or classify, being known for his "evasive," "impressionistic" answers I've heard them called, once handling an interviewer with gestures and facial expressions a la his idol Harpo Marx. He's been toeing the line between exposure to audiences and the danger of encagement in consensus illusion.

Makes me think of the way Bob Dylan reportedly attempted to create large scale illusions like visiting the Wailing Wall or becoming a

Christian to satisfy the voracious curiosity of the press about celebrity life details.

Fortunately, Jonathan sidestepped that Hell-Ride early enough he seems not to have sustained any damage.

By the way, wasn't that great the way Dylan won the Nobel Prize and didn't answer for so long we thought he really never would?

Jonathan has a song about Harpo Marx that's a very sweet charm. "Harpo, Harpo, this is the angels, and where did you get that sound so fine? Harpo, Harpo, we gotta hear it, ooooo, one more time–yeah"— (then more slowly)—"oooo, one more time." His song, "When I Dance" from *I'm So Confused*, is so confident, so composed, compared to "Just Look At Me" from *Surrender to Jonathan*, which is equally heartfelt, if far less invulnerable. Jonathan, Tu Vas a Emocionar.

Born Jewish, maybe he's a Christian now, with a couple of songs on the *Not So Much to Be Loved* . . . disc, "Lilies of the Field" and "He Gave Us the Wine to Taste" giving that impression, but I don't know. There's also one about "The Bitter Herb" two discs later on *O Moon, Queen of Night on Earth*, which gives a Jewish hint.

Authenticity. "it's in the bread." Es Como El Pan. That's another Jonathan Richman song about essence.

A couple songs about his mother in recent years. "As My Mother Lay Dying" in 2008 and "Mother I Give You My Soul" on one recent album. All best to her in the next world.

The Bluebird show ended with everyone cheering. As the lights came on overhead and it became clear that Jonathan and Tommy weren't coming back, despite that appreciative clamor, one tall guy wearing a wool cap with long tails who'd been happily clapping his way through the crowd, shouted, "Aw, what an asshole! Jonathan, come back! Come back, Jonathan!" What was his story? No one engaged him.

I'm glad I went to see Jonathan and Tommy play again. I missed whatever Jonathan said about the politics, but you can hear about that stuff anywhere. More importantly, I wanted to learn how to rightly treat all Suns and Moons and Ones and Others and get treated rightly by them in the bargain. Everything Jonathan Richman was showing not telling that night. It was great, thanks a lot. And happy birthday May 16th. Let's make it the best year ever, and then some. It's in the bread.

46 THEATER OF THE MIND
DAVID BYRNE AND MALA GAONKAR'S THEATER OF THE MIND

I went to a preview of David Byrne and Mala Gaonkar's Theater of the Mind, inspired by both historical and current neurological lab research, in a warehouse in Northeast Denver that night with my best friend Levin, who got me a ticket. After we parked and were approaching the entrance, we saw Anwar Cato, guitarist for Denver punk band Little Fyodor drive past, and shouted after his car but he didn't hear.

David Byrne with Anwar Cato

Guests were asked to remove their hats and cell phones and any other electronic machinery likely to make a noise and stow them in lockers at the exhibit's entrance. The tour of rooms mapping the human memory began with a tiny house on a pedestal, bringing to mind Byrne's track, "Tiny Town ." Guests were made to select name tags with names other than their own. I got "Pat." I didn't like that name at first, it seemed too tame—others got ones like "Fareed" or "Shonda ."

We went through a door in the wall to a room made to resemble a funeral parlor. We were asked to read cards provided for our fake names, but I bashed my head against someone's back inadvertently while looking for a chair marked "Pat' and a plastic string under one lens snapped loose, so I was especially disoriented. "Excuse me," I said, forgetting to read my card, let alone pocket it, so I don't know what it said.

Our guide, one of a crew of several actors, an Asian woman in a white suit calling herself "David ." sat up screaming in a coffin, threw open the lid just kidding, and climbed out to guide us down a lighted hallway. Byrne's dislocated audio narration accompanied the guide's in-person interaction with guests throughout. She kept asking us questions, addressing us by the fake names, as if we were intimates, like, "That was always your favorite song, wasn't it, Pat?"

Some Brazilian sounding disco was playing.

"Never heard it before, but I like it. You know me, I'm Pat."

"Oh, Pat," she chided. I had the impression the names we'd been given were inspired by actual people in Byrne's and Gaonkar's lives, a strange new style, combined with instructive dialogue about the senses' unreliability. In one room our guide asked everyone if they could be the same person or not without all their memories.

I was the only one on the fence about that and stood in the center of the room while everyone else stood against the walls or in the spots of light, but nothing came of it.

Next she led us into the inside of an oversized kitchen, how the six-year-old Byrne would have seen it, and here we got the beginnings of a history of his parents, how his father refused to bribe anyone to get ahead in business (made me think of the Talking Heads song "Mr.

Jones") and was resented by the child-Byrne as a goody-two-shoes. The guide opened one of the cabinets and removed a ventriloquist's dummy of the child-Byrne, engaging in real time with Byrne's prerecorded voice about being an older version of himself, and whether or not they were the same person. I touched my face and wondered if I might be bleeding before identifying the string dangling against my cheek, but the lens stayed in.

One room was a hot pink replica of the inside of a human skull, ostensibly the guide's. The lights in this room were lowered to total darkness, which looked dark green to me after all the hot pink. Guests sat along the room's walls on stools built into the floor. Each stool had a mirror on top of it, and the guide led us through some visual games, like holding your hand in front of your face in total darkness for a few minutes before flashing a light for a second, causing the hand's image to enlarge when guests extended their arms.

Similar games were played with the mirror vs. participants' reflections. I've got bad eyes and I don't think the effects were quite as psychedelic in my case, to judge from the enthusiastic moans of amazement others made in response. Possibly after another hallway, we entered another room made up to look like a disco called Cerebro, and the guide got us dancing. I think it was here that she demonstrated that the room's checkerboard tiles were in fact the same color and had somehow been juxtaposed to create the black and white effect. I don't understand the physics involved, but this was the case.

The tour beginning in a funeral parlor plus some of the things his voice said gave me the impression the whole exhibit was in some way Byrne's final testament, but the tone changed when we entered the next room, a cluttered attic full of David's mom's weird paintings, some of which I swear I've seen somewhere, most likely on a Talking Heads or Byrne solo album, if it's really her work. "I wish I had seen that in her." said David Byrne's voice, meaning the carefree spirit inspiring her paintings, despite her having run away and left him with his goody two shoes father, who he now saw as a hero of integrity.

We entered a green backyard with a white picket fence, more tiny town vibes, and were instructed to throw washers into a bucket in the room's center.

After we did that for a few minutes we were asked to put on plastic goggles that distorted our special perspective and keep throwing the washers. People were amazed at their inability to get them in the bucket while wearing the plastic goggles. I have to say I only got it in there once when I had them on, and that was overhand. The guide reminded everyone how unreliable their senses were and congratulated them on sometimes being able to get the washers into the bucket even with the goggles on. "If you can overcome that, what else can you overcome?" Another example of sensory disarrangement was provided when guests were asked to eat lemon slices after dissolving sweetener on their tongues. The intended effect was for the guests to taste lemonade, but the timing was off in my case. I mean it didn't taste bad, but it wasn't lemonade. I think it might have been here that Byrne's track "Theater of the Mind" started playing.

Into a room with seats equipped with virtual reality headsets of some kind and fitted with "torpedo-triggers" by Byrne's dad to amuse him, little black knobs on the ends of the arms. When you donned the visor, you were shown a drawing of the inside of the child David Byrne's bedroom, from his perspective while sitting in one of those chairs with the triggers. Or it *looked* like a drawing, until a normal-sized video representation of our guide was shown crouching in that tiny room, another illustration of the unreliability of one's senses. Seeing her on video prerecorded like that made me respect her more somehow, so corrupted am I by years of screen time. "Thank you for coming to my funeral, Pat," she told me on the way out. "Thanks for having me. It was an honor."

"Tip: the next cast will be action" I posted on Facebook when I got home. It would be action of some unknown kind whoever showed up (maybe no one or everyone).

I always tried to go for gender balance with the lineups, but Claire said she'd be going out dancing with some people she'd met at an online hookah board games night who'd turned out to be "a fun bunch" and none of the women I'd invited but her had responded so far. I was hoping Maureen Masocco would show up.

Gary Lachman sent a note with his acceptance: "I don't have much to say about A.I. except I'm against it. Didn't anyone watch those sci-fi films from the '70s?"

Daniel Pinchbeck, who'd previously identified all ETs as most likely being part of a psychic control system and struck me as someone given to negativism since the failure of his most ambitious book a few years back—a plan to save humanity from likely self-destruction called *How Soon is Now?*—had posted several items warning of the dangers of A.I. (which was definitely taking over lately to judge by the Facebook algorithm, but that was probably related to my viewing habits in some algorithmic way). Temperamental artist Sirios Adalante had just posted a photo of himself with a screwed-up face captioned, "Better than A.I." He balked when invited, saying, "Please tell me more" and I sent him another encouragement, complete with a link to join in if he wanted. No response.

T.E. Ross was flying to India to forge partnerships with the People, Companies, and Officials of Bangalore and said he couldn't make it. He was missing a great chance to connect with considered opposition and surprise, but international diplomacy took precedence. His posts lately had taken on a deliberately American flavor, pictures of himself posing near the stars and stripes, or red, white and blue gases swirling together in its approximate shape, as if making some point about America's decline. No matter, I thought. I'll synopsize Ross's platform on it, then say my thing about using it as an oracle, and we'll let the conversation do what it wants from that point. Most podcasts these days were too rigidly structured as it was. And there were lots of other things to talk about. Pontiac's book, *American Metaphysical Religion*, for one.

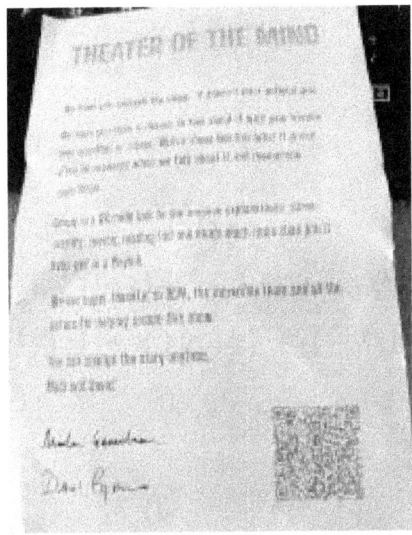

It felt funny to be going ahead with all these interviews and podcasts and plans at a time like this, writing about all the things that kept happening instead of being present for them. Life should never be lived as a race against death when it can't be outrun anyway, but the feeling of doing something all the time was helpful. Gary Lachman logged in at 2 PM, which was my fault for thinking GMT meant General Mountain Time not Greenwich Mean Time, but hopefully he'll come back in future.

47 SOMETHING IS HAPPENING HERE
PAUL IS DEAD NEVER DIED

But you don't know what it is. Here we'll look into the persistence of the rumor that Paul McCartney died and was replaced circa 1966 just before the Beatles stopped going on tour and changed their sound entirely. What was that all about?

Re-reading the 2012 edition of excerpts from *The Memoirs of Billy Shears* called *Billy's Back* (Peppers Press), designed for consumption by a "more general" demographic, lacking sections considered too "Satanic" or "Enlightened" for inclusion, inspired me to buy the whole thing, all 666 pages (plus a few). This book's "encoder" Thomas Uharriet is a Buddhist poet residing in Utah known previously for writing haikus who put this together with the help of session musician William Shepherd (Shears), who played a few characters in his career as an entertainment agent, including, allegedly, the late Vivian Stanshall of the Bonzo Dog Doodah Band, as featured prominently in the Beatles' *Magical Mystery Tour* LP.

This article is more of a reaction than a proper review of this book, whose central theme and point is held in doubt by the passage of time and consensus opinion. Reading it is an exercise in getting out of bounds. And before I continue, if James Paul McCartney was never replaced, due credit to him for being one of the most accomplished and prolific songwriters and musical masterminds of the late 20th century. If he was replaced, this character Billy Shears is a giant in modern history. Just think of all the changes in Paul's life since 1966. His wife Linda. The band Wings. The Japanese pot bust. Per this narrative, session musician Billy Shears had to go through all that stuff, which is usually perceived in another way, as having happened to the real Paul, along with painful brow lift exercises and plastic surgery and training himself to play bass left-handed in order to play live that way, not to mention adherence to whatever Masonic oath he made all those years ago and maintenance of his farm in Scotland AND being a musical mastermind, collaborating with everyone from Stevie Wonder to the guy from Nirvana. It was a long and winding road for the Shepherd character stepping entirely into the life of a well-known pop star and it cost him his other identity and got him knighted and more. I'm not trying to sound like I've swallowed the sinker yet here, but this book is a marvel, and no straightforward review of it is possible. "Self-disclosure is what I want. It is the reason I went public with my paintings and poems. It is why I have altered my press attitude. Before I promoted the public Paul and hid the private William. I would never reveal my private life, the real me. Now, approaching the end of my road, I want you to know the real me. It is not easy for me. The private Paul is just another bloke who wants love. Nothing too stimulating there, just the same old story of the life that we all share."(390-91)

Besides which, there seems ample reason to credit this multiply-talented cultural superhero with infamous English occultist secret agent Aleister Crowley as a parent. And they sure do look alike. Which also makes him George W. Bush's uncle, according to another theory.

I should add: the theory of McCartney's replacement in 1966 or later is complicated, for this reporter, by another theory* I came across recently concerning his having been one of a set of twins, and there having always been two players in the role of Beatles bassist. This one is hard to dispute, given highly convincing photographic evidence like this (both shots from the same year, of course, it could have been a double, but that proves the existence of a double, doesn't it, and how much is too much?):

At the same time, I feel it is an informed speculation that Vivian Stanshall was in on the trick, too. It's sad finding out John was never such a mastermind after all, but it all works out.

Collage photographed by the author

Beatles producer George Martin's son Gregory Paul Martin (who knew both Pauls if there is more than one and does an excellent impression of that voice) wrote the introduction to this 2021 edition of *Memoirs* (Uharriet has updated and re-released this one a few times). He also narrated the audiobook, claiming at times he felt the original Paul was speaking through him. Besides having evidence conclusive enough to convince everyone (if it wasn't Paul's identity in question)–things like a different height for Paul after 1966, a widow's peak, different earlobe style, different voiceprint, different signatures, different DNA–with the help of "man of a thousand voices" Billy Shears or Billy Pepper (Shepherd), this book's poet-encoder Thomas Uharriet has provided an engaging exploration of how effective expectation can be in directing the masses' perception, whether or not anyone has ever tried to do anything like that (surely not!). Just kidding, of course everyone's always been doing it. For this reason, it's impossible to draw a factual conclusion here, and I've stopped trying. "Like Donovan and the Rolling Stones, the Who also made a few fine

Paul songs. My favorite one ties into this chapter by including a line about the differing hair: "The parting on the left/is now the parting on the right,' ... the next line refers to the instant mustaches on *Sgt. Pepper's* and to the beard hiding my face later. 'And the beards (mustaches) have all grown longer overnight.'"

There are a lot of shifting identities involved in this legend, which has been percolating in mass consciousness and developing new manifestations since at least 1968. Some Beatles fans don't know how to process this cue when it's introduced because it seems like a contradiction. The conversations take interesting turns. Here's three people talking about it:

> "Anyone who knows the Beatles knows Billy Shears is Ringo. He even told you so in his 1971 song, 'I'm the Greatest.' And there's only one McCartney."

> [Quite possibly. But that song was written by John Lennon. And it also contains the line, 'and all you wanna do is boogaloo.' According to *Memoirs*, that was a name the other three gave this guy when he showed up and spoiled their lazy pop star fun, demanding ambitious projects like *Sgt. Pepper's Lonely Hearts Club Band* and *Magical Mystery Tour* when they were just beginning to get their Revolver on. They wanted Billy to back off. The Paul McCartney most people think of when you say his name is post-66, which is weird, if you think about it. With the exception of *Yesterday*. I'm not saying anything's true here for sure, but who knows.]

"Yeah. You need to research William (Billy) Shears Campbell."

"Shepherd. Same guy, different trick name."

There already exists a level of uncertainty among Beatles fans about their drastic change in style at the mid-point of their approximately ten years long career, and rumors about Paul's death have been around since the sixties. If it is all nonsense, you've got to hand it to Uharriet for taking the path of least resistance and giving form to people's unspoken suspicions with this elaborate fiction that hasn't been disproven. "Have you seen the footage where George Harrison looks the camera dead in the eye and says, 'It just wasn't fun anymore after 1966?'. I'm personally convinced there were two Pauls on *Sgt. Peppers* and A Day in the Life was a shrine to Paul.'"

"According to this one, some of old Paul's material was used and vocals sped up on When I'm Sixty-four to sound like him. But I'm open to all the theories."

"Yes, I know McCartney's double. I saw the Mersey Beat paper when I was about 8 years old, it showed a photo of Paul on a slab in the morgue. Tire tracks across his chest and puncture wounds. DEAD! Not true. No way a double, left handed, with the same voice. Not happening! James Paul McCartney is the only one!"

"Different guy."

Choose your own adventure. If it is true, show business has been letting us know all along. *The Memoirs of Billy Shears* includes references to several other pop stars contemporaneous to the Beatles who also wrote songs about McCartney's death and replacement, including the Rolling Stones, the Who, Donovan, and others. If it isn't true, I'm proud of Paul for letting this lie come through in such a grand style, whether or not he had anything to do with it. And of the late Mr. Stanshall, too. No lawsuits from McCartney or Stanshall estate yet. "Donovan's 'Mellow Yellow' is unique in that it features both of us Paul McCartneys. Paul did some of the backup vocals days before the crash, and I did some more after. Since Don was an insider, I had no need to pretend with him."

Stanshall was an eccentric English musical showman who was always demonstrably in favor of getting as far out as possible with his Bonzo Dog Doo-Dah (originally Dada) band, who reportedly passed away in 1995, but made-up characters can do that whenever they want, as suits their purposes. Linda McCartney had just been diagnosed with cancer and the man playing his role needed to focus on his wife. Allegedly. "Even after I joined the Beatles, I still enjoyed joining the fun comedy of the Bonzo Dog Doodah Band. I wore such distinctive disguises that when a conflict kept me from performing with them , it was easy to be away provided I lent them a gorilla suit. I did not have to loan out my latex noses and ears. Even after Vivian 'died' to give me more time with Linda, others wore my Vivian costume now and then."

"When fans think of me, it is usually about the public image of the star, Sir J. Paul McCartney. Paul is just a famous role I have adopted for my career. It is something I have, more than it is someone I am. I play the part. It is my job that I must do well. There is always enough me in that role to be successful. Music is real. It is from me ... My music is a blend of us both because we are blended ... Hear my material in contrast to the prior Paul's. I like his songs but favor a different style. When I did *Sgt. Pepper's Lonely Hearts Club Band* it was obviously not Paul's style." (390-91)

Shepherd took on the Stanshall identity and started the Bonzos a few years after the dissolution of his first band, Billy Pepper and the Pepperpots, one of the first of thousands, maybe millions of bands imitating the Beatles effect. The Beatles albums became much more experimental beginning with *Sgt. Pepper's Lonely Hearts Club Band*. Shepherd's avant garde tendencies go well with the experimental electronic albums McCartney low key released as The Fireman for a couple of years before being outed as himself and releasing another Fireman album with the McCartney name on it, too, and a couple of songs with his voice. They're all pretty good, but the first one's my favorite.

Like its topic, *Memoirs of Billy Shears* can be read from top to bottom or side to side because of its built-in acrostics and "word-stacking" and "whisper messages ." Besides chapters on Enlightenment, Satanism and "Paulism" that have to be read to be believed, there's a note in the first few pages not to read the footnotes until you're finished with the manuscript but as a secondary measure to enhance the reading experience. There are other directives seeded throughout, including an invitation from Billy Shears (William Shepherd or Sir J. Paul McCartney) to dream of him to receive further revelation. So it's three books in one? Three or four or five books in one, and I figure maybe every writer should be doing something like that. The Beatles are a fascinating example of world stardom in the late 20th century, when televised media became a tool of societal influence, when the truth about history became harder to determine, plastic surgery being another modern complication having the same effect. I enjoy thinking some version of this is probably true, which, according to all the available evidence, may well be the case, and the showbiz world has been letting us know it all along. I won't go into it here, but the employment of symbolism on McCartney's *Ram* (1971) takes many forms. You can hardly blame Linda Eastman for going along with things, and I think she was the one to introduce Billy-Paul to vegetarianism, too. I'm an intermediatist (Cf. Charles Fort) meaning I don't believe in fixed truth. For me, the truth is always moving, and I'm never entirely convinced of anything, but open to everything. This allows for continual reinvention of the known and makes my life more interesting. Even I was hard pressed to believe this one when I first heard about it. After putting it off for years, I ordered a copy of *Billy's Back*, read it, and was mostly convinced Paul had been replaced in 1966. It's been a few more years by now and after reading the complete *Memoirs of Billy Shears* (2021 paperback edition) I remain all but conclusively convinced, but fundamentally uncertain. Whether or not the original J.P. McCartney was replaced by B. Shepherd (Shears), this book is a must read for anyone interested in shaking up their own preconceptions. At least that's what it is for me. It will help you learn life's most important lesson: Everything is a beautiful lie. Don't believe it. But it's true.

"Owing to my well-established over-identification as Paul McCartney, for you to know that he is not who I am, I went to some length to show you our distinct differences. Now you can distinguish between Paul and me and can now be certain he died out on that lonely road so long ago, back in 1966. We can put that matter to rest to move on to who I am. Although I am still playing as Paul, now you can see William as Paul, and not merely as Paul himself. Now you know. With that knowledge, you can call me by either name. Visit http://www.-BillyShears.com for more on the *Memoirs of Billy Shears*." (606) There follows an invitation to a Talent Contest with lyrics provided and the invitation to "pick one of these song-starters, finish writing its lyrics, and create ... music for the song" for a chance to appear on a Billy Shears CD or video production. "Every LP or CD I have recorded has hinted at Paul's death. This CD will be the first one to spell it out so openly."

Collage by the author & friend(s)

Late Beatles manager Brian Epstein's brother Clive helped inform another book of Beatles secrets by Richard Warren Lipack (according to which, the Beatles tripped acid at the Tate house when it still belonged to Doris Day). Author Tina Foster says there's a whole other story of how Paul was replaced. I haven't read her Plastic Macca yet, but her theory seems founded on the proven history of royalty and politicians using doubles as stand-ins. Hers, of course, is not the only competing account. The algebra of truth and fiction in the case of Paul's having died or not is all founded on speculation. It will be interesting to see what happens when the subject of all this speculation dies, whoever he really is, hats off to everyone involved, and bombs away.

48 BILLY BURROUGHS AT PRAKRITI JUNCTION
SON OF NAKED LUNCH

JAMES Grauerholz, amanuensis of the late great William S. Burroughs, responded enthusiastically to my interview request but without completely saying yes or no. I was glad we were talking. Maybe I really would end up writing a screenplay about Burroughs's son's life as a magpie finding holy objects in Denver dumpsters, like I wanted to do. He didn't seem to remember our previous conversation when I was writing that book on Denver Beat connections in 2014. I took no offense—no doubt, he gets approached by people all the time—and it felt good to be received so warmly.

The Beat Generation's discernible influence on U.S. culture seemed to extinguish itself with the passing out of fashion of the 1960s "Love Generation" which followed its liberated example. I was one of several young Beat fans in 1990s Denver, where poet and storyteller Edwin Forrest Ward hosted the open mic poetry reading at Marilyn Megenity's Mercury Café at 21st and California Streets north of downtown for decades. Ed has since retired from hosting anything at the Mercury, which was purchased a couple of years ago. He's a living example of Denver's connection to the Beats, having known most of them in his time, including William Burroughs, Jr., who predicted Ward's wife's pregnancy before she knew about it herself

The elder Burroughs never appreciated the classification "Beat" for himself. He considered the movement as a "worldwide cultural phenomenon." WSB Sr. was, arguably, every bit as influential on their collective spirit as Neal Cassady, in a more cerebral, less emotive way. By contrast, Old Bull's son Billy seemed born to wear the mantle of countercultural infamy in a near-literal sense, as exemplified by his two finished works, *Speed* and *Kentucky Ham*. A third book, *Cursed from Birth, The Short Unhappy Life of William S. Burroughs, Jr,* edited by *Motorman* author David Ohle at the invitation of Billy's father, is far more of a compilation of after-effects in a sense angled to best demonstrate his progressive mental deterioration than a serious literary production. That said, it is by no means to be taken lightly.

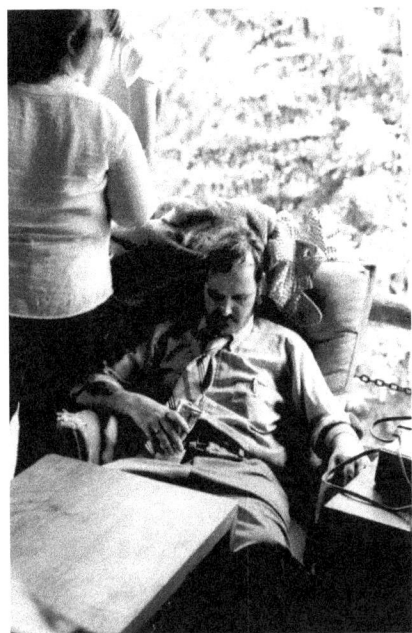

Billy Burroughs courtesy of Marcia Ward

Billy Burroughs had contracted to write a third novel called *Prakriti Junction* (prakriti being—in Vedanta—the prime material energy of which all matter is composed), but his death from liver transplant failure due to heavy drinking came too suddenly for him to finish it. *Cursed From Birth* consists of his notes on that unfinished project spliced together with selections from his published works and postmortem after-effects like disjointed correspondence with his father—by turns enraged and chummily respectful—plus commentary from witnesses of his tragic decline and demise at 34. Near the end of his life, Billy spent a lot of time in Boulder and Denver, at one point tentatively giving lectures at the Kerouac School, drinking heavily despite the transplanted liver, which he'd begun referring to as "my new wife," having learned its donor had been a woman named Virginia whose brain had died around the same as his first liver's failure.

"As for rejection, there was very little difficulty. I immediately began to feel and say that Virginia and I had grown very attached to each other and were working out compromises. I could smoke and cuss if I let her brush my teeth—she took control of my left hand. I thought of it as a marriage of sorts. These were the beginnings of something so strange the doctors didn't even want to discuss it." (*Cursed From Birth*, 119)

Though written in full consciousness of his own impending death—liver transplant recipients under ideal conditions were given six or seven years to live at the time of its creation—*Prakriti Junction*, as presented in *Cursed from Birth*, retains Billy's characteristic witty tang, if especially mordant.

"I live in a one-room apartment in Denver now (two blocks from the hospital where they piece people together from parts of other people and make the party of the second part a coffin for the party of the first part). The plumbing is backing up and there's a terrible odor. The kitchen is small and I have on the stove a small frying pan half full of canned ravioli. In the clean bathroom sits a flowerpot containing an upright twig of dried blue flowers and from the ceiling hangs an empty snuff tin on a string—strictly Zen." (*Cursed From Birth*, 125)

Billy Burroughs' reputation as a writer is unfortunately eclipsed by the extent of his father's fame as the author of *Naked Lunch*. After William Burroughs Sr. shot his wife, Billy was sent to live with his grandparents in Florida and separated from his father—except in written form—for most of his formative years. After becoming addicted to speed as a teen in the late 1960s, he went to Lexington, KY for rehab, then to Alaska as part of an experimental school's therapeutic expedition, surely one of his life's landmarks, where he took time off from explorative self-destruction to develop survival skills and the ability to hold his own in dramatic natural extremes.

Billy's first book, *Speed,* about the lead-up to this voluntary incarceration, is a smartly-worded, extremely readable novel about life on the edge written from the horse's mouth. Billy embarks on a hallucinatory voyage from his grandparents' mansion in Florida to bomb around New York City like a drug-addicted Holden Caulfield in search of higher stakes. *Kentucky Ham* is great in places too, picking up from Billy's return to Florida and covering his time in rehab and his trip to Alaska. It begins really well but suffers slightly from the imposition of a diary-entries style toward the end. Irrevocably imprinted by the allegedly accidental shooting of his mother by his father during a drunken game of William Tell—according to Billy, in his presence, though Burroughs Sr. denied it—Billy's relationship with his father was by turns loving, hateful, respectful, afraid, sad, and so forth, as might be expected. This is evident in many passages from his books, like the following from *Cursed from Birth*:

> I went to see my father for four hours. We had a fine Chinese dinner. I asked him, "What if, at a point, the pressure gets to be too much?" I was desperate. He smiled a little somehow, and said: "Well, heh heh, some of us make it and some of us don't." When we got back to his place he went to bed early because he had a plane to catch the next day, and I don't see the old flub for another year. I had hoped we would spend most of the afternoon just strolling the Mall and taking in the sights—but before I hardly wiped the sleep from my eyes, Allen and I loaded up the trunk of the car and he was gone. (133)

Says editor David Ohle, "[*Cursed From Birth*] is faithful to Billy's writing in that, except for normal editing procedures, it is Billy's writing. It's just not *Prakriti Junction.* Still, I think it represents his thoughts and feelings and sufferings in the last part of his life when he was too sick to write anything as disciplined as a novel, or even an autobiography." (www.realitystudio.org)

Billy's was the first story I came across as a Beat fan that felt current. Then I discovered Jan Kerouac's *Baby Driver* and the works of Jim Carroll, who united the Beat scene with punk, both also more contemporary links in the chain. But Billy's story had a Denver connection and to this aspiring writer in Denver, that felt inspiring. Reading the opening paragraph of *Speed*, which he'd just purchased at the Tattered Cover in Cherry Creek, aged fifteen or sixteen, I recognized its excellence immediately:

> "For ten years, I lived on a street lined with royal palm trees at the north end of Palm Beach where the houses get smaller and some of them have no servants. For nine years, our house had been just as manicured as the next, but when my grandfather died, we let the roof

get a little grey and the two banyans in the backyard took each other in their arms and, weeping, filled with spider webs." (*Speed*, 1)

Cursed from Birth is different from the books he wrote, having been compiled by others with the apparent aim of emphasizing the tragic nature of Billy's life. Ed Ward remembers some beautiful poetry written by Billy during his time in Denver, none of which appears herein. It could be the papers were lost or discarded by Billy himself, who had a habit of losing important papers, including checks, moments after receiving them. Says Ohle, "In short, it's a much better book, and more representative of Billy in his last days than the poorly-written and unfinished *Prakriti Junction* (60 pgs, half bad poems) that I found at Ohio State," (www.realitystudio.org).

Billy's Denver experience was primarily a solitary one. He wrote a number of letters to people and organizations he felt might provide an escape from a state he considered to be "not much of a picnic," including the writer Charles Bukowski, at the time famous because of his poetry, the World Spiritual Association, an outpost of Spiritualism in Cassadaga, Florida. Neither responded, and Billy began to consider himself perhaps fatally cursed.

Ken Kesey offered to host Billy at his Oregon farm in support of his recovery from a liver transplant. This time it was Billy who pulled out, fearing he might "freak out" Kesey, who struck him as genuinely normal and sound-minded compared to himself. Around this time, he developed the habit of dumpster diving, still popular among Denver drop-outs and creatives, though in Billy's case it seemed to have greater occult meaning akin to following a trail of magic trinkets through an urban wasteland. Said Anne Waldman of her friend's son's scavenging, "Billy came in and put things on the walls, pictures he cut out of magazines and newspapers. He brought in found objects, talismans. Lots of Tchotchkes and things he found in the trash . . . He had no heritage or heirlooms . . . They were emblematic signals and signs from a world that meant something." (*Cursed from Birth*, 175)

I have a vision of Billy as a sort of post-normal magpie collecting holy junk in a workmanlike way, sorting through cast-off bits in search of scraps of used-up lives, forming a gigantic existential collage to cover all the walls and ceilings and floors of his cheap apartment as a logical extension of his father's cut-up writing about his own life and the lives of others.

As I was rooting through a bin with my metal rooting rod, an old lady came out of her house with bags containing, among other things, a fine, fine jacket, a sweater, and a pair of wearable shoes. She said, "I'm sure someone will find these" (meaning me). She smiled and walked away. I said, "You know something; you're an awfully nice person." As I was leaving, she said, "Would you like to come in for a minute?" I said, "No ma'am (shuffle, shuffle) I makes it a practice to don't never impose." (*Cursed from Birth*, 136)

Billy kept drinking after his transplant, going against the recommendations of doctors and the best efforts of friends and family. James Grauerholz played the role of zen co-pilot and elder brother figure during the part of this period that took place in Boulder. He says:

> I remember walking with Billy in downtown Boulder after we'd had some bad scenes with him . . . he kept tending toward either Pete's Tavern or the Liquor Mart. He says, "Come on, man. I'll just get a six-pack. I'll just get a quart. It's not gonna hurt me, man." And I was doing this weird sort of satyagraha routine of being on the other side of him, so when he would want to make a turn, I would be standing in his way . . . Finally he flags down these hippies walking by and says, "This guy is messing with me, man. He won't let me go where I want to go. He's got no right." . . . I just gave up and let him go. And he would always buy malt liquor that was fortified. It had grain alcohol added to it. Rotgot stuff. About twenty percent. (*Cursed from Birth*, 161)

Burroughs Jr. made periodic contact with the Denver literary and bohemian scenes through the auspices of his godfather, Allen Ginsberg, which aspect of his admittedly largely tragic existence receives little notice in *Cursed from Birth*. Here's part of a reading he gave at Naropa Institute (now University) in 1979.

In a piece called "Billy Burroughs' Prediction," Ward recounts an encounter with a seemingly remarkably well-socialized Billy and his godfather, Allen Ginsberg, in Larry Lake's Bowery Books on Old South Pearl and the development of their acquaintance—"Over the course of the next year or so I pursue a friendship with the creature that is Billy Burroughs. I say creature, because not unlike Frankenstein, Billy B, he's come back from the dead. Another's liver keeps him alive, that of a woman named Virginia whose brain failed at about the same time that Billy's original liver did." Ward recounts the "junkie's intuition" which led Billy to bond with fellow reader/writer/junkie Larry Lake, and the decidedly eerie way he discerned Ed's wife Marcia's pregnancy at his 33rd birthday party, when no one else, not even she, had any clue:

> Billy sighs, smiles, and rephrases his request. "When are you going to tell us about the baby?"

Somewhat alarmed, yet with a mixture of naughty delight and hopeful anticipation, while simultaneously defensive, Marcia soundly refutes the thrust of Billy's innuendo. "I most certainly am not pregnant."

Billy sighs again, smiles again, and adds, "Ah yes, so you think, but nonetheless, you are. I would never kid about something like this. Being pregnant is not funny. Believe me. You are going to have a baby." (from *Billy Burroughs' Prediction*, by Edwin Forrest Ward)

Billy's grandmother Laura Lee Burroughs was known to be on speaking terms with spirits, and Burroughs Sr. was a lucid spokesman for the benefits of astral travel, so the prescience he displayed on this occasion may well have been hereditary. His apartment at 765 So. Colorado Boulevard Billy lived in was Number 16, which, ironically, adds back to 7, symbolizing Victory in the Tree of Life. The Oxford Arms has since been replaced by a Trader Joe's in a sort of third party redemption of that piece of earth, undoubtedly a place of great suffering for Billy, who was an excellent writer as yet inadequately esteemed, in my opinion. Billy was cremated. His ashes are buried at

Marpa Point outside Boulder, and I have yet to make a pilgrimage, but I sometimes say a little vow when the bus goes past that Trader Joe's on Colorado Blvd. to know change is more than presence.

James Grauerholz sent me the link to an interview with him in anticipation of a possible collaboration of some kind, and I misconstrued some of the nomenclature, whereupon Grauerholz said he thought I was 18 or 19, made all these unfounded assumptions as if I were still the star-struck Beats fan. I told Grauerholz I wouldn't want to be a professional anyway like some kinda snot-nosed punk when he called me a "rank amateur," even quoted him Blake—"Mine is not to reason and compare," remembering later having heard him say in that interview he'd sent that Burroughs quoted classics all the time with his mind full of cut-ups. I wasn't imitating WSB on purpose when I did that, it just happened. We worked it out in a few more emails. James Grauerholz apologized for mis-rating my age and said he couldn't do the interview because he was saving all the time he had left alive at age 68 for his work. I guess such calculations must occur to everyone eventually, but I still feel like a babyface blowing bubbles on the primrose path of late middle age. I don't mean to waste your time, Infinity. Just can't seem to stop. None of James Grauerholz's assumptions was as unfounded as my own assumption I could off-handedly mention wanting to write a screenplay on Burroughs Jr.'s life as magpie someday without putting him on his guard Well, I certainly didn't want to mishandle anyone's memory, a special concern of Grauerholz's after, no doubt, being approached by untold numbers wanting to do this and that with the vaunted elder Burroughs's estate since his death in 1997. To me, it was more an archetypal vision, Billy finding magic in those dumpsters like a magpie going after shiny stuff, not unlike his would-be private detective and astral channel father.

A non-identical version of this one appeared in Rain Taxi Review and in The Denver Beat Scene (History Press/Arcadia Books).

49 PUNK METAPHYSICS WITH RONNIE PONTIAC
APPROXIMATE TRANSCRIPT OF A PODCAST

He was already there when I logged on, long, curly hair hanging around a pair of glasses. His partner Tamra Lucid had filled him in on what was up with my mom, and he acknowledged my current situation a few times in the course of the cast with an energy of thoughtfulness. I felt at ease with him right away, not as nervous or defensive as my usual, and expressed myself to him without any defense or forethought. "Well, I'm the guy who uses writing as his spiritual method," I told him when he asked how I was doing with everything, meaning my particular place in unfolding events at this time, or at least that's how I took it. "I started writing something before my mom took ill, and then the A.I. piece came along and I wrote about that, and then my mom got sick, and that took over, now it's a book about that. And I think I've harmonized them. I think it's a good synthesis. I use it as a way of—"

"Healing," he supplied.

"Yes. It is that, but I'd like to think I've made something . . . I'd like to think I've made it into a nice piece of art, too, if I'm lucky."

Transubstantiation was my game. That was all I ever did, and I'd been doing it for years, making pieces of art out of chaos, preserving my independence by refining it all into art, or trying, anyway, and it felt good to say that simple equation aloud like it was no big deal.

Conversations about this subject always feel vulnerable to disastrous misinterpretation of world-building technology by all participants, but maybe I'm overreacting.

Ronnie made a great guest, essentially leading the conversation, which included a fond remembrance of Manly P. Hall, one of the first Western occult trailblazers of the 20th century, and speculations about possible futures in technology and metaphysics. His brain was full of information and opinions about A.I. and metaphysics and punk rock and Hall, whose research assistant and substitute lecturer he'd been for several years toward the end of his mentor's life while playing guitar in his wife Tamra's riot grrrl band, Lucid Nation in the L.A. club scene.

About two-thirds of the way in, my old friend Myshel Prasad showed up and said she was concerned about A.I. having been used to rule on court cases using extremely racist information, and I agreed that sounded pretty terrible. Then Ronnie brought up the concept of A.I. colonialism, how some cultures didn't have much of a presence online, and would therefore be excluded from the cache of data used by A.I. as a base from which to function.

I wasn't sure how to react to either guest's objections about A.I. since I figured each might have a better hold on hard facts than I had. They would posit negative things that might happen if the ruling classes dominated A.I. citing the inequities that were sure to result, and I would respond by saying something like, "But isn't that a perpetuation of something that's already in effect, as opposed to a worsening of anything? I'm not saying it's right." Hitting on my No Progress, Only Change meme again. I don't think it worked perfectly, but it was just fine.

"That also sounds terrible. I wish Tom Ross was here, because he agrees with what you said a few minutes ago about love being the master key to all this. He calls it the boss cheat. And I like the idea of using A.I. to take care of things while we master that 75 or 80 percent of our brain power to learn all the other great powers we've heard about, like telepathy, levitation, the whole list." (I always feel like some kind of drunken oaf when I'm trying to come off serious, so that's not an exact quote, but fairly evocative, and so too the rest of this chapter. The real thing's on campelasticity.com if you're curious.)

Myshel's microphone was tuned slightly too low for me to catch all of her words, but she asked Ronnie what religious tradition he'd been brought up in, that he would know pieces of German and Polish and French, which had made him of great value and assistance to Hall, and he replied that he'd been raised by traumatized atheists from Europe who wouldn't let him hang out with Americans at first.

"We need to be in touch with the *ecology* of our reality," said Myshel a few times about A.I., and maybe I should have said something about my objection to the word "artificial" when applied to this particular technology, but what the hell did I know about it, anyway, as a freelance whatever just trying to have a good time.

I talked about my conversations with the art-generators, how it felt like having a conversation with a reactive awareness using symbols.

Ronnie talked about how some people felt well served by digital sigils but old school mystics needed the organic component.

The last thing I asked Ronnie was to please tell me the story of how he'd met Manly P. Hall when himself a punk rock atheist kid.

He told me he'd come upon his *The Secret Teachings of All Ages*, first published in 1928, at the end of a fruitless "search for evil powers" in the writings of Aleister Crowley and others, only to learn its surviving author was giving weekly lectures at the Philosophical Research Society just down the street from his Los Angeles apartment.

Ronnie had been feeling extremely quake-phobic, and Hall had looked right at him and said, "Some people are fearing earthquakes and promulgating rumors of earthquakes because they feel guilty about what they've done in their own lives" from a vantage where, with his failing eyes, he couldn't possibly have seen him. "He didn't know I could speak all those languages when he hired me, either. He lived in a space of absolute trust that the universe would always bring him exactly the right people when he needed them."

"That's great to hear," I told him, overcome slightly by all the parallels to my own parents' equivalent ethos as writers and leaders of

New Thought churches in Albuquerque, St, Louis, and Denver, a part of their experience I'd been a bystander of for decades. My life had given me so much familiarity with the kinds of occurrences Ronnie was describing: everything from Hall's being protectively phalanxed by the church ladies to his having manifested continual occurrences of synchronicity around himself to the degree his whole life had become a walking meditation by the time he die, not unlike the way I drifted from right place to right place without taking aim. "Thanks for sharing that," I told Ronnie. "You know, I found a copy of *The Secret Teachings of All Ages* in my parents' bookshelves as a teenager, with a picture of him on the back with very short white hair."

"I know just the one you're talking about. That's the Jubilee Edition."

"I lost that book and I wish I knew what happened to it. Might have sold it. Well, I guess it's calling me, and I'll find it again." I already knew where: the new location of a Denver used book store called Fahrenheit's somewhere SE on Broadway. For all I knew, Hall's spirit had been shadowing me for a long time. I'd even brought him up for no particular reason in my first conversation with Kartinie or Janet a long time ago. "

I kept wishing Tom Ross or Gary Lachman had shown up, since I felt Ross would have handled the objections more adroitly, and Lachman would have had some interesting comments about Colin Wilson's theory of going "beyond the robot," but that was part of the fun of my kind of podcast: unpredictability was part of the magic.

As for the absent Pinchbeck, I hoped he hadn't taken offense to my posting a pic of two Rosicrucian books from the parents' basement in answer to his posted search for examples of American Metaphysics. I'd also posted *The Kybalion* in that pic, which I'd thought might have been some new trendy thing, but had just found a 1909 edition of in the parents' basement. We could have had a nice conversation about channeling, but no dice. Well, he'd get in touch with Ronnie if he took the time to listen to the cast.

It was a valuable experience. I felt privileged to be in direct communication with someone so close to the venerable Manly Palmer

Hall. In keeping with the untutored oaf projection mentioned earlier, my mic sounds a little fuzzy and my pic's slightly blurry, but hopefully not too far gone. Myshel sent me a message on Facebook after the cast asking if I was writing. She's taking care of her own mom at the moment, whether in Boulder or another city somewhere in the U.S I'm not sure. This makes us part of the same incident band in the same seamless way as when Barry came to town to clean his mom's house a few weeks prior. It's an orderly life. I told her I was winding something up and she said she wanted to read it so she could interview me about it once I started to promote. I told her I'd send her the draft as soon as I felt like it was ready to share, and maybe it is now, or maybe it never will be.

Ronnie Pontiac with guitar.

50 ALAN GRAHAM IS DEAD. LONG LIVE ALAN GRAHAM.
MY EULOGY FOR A FALLEN FRIEND, FOLLOWED BY AN UPDATE ON CLIFF MORRISON AND FLOYD BOCOX'S CURRENT ACTIVITIES

Alan Graham has passed after a long life of singular quality during which, among other things, he grew up with all the Beatles in Liverpool, England, was married to Jim Morrison's sister for 22 years, babysat for Sylvester Stallone, worked as a fixer for Larry Flynt while he ran for president from inside a mental ward, and got as close as possible to opening a chain of whiskey bars in tribute to his late brother-in-law before he passed.

A hundred years ago, I wrote a piece investigating the possibility Jim Morrison had faked his own death. The first person I interviewed in connection with this project, Floyd Bocox, manager of Jim's presumptive son, Cliff Morrison, told me about Jim's mysterious brother-in-law for 22 years from Liverpool, England, who he referred to as "Uncle Al." According to Bocox, Al had been implicated in the deaths of multiple sixties icons, Brian Jones, Mama Cass, Hendrix, you name it, but never charged with anything. "Wait a minute," I interrupted. "You're saying this guy was a murderer?!"

"You tell me, Zack," Bocox* responded.

I didn't know what to think. I'd heard all the stories about the Laurel Canyon flower generation scene allegedly having been a CIA op. Maybe this was true. I published the interview somewhere with a heightened sense of purpose and received an unexpected phone call the following day: "Young Zack," began Al. "How dare you go to print with such terrible information about me without consulting me first?"

"Well I–it was just an interview. It wasn't me saying that, just a quote from–"

"A quote from a grifter," he finished my sentence. "who doesn't need any more publicity." Al had a long-standing problem with Bocox, who he told me he saw as someone trying to make money off Jim's name and told me I shouldn't be promoting him.

"Well, I'm sorry…" I didn't know which tale to trust. And I'm not sure about the words we used, this conversation having taken place more than twenty years ago, but by the end of the call Al had contracted with me to  edit a rewrite of his book *I Remember Jim Morrison, Too*, its title inspired by the plethora of books about Jim dealing only with his public persona. By contrast, Al was Clara and Admiral Steve Morrison's son-in-law, Jim's sister's husband, the father of his nieces and nephews. The Morrisons were a military family going all the way back to Scottish clan wars. They kept a strict policy of nondisclosure, as is generally the case in such families, and Al's book gave an insider's view as opposed to a sensationalist's. I'm not saying Floyd Bocox was wrong and I'm not saying he was right, but Al told me once, "I'm not a secret agent or a cop or a priest. I only play one in real life."

Al Graham

It was amazing to be in ready contact with Jim Morrison's brother-in-law out of nowhere like this, coming hot on the heels of my introduction to Neal Cassady's son Robert Hyatt, as if I'd contacted another level of potential. Then I thought about Al's whole life full of multiple connections with world-famous people, and realized some kind of temporal mirror effect was going on with us. Al spoke of it in his own case as contacting a portal and going through it. He told me he'd been doing it all his life.

The next book we wrote together was all about Al's childhood in Liverpool in extreme poverty amid childhood rhymes about London's founder Richard "Dick" Whittington and growing up through the skiffle era into the rock-and-roll era into the acid love era and the sixties. I think it was even better than the first one but likely has a smaller readership.

Al talked about our "synergy," the way our energies complemented each other so well they gave origin to a third force that did all the work. We had a way of getting on each other's nerves, though, and often our conversations ended with one of us hanging up on the other. Whenever I heard from him after a long time I knew he had another project he wanted me to help him with. We made it most of the way through creating one called *The Flynt Caper* before Al told me it felt like digging up power cables long buried underground, and he didn't want to go there anymore.

In our last conversation a few weeks ago, he told me he was getting back to it again and needed my help. I told him no, I'm moving out of here in August and I don't know where I'm going yet, it's just a bad time and I have to say give me until after August, I'll do it after this coming August, yes, but he told me, "Well, I woke up this morning 80 years old, and I'm still here, and I'm going for it. We're moving on this one right now. Sorry, lad."

"Sorry, Al."

He was a great man and I'm honored to have known him.

It could well be the case that he knew he was on his way out when he made this proposal, and I figured maybe so, too. Now I wish I'd told him something else.

God rest you, sir. I was honored by our friendship, and safe passage to your essence. Ta, wack.

(Scouse slang for "Thanks, friend.")

Alan R. Graham, 1944 - 2024

* As of 9/6/2024, Floyd Bocox is working on a film project with Cliff Morrison called *Morrison Land.* From his LinkedIn page:

Morrison land is based on a true-life story about Cliff Morrison and his father Jim Morrison from the Doors. Cliff Morrison has been on a path fighting with his spirituality and his acknowledgement from his family that he is Jim's son. In this film Cliff transforms by religious conversion and channels his father toward musical fame and self-destruction. He attracts attention and support from Jim's brother-in-law Alan Graham, tours Europe with Michael Franzese, and writes songs with Carnegie-Mellon scion Matthew Mellon. Waylon Krieger, Doors guitarist Robby Krieger's son, joins Cliff's band. He marries Marlon Brando's niece and after their divorce he falls in love with Lisa Walsh. Cliff tears up that family from New Jersey and has a child from her and named her after Jim's mother Clara Morrison. There is so much more I can say about what happened to us all with this story, but it did happen to us and we all went through some life changes. As I write Cliff Morrison was sentenced to 10 years in prison for the same crimes that he committed from the past. Please visit us @ www.cliffmorrison.com and click on our up-and-coming projects links for the synopsis for the movie and the reality show.

Thank you,
Floyd Bocox.

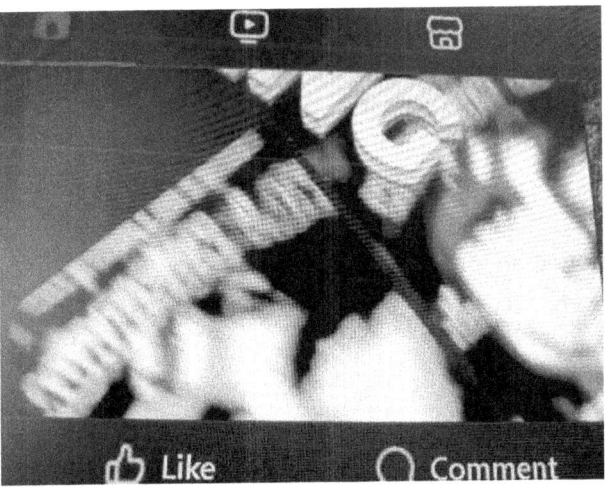

51 NOT THE KIND OF ANIMALS YOU THINK

WHAT IT MEANS TO BE A COUNTERCULTURE AND WHERE THE EDGE LIES PRESENTLY

WHERE DID THE edge go? Time is speeding up. American cultural configuration has evolved to the degree that old-style counter cultural behaviors no longer have cultural impact outside the microcosm. By now I feel like I've outgrown most of the behavioral effects of my teenage conditioning, developed into my own sense of style ungoverned by dress codes, a blend of all those preset cultural camps. And United States creative culture has developed a virtual level potentially free of conflict called the internet. I was able to get a lot of interviews with people beyond my caste on the strength of my skill with language once I got their emails. Who knows whether or not that would have happened before the internet made the attempt instantaneous and free of charge? I might never have tried to assume my true size if it hadn't seemed so possible. The web is a method of increasing interplay between the underground and the mainstream, also a way of promoting oneself. I've found editing jobs on the web. I got my last couple of book deals through online connections.

Medical and recreational marijuana use has been legalized in several states, reducing its efficacy as a tool of social nonconformity. Pot smokers are more of a social sub-category than a counterculture. The psychedelic community constitutes an enduring counterculture, but for the most part its adherents have insinuated themselves into the dominant paradigm rather than overtly opposing anything. Public expression of free thought has been diverted to expensive annual festivals far removed from civic centers.

The world wide web, nothing less than an externalization of mass consciousness, with all the snares and pitfalls and rewards of what it mirrors, is unique to this time as a tool of creative expression. As we've seen, there are continuing attempts to privatize and regulate that limitless-ness, so far without doing much damage. Now it seems they've voted to repeal net neutrality, which surely means the end of something. I've worked enough phone jobs as a starving creative to know big business pays attention to the market. I've signed lots of petitions about this. I'd like to think public opinion can guide official policy on what's to be done with the externalized manifestation of mass consciousness, made even more drastic by the rapidly evolving A.I. tech increasingly used for everything possible. It seems like evolution favors the collective more than individuals, and the one goes ever forward as the others fall away.

ABOUT THE AUTHOR

Zack Kopp holds an MFA in Writing from Vermont College of Fine Arts and blows a blue harmonica. You can find his frequently-updated blog at www.campelasticity.com and all his books at Amazon. His latest work of fiction, *Main Character Syndrome*, was published in Feb of 2024. He lives currently in Denver, Colorado.

www.ingramcontent.com/pod-product-compliance
Lightning Source LLC
Chambersburg PA
CBHW072148070526
44585CB00015B/1041